How to Form Your Own Corporation Without a Lawyer for Under $75.00

Ted Nicholas
Sean P. Melvin

DEARBORN™
A **Kaplan Professional** Company

W9-ANG-058

Library Friends of
Lake County Public Library

LAKE COUNTY PUBLIC LIBRARY

3 3113 01889 2341

This publication is designed to provide accurate and authoritative information in regard to the subject matter covered. It is sold with the understanding that the publisher is not engaged in rendering legal, accounting, or other professional service. If legal advice or other expert assistance is required, the services of a competent professional person should be sought.

Hard Cover Printings:
©1972 by Ted Nicholas
First Printing January 1973
Second Printing May 1973
Third Printing December 1973
Fourth Printing December 1973
Fifth Printing (Revised April 1974) ©1974 by Ted Nicholas
Sixth Printing (Revised September 1975) ©1975 by Ted Nicholas
Seventh Printing (Revised September 1976) ©1976 by Ted Nicholas
Eighth Printing (March 1977) ©1977 by Ted Nicholas
Ninth Printing (Revised November 1977) ©1977 by Ted Nicholas
Tenth Printing (December 1977) ©1977 by Ted Nicholas
Eleventh Printing (April 1978) ©1978 by Ted Nicholas
Twelfth Printing (July 1978) Special Edition ©1978 by Ted Nicholas
Thirteenth Printing (Revised April 1979) ©1979 by Ted Nicholas
Fourteenth Printing ©1980 by Ted Nicholas
Fifteenth Printing ©1980 by Ted Nicholas
Sixteenth Printing ©1981 by Ted Nicholas
Seventeenth Printing ©1981 by Ted Nicholas
Eighteenth Printing (Revised September 1981)
©1981 by Ted Nicholas

Sixteen Quality Paperback Printings:
(Revised January 1982) ©1982 by Ted Nicholas
(Revised February 1983) ©1983 by Ted Nicholas
(Revised November 1983) ©1983 by Ted Nicholas
(Revised February 1984) ©1984 by Ted Nicholas
(Revised February 1985) ©1985 by Ted Nicholas
(Revised September 1985) ©1985 by Ted Nicholas
(Revised May 1986) ©1986 by Ted Nicholas
(Revised November 1986) ©1986 by Ted Nicholas
(Revised May 1987) ©1987 by Ted Nicholas
(Revised March 1989) ©1989 by Ted Nicholas
(Revised February 1990) ©1990 by Ted Nicholas
(Revised February 1991) ©1991 by Ted Nicholas
(Revised November 1991) ©1991 by Ted Nicholas
(Revised March 1992) ©1992 by Ted Nicholas
(Revised May 1996) ©1996 by Ted Nicholas
(Revised May 1999) ©1999 by Dearborn Financial
   Publishing, Inc.

Published by Dearborn,
a Kaplan Professional Company

All rights reserved. The text of this publication, or any part thereof, may not be reproduced in any manner whatsoever without written permission from the publisher.

Printed in the United States of America

99 00 01 10 9 8 7 6 5 4 3 2 1

Library of Congress Cataloging-in-Publication Data

Nicholas, Ted, 1934-
     How to form your own corporation without a lawyer for under $75.00
/ Ted Nicholas, Sean Melvin—26th ed.
       p.   cm.
     Includes index.
     ISBN 1-57410-125-0 (pbk.)
     1. Incorporation—Delaware—Popular works.   I. Melvin, Sean P.
II. Title.
KFD213.Z9N5   1999
346.751′06622—dc21   99-20575
                                                                              CIP

Dearborn books are available at special quantity discounts to use as premiums and sales promotions, or for use in corporate training programs. For more information, please call Dearborn at 800-621-9621, ext. 4529, or write to Dearborn Financial Publishing, Inc., 155 North Wacker Drive, Chicago, IL 60606-1719.

LAKE COUNTY PUBLIC LIBRARY

DEDICATION

To businessmen and women who have successfully incorporated by using this book, and to all of you budding entrepreneurs who will soon be incorporating your dream business.

ACKNOWLEDGMENTS

I'd like to thank my friend, Sylvan N. Levy, Jr., for his useful suggestions after spending many hours reviewing the manuscript.

Additionally, the entire staff of Upstart Publishing Company, as well as reviewer Robert Friedman, have been of enormous assistance in the preparation of this book.

Special acknowledgment is given the Corporation Department, Secretary of State's office in Dover, Delaware, and its capable staff. In particular, I deeply appreciate the efforts of the Assistant Secretary of State, Richard H. Caldwell, for his personal assistance and helpful comments in reviewing this book.

Since the first printing of the hardcover edition in January 1973, Robert Reed, Secretary of State appointed by Governor Sherman Tribbitt; Grover Biddle, the Assistant Secretary of State; and Marie Shultie, Director, Corporation Department, and her staff have been of enormous assistance in helping to process smoothly and efficiently the large volume of new corporations from all over the world that have been formed as a result of this book.

In 1996, Secretary of State Edward J. Freel continued the fine work that historically has been done by the Corporation Department.

T.N.

A BRIEF HISTORY OF THE CORPORATION

Most of American law has its origin in England. The corporation as a legal entity under English law dates back to the late fourteenth century. In the early 1600s, again in England, a number of joint stock associations were formed in an attempt to gain the same advantages as chartered corporations. In all contractual dealings, these companies were able to offer their shareholders liability protection. As a result, investors in such companies were in a more favorable position than partners whose liabilities for partnership debts were unlimited.

Corporations have been a part of North America's history for over 300 years. The Massachusetts Bay Company was chartered in 1629 by Charles I of England. Its purpose was to colonize the area near Massachusetts Bay. In 1630, it founded the city of Boston. The Hudson Bay Company of Canada was chartered in 1670 and continues to operate trading posts there today.

During the early stages of the American Republic, it took a special act of a state legislature to grant a corporate charter to a business enterprise. The first state to permit incorporation under a general law was New York in 1811. By 1900, nearly all the states had constitutional provisions forbidding the granting of corporate charters by legislators.

Until the Delaware General Corporation Law was adopted in 1899, Delaware too had granted corporate charters by an act of the legislature. Delaware was the pioneer state in creating an attractive climate for free enterprise. Many of the corporations begun during America's great industrial revolution of the 1800s were chartered in Delaware. Its friendly and accommodating atmosphere toward business enterprises still exists. Low taxes, fast service, simplified requirements, and the Court of Chancery, the only separate business court system in the United States, combine to attract both small one-person corporations and large corporations to Delaware. One-third of the companies listed on the American and New York Stock Exchanges are chartered in Delaware.

Corporations in America in the early stages were burdened with sharp restrictions on longevity and size. Terms were fixed to a specific number of years, 20 to 50 years being common. There were also ceilings on authorized capital. These and other limits were abandoned over time.

In the 1700s corporations carried on a large part of world commerce. By the late 1800s corporations had multiplied enormously. Nearly every business owner that required capital or a union of large numbers of people, or desired limited liability, incorporated. The wealth and business holdings in the country to a great extent were and still are controlled by them.

At present the states compete with each other to attract business. Some are more aggressive than others, which creates a healthy atmosphere. Many have attempted to model sections of their law on the General Corporation Law of Delaware. However, while there are some similarities, no state has been successful in achieving all of Delaware's benefits.

Today, more than 2 million active corporations exist. About 800,000 of these have elected to be taxed like partnerships. According to *The Wall Street Journal,* more than 50,000 new corporations are formed each month in North America. This book is and will be used by a growing number of them—500 to 600 each month, or nearly 2 percent of all the corporations formed each month in the United States.

CONTENTS

Definition:

> **Corporation. An artificial person or legal entity created by or under the authority of the laws of a state or nation, composed, in some rare instances, of a single person and his successors, being the incumbents of a particular office, but ordinarily consisting of an association of numerous individuals. Such entity subsists as a body politic under a special denomination, which is regarded in law as having a personality and existence distinct from that of its several members, and which is, by the same authority, vested with the capacity of continuous succession, irrespective of changes in its membership, either in perpetuity or for a limited term of years, and of acting as a unit or single individual in matters relating to the common purpose of the association, within the scope of the powers and authorities conferred upon such bodies by law.** *Dartmouth College v. Woodward,* **17 U.S. (4 Wheat.) 518, 636, 657, 4 L Ed. 629.**

"For many years, even decades, the Delaware General Corporation Law has been the pacesetter for American corporation statutes. Indeed, viewed realistically, Delaware Corporation Law is national corporation law."

"The fact is that states cannot effectively exert controls and restrictions even over enterprises organized under their own corporation statutes. If they attempt to do so, enterprises merely incorporate in some other state with a more 'liberal' statute since the federal system permits individuals to incorporate wherever they wish in order to do business on a local, state, national, or international level."

From *The Delaware General Corporation Law*
by Ernest L. Folk III, Professor of Law,
University of Virginia, and published for
Corporation Service Company by
Little, Brown and Company, Inc.
34 Beacon Street
Boston, MA 02106

"Anyone may so arrange his affairs that his taxes shall be as low as possible; he is not bound to choose that pattern which will best pay the Treasury; there is not even a patriotic duty to increase one's taxes."

Judge Learned Hand

PREFACE

People from all 50 states and several thousand readers from other parts of the world have already used this material to form corporations.

This book enables the reader to incorporate at the lowest possible cost. The necessary forms are in tear-out form, complete with instructions.

Ted Nicholas is the founder of The Company Corporation. This corporation provides various low-cost services to persons who form a corporation (See Section VIII).

Lawyers' fees for incorporating range from $300 to $3,000 or more. The system enables anyone in the United States to form a corporation without a lawyer at the lowest possible cost, and includes other money-saving and tax-saving ideas.

A little-known fact is that an individual can legally incorporate in many states without the services of a lawyer. Lawyers provide important professional services to their clients. However, incorporation is a relatively simple task that does not require professional services. Forming a corporation usually involves minimum legal fees of at least $300.

Before this book was written, it was difficult for an individual to incorporate without a lawyer because there was no such publication on the subject written in everyday English. In addition, companies that assist individuals in forming a corporation work only through lawyers who prepare the corporate documents. Legal fees for incorporation prior to this book were almost completely unavoidable.

Delaware is emphasized as the state in which to incorporate. Regardless of where a person lives or has a business, this book enables a person to incorporate and take advantage of Delaware's corporate laws. In Delaware, anyone can form a corporation so long as he or she completes the forms provided for that purpose. You can find the reason for this in Section II. Delaware is the state of incorporation for over 200,000 corporations that range from small one-person operations to the largest in the United States. Because of the advantages to corporations of Delaware's corporate laws, more than one-third of all corporations listed on the American and New York Stock Exchanges are Delaware corporations. This is a much higher percentage than any other state. Yet you may also find that incorporating in your own state is more advantageous in some cases. If so, this book provides the forms and filing requirements to form a corporation in *any* of the 50 states.

Most of the corporations formed in Delaware are headquartered in other states. The individuals who own these corporations almost never visit the state.

More than 30 companies act as a *registered agent* and provide such services as a Delaware mailing address for the corporations formed in Delaware.

In most cases, the needs of an individual or company that wishes to incorporate involve a simple corporate structure. The goal of this book is directed toward the simplest and lowest-cost method of forming a corporation. A person with a business of any type or size who wishes to incorporate and conduct business anywhere in the United States can beneficially utilize the elements in this book.

Many thousands of new corporations have already been formed by using this book.

Prices and fees quoted in this book may be increased without notice by the various states and other bodies, and should be used only as a guide.

ADVANTAGES AND DISADVANTAGES OF INCORPORATING

SECTION I

Before you decide whether to incorporate, review other alternatives. You can choose from two other fundamental ways to operate a business—sole proprietorship and general partnership. (**Note:** The comparisons in Section I apply only to general partnerships, not to limited partnerships or limited liability partnerships.) Both have similar advantages and disadvantages. In general, the primary advantages to choosing a sole proprietorship or partnership entities are that they are (1) slightly less expensive to organize, and (2) relatively informal.

In essence, a sole proprietor is a one-person business which is an extension of the individual. A general partnership is two or more persons operating a business in context.

ADVANTAGES OF GENERAL PARTNERSHIPS AND PROPRIETORSHIPS

1. The cost to organize is lower because there are no incorporating fees.

2. Record keeping is less formal.

3. The owners file one tax return.

4. Owners can deduct losses that might be incurred during the early life of a business from other personal income.

5. The limit of tax-deductible contributions to Keogh-type pension and profit-sharing plans has been increased to the smaller of 25 percent of the participants' contributions or $30,000. This has reduced the tax advantage of benefit plans previously available to a corporation.

6. Profits of a partnership, unlike dividends paid by a corporation, are not subject to a second federal income tax when distributed to the owners. Rather, the owners pay it at their individual tax rate (known as pass-through taxation). However, whether this is a tax benefit depends on certain other factors, namely:

   a. The individual tax brackets of the owners as compared with that of the corporation

   b. The extent to which double taxation of earnings of the corporation is eliminated by deductible salaries paid to owners and by retention of earnings in surplus

   c. Deductions for fringe benefits that are unavailable in partnerships but fully deductible in corporations

   d. The availability of the S corporation, which offers the tax advantages of a partnership and the liability protection of a corporation

SOME DISADVANTAGES OF PROPRIETORSHIPS AND GENERAL PARTNERSHIPS

1. Unlimited personal liability. The owner(s) are personally liable for all debts and judgments against the business, including liability in case of failure or other disaster.

2. In a partnership, each member can legally bind the other so that one partner can cause others to be personally liable.

3. If the owner(s) dies or becomes incapacitated, the business often comes to a standstill.

4. The owner(s) does not have the full tax benefits of tax-deductible fringe benefit plans, including pension and profit sharing that are available to a corporation.

ADVANTAGES OF INCORPORATING

1. The personal liability of the founders is limited to the amount of money put into the corporation (with the exception of unpaid taxes).

2. If a business owner wishes to raise capital, a corporation is generally more attractive to investors. Owners may raise capital easily by selling company stock to the investor.

3. A corporation does not pay tax on monies it receives in exchange for its stock.

4. Many more tax options are available to corporations than to proprietorships or partnerships. One can set up pension, profit-sharing, and stock option plans that are favorable to the owners of the corporation.

5. A corporation can continue its existence in the event of the death of its owners or principals.

6. Shares of a corporation can be readily distributed to family members.

7. The owners (shareholders) of a corporation that is discontinued because it is unsuccessful can have all the advantages of being incorporated, yet be able to deduct from personal income up to $50,000 on an individual tax return or $100,000 on a joint return of the amount that was invested in the corporation as a loss. (See Section XVII.)

8. The shareholders of a corporation can operate with all the advantages of a corporation, yet be taxed at their individual income tax rates if this option provides a tax advantage. (See Section XVIII.)

9. Owners can quickly transfer their ownership interest represented by shares of stock without dissolving the corporation.

10. The corporation's capital can be expanded quickly by issuing and selling additional shares of stock.

11. Shares of stock may be useful for estate planning and family business succession planning.

12. The corporation can ease the tax burden of its shareholders by accumulating its earnings if the accumulation is not unreasonable and is for a business purpose.

13. A corporation is a legal entity. That is, a corporate entity will be separate and apart from its owner(s) (known as "shareholders"). It can sue and be sued, enter into contracts, and be subject to regulatory penalties.

14. A corporation may own shares in another corporation and receive dividends, 80 percent of which are tax free.

15. A corporation's federal income tax rates may be lower than the owner's individual tax rates, especially for a company with annual taxable income in the $28,000 to $100,000 range. As of this printing, income tax rates on companies are as follows:

Taxable Income	Rate of Tax
Up to $50,000	15%
$50,000–$75,000	$7,500 plus 25% of the amount over $50,000

$75,000–$100,000	$13,750 plus 34% of the amount over $75,000
$100,000–$335,000	$22,250 plus 39% of the amount over $100,000
$335,000–$10,000,000	$113,900 plus 34% of the amount over $335,000
$10,000,000–$15,000,000	$3,400,000 plus 35% of the amount over $10,000,000
$15,000,000–$18,333,333	$5,150,000 plus 38% of the amount over $15,000,000
Over $18,333,333	35%

DISADVANTAGES OF INCORPORATING

1. The owners of a corporation file two tax returns, individual and corporate, which may require added time and accounting expense. (The owner of a proprietorship files one return; a partner in a general partnership files only one return, and the partnership files an information return.)

2. If the net taxable income of a business is substantial (i.e., $75,000 or more), there may not be tax advantages. However, the S corporation option allows corporate income to be treated as the income of the individual owners, and the income is taxed at their individual rates, not at corporate rates. Furthermore, in businesses where there is personal liability on the part of the owners, it may be desirable to incorporate even if the income is modest.

3. Maintaining corporate records will require added time. (See corporate forms, Section XXIII.)

4. If debt financing is obtained by a corporation (e.g., a loan from a bank or individual), the fund source may require the personal guarantee by the owner(s), thereby eliminating the limited-liability advantage of a corporation, at least to the extent of the loan. But as the business continues to operate and demonstrates a sound financial history, many lenders will accept a corporation's promise to pay without requiring its owners to guarantee payment.

NOTE: Probably the biggest single disadvantage to incorporating prior to the publication of this book was the high initial cost of legal fees.

REASONS FOR INCORPORATING IN DELAWARE

SECTION II

THE ADVANTAGES OF INCORPORATING IN DELAWARE

1. There is *no* minimum capital requirement. A corporation can be organized with zero capital, if desired. Several states require that a corporation have at least $1,000 in capital.

2. *One* person can hold the offices of president, treasurer, and secretary, and be the entire board of directors. Some states require at least three officers and/or directors. There is no need to bring other persons into a Delaware corporation if the owner(s) does not desire it.

3. An established body of law that governs corporations has been tested in the Delaware courts over the years. There is therefore a high degree of predictability of the outcome of any legal proceedings in Delaware based on past history and experience. This can be meaningful to investors in a corporation. The Court of Chancery in Delaware was the first separate court system in the United States which decided business related cases exclusively. The Chancery Court has a long record of promanagement decisions and is the model used by other states that have adopted a similar system.

4. There is no corporate income tax for any corporation formed in Delaware that does not do business or derive any revenue in the state.

5. The franchise tax on corporations compares favorably with that in any other state.

6. Shares of stock owned by a person outside the state are not subject to any Delaware taxes.

7. A person can operate as the owner of a Delaware corporation anonymously if desired. (See Section XVI.)

8. One can form a corporation by mail and never visit the state, even to conduct annual meetings. Meetings can be held anywhere at the option of the directors.

9. The Delaware Division of Corporation welcomes new corporations and is organized to process them the same day they are received.

10. Delaware is the state friendliest to corporations because it depends on its Division of Corporation as a prime source of revenue. The corporation revenue is exceeded by income taxes. The state therefore depends on attracting a high volume of corporations. It has historically kept its laws and fees relevant to corporations favorable and at a low cost.

11. There is no inheritance tax on shares of stock held by nonresidents. These shares are taxed only in the state of residence of the corporation owners and/or by the federal government in some cases.

12. Directors may fix a sales price on any stock that the corporation issues and wishes to sell.

13. Shareholders, directors, and/or committee members may act by unanimous written consent in lieu of formal meetings.

14. Directors may determine what part of the consideration received for stock is capital.

15. Corporations can pay dividends out of profits as well as from surplus.

16. Corporations can hold stocks, bonds, or securities of other corporations, real and personal property, within or without the state, without any limitation as to amount.

17. Corporations may purchase shares of their own stock and hold, sell, and transfer them.

18. Corporations may conduct different kinds of business in combination. If the corporate documents filed with Delaware have the broadest type of purpose clause as outlined in this book, any business activity of any kind may be conducted. More than one type of

business can be conducted by the same corporation without any changes in the documents filed with the state.

19. Corporations have perpetual existence (unless specified otherwise in the Certificate of Incorporation).

20. The directors have power to make or alter bylaws.

21. Shareholder's liability is limited to stock held in the corporation (with the exception of taxes and assuming the business is conducted in a legal manner).

22. Only one person acting as the incorporator is required, whereas many states require three.

23. Directors' personal liability is strictly limited, or in some cases, eliminated entirely.

24. The Delaware legislature has provided a balance between the benefits of an unfettered market for corporate shares and the well-documented and judicially recognized need to limit abusive takeover tactics.

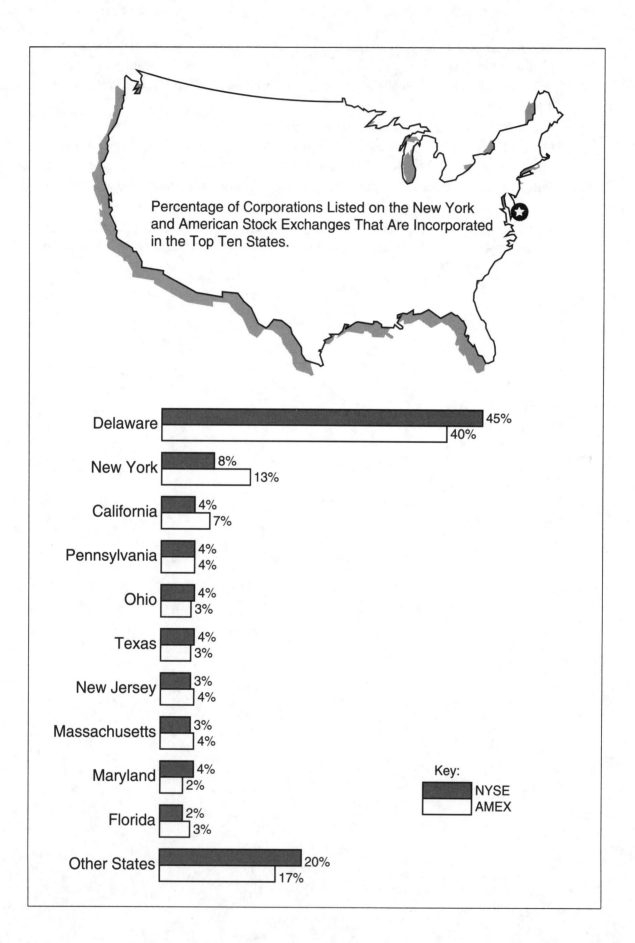

Percentage of Corporations Listed on the New York and American Stock Exchanges That Are Incorporated in the Top Ten States.

State	NYSE	AMEX
Delaware	45%	40%
New York	8%	13%
California	4%	7%
Pennsylvania	4%	4%
Ohio	4%	3%
Texas	4%	3%
New Jersey	3%	4%
Massachusetts	3%	4%
Maryland	4%	2%
Florida	2%	3%
Other States	20%	17%

Key:
NYSE
AMEX

TYPES OF SITUATIONS IN WHICH INDIVIDUALS MIGHT WISH TO INCORPORATE

SECTION III

A few examples of situations in which individuals may wish to incorporate a business activity or profession either planned or presently in operation are as follows:

1. A professional person (or partnership) such as a Certified Public Accountant (CPA), engineer, physician, dentist, architect, attorney and other regulated professions

2. A franchise owner

3. A person or company planning to conduct a private or public stock offering

4. A manufacturing service or retailing business that includes a manufacturer's representative or a distributor (many of whom operate out of their homes)

5. A personal real estate investment, such as an apartment building, store, or any commercial-building project

6. A business endeavor involving the ownership of one or more shareholders (sometimes erroneously called partners)

7. An activity or organization formed for nonprofit purposes, such as a foundation, association, charitable organization, or volunteer organization

8. A company that invests in securities or other companies

9. A person who forms a business that creates exposure to liability (e.g., businesses that operate vehicles, perform construction work, offer food, or offer such personal services as physical training or hair care).

It often makes good sense from both a tax and personal liability standpoint for certain interests of an individual, such as a real estate investment, to be incorporated into separate entities.

CERTIFICATE OF INCORPORATION

SECTION IV

When a Delaware corporation is formed, a certificate of incorporation is filed with the Secretary of State's office and with the Recorder of Deeds. It is also necessary to prepare minutes of the first directors' meeting, bylaws of the corporation, stock certificates, and the corporate seal (forms for everything except stock certificates and the corporate seal are supplied in this book).

Any person or his or her registered agent (see Section VII) may file the Certificate of Incorporation.

An individual or registered agent can also arrange to provide the corporation with a Delaware address. Preparation of minutes of the first directors' meeting, bylaws, stock certificates, and corporate seal can be ordered and completed by the person incorporating. Minutes and bylaws in standard form can be removed from this book and used for this purpose. A complete sample specimen and blank certificate of incorporation are shown in Section V. Forms for bylaws and minutes are in Section XXIII.

A very important element of the certificate is the purpose clause in paragraph three. The broadest clause enabling the corporation to engage in any business activity is used in this book. No matter what businesses the corporation engages in, this clause should not be changed. The broadest powers are given to the director(s) and officer(s). The only types of corporations to which this clause does not apply are institutions, schools, insurance companies, professional corporations, and banks.

Fifteen hundred shares of stock, which is the maximum number for the minimum state fee, are used in the sample specimen. This premise takes into consideration the annual corporate franchise fee, which is only $30 for 1,500 shares. If this number of shares or any lesser number is selected initially as the number authorized by the corporation, it can easily be changed at any time if more shares are to be issued later. More shares, stock splits, or a new capital structure require only a simple form to be filed with the state. A schedule showing the fees for these types of changes is available from the Secretary of State, Dover, Delaware. A Delaware registered agent can file the forms involving these changes, or they can be filed by an individual residing anywhere in the United States.

FORMING THE CORPORATION WITHOUT ENGAGING A REGISTERED AGENT

SECTION V

Any person can form a Delaware corporation. The owner(s) never has to visit the state. Annual meetings may be held anywhere the Directors choose. Below is the least costly way to accomplish the incorporation. (This approach, while the least costly, does not include the benefits of the services a registered agent can provide.) The following are the steps involved:

1. Establish a street mailing address in Delaware; (P.O. Boxes are *not* acceptable). This can be a private home or office. (Without engaging a registered agent's services to provide assistance, this is usually the most difficult problem to solve.) (See Section VII.)

2. Decide whether to form a regular corporation or close corporation. (See Section VI.) Complete the blank certificate of incorporation on the following pages, using the same format on the succeeding page. The language in this certificate has been prepared by the Secretary of State, Dover, Delaware. Be sure to fill in the name and address of one incorporator who resides in any state.

   Send two copies of this certificate (with *original* signatures) to the Secretary of State, Division of Corporation, Townsend Building, Dover, Delaware 19901. Include a check for $50, which is the minimum cost of the incorporation. It is an additional $21 for a certified copy of the articles of incorporation. If the corporate name you pick is not available, you will be notified. Otherwise you will receive notice of the date that your corporation has been filed.

3. When you receive one certified copy of the certificate of incorporation plus a receipted bill from the state, file this copy with the Recorder of Deeds' office in the county where the street mailing address of the corporation is located. There are three counties in Delaware. The addresses for the Recorder of Deeds' offices in the three counties are as follows:

   Kent County–County Courthouse, Dover, Delaware 19901

   Sussex County–Box 505, Georgetown, Delaware 19947

   New Castle County–800 French Street, Wilmington, Delaware 19801

   Enclose a check for $24.* (The charge is $9 *per page* submitted with a minimum of $18 to record a one-page certificate and certification page plus a $6 document-recording fee. Conventional certificates prepared and typed on legal-size paper are from four to ten pages, costing the person filing from $42 to $96. This is the reason that all certificates of incorporation except nonstock are printed on one page and are available from The Company Corporation.)

   In some other states, a similar incorporation procedure applies. If you are interested in forming a non-Delaware corporation, obtain specific information by writing to the corporation department of any state. However, no state has all the benefits of incorporating in Delaware.

   Standard forms are provided in Section XXIII for bylaws and minutes of the first meeting.

---

*Applies to New Castle County only.

11

There are also legal-stationery companies that can supply a complete kit of the above forms at a cost ranging from $60 to $99. A corporate seal and stock certificates cost $25 to $30.

The Company Corporation provides a kit that includes a corporate seal, stock certificates, and forms for minutes for Section 1244 of the Internal Revenue Code (see Section VIII) for $75.00, plus tax.

If you prefer to engage a registered agent to act in your behalf, such services can easily be obtained. (See Section VII.)

CERTIFICATE OF INCORPORATION
of

JOHN DOE, INC.

FIRST: The name of this corporation is _____ (repeat name exactly as above) _____

JOHN DOE, INC.

SECOND. Its registered office in the State of Delaware is to be located at 1013 Centre Road in the City of Wilmington, County of New Castle. The registered agent in charge thereof is (name and address of your registered agent) The Company Corporation at same as above.

THIRD: The nature of the business and the objects and purposes to be transacted, promoted, and carried on are to do any or all the things herein mentioned as fully and to the same extent as natural persons might or could do, and in any part of the world, viz:

"The purpose of the corporation is to engage in any lawful act or activity for which corporations may be organized under the General Corporation Law of Delaware."

FOURTH: The amount of the total authorized capital stock of this corporation is 1,500 shares of no par value.

FIFTH: The name and mailing address of the incorporator is as follows:

NAME: ADDRESS:

(leave blank if using The Company Corporation as agent; otherwise your name and address)

SIXTH: The powers of the incorporator are to terminate upon filing of the certificate of incorporation, and the name(s) and mailing address(es) of persons who are to serve as director(s) until the first annual meeting of shareholders or until their successors are elected and qualify are as follows:

Name and address of director(s)

John Doe, 1 Main Street, Atlantis, CA   [fill in name(s)
Jane Doe, 1 Main Street, Atlantis, CA   and address(es)]

SEVENTH: The directors shall have power to make and to alter or amend the bylaws; to fix the amount to be reserved as working capital; and to authorize and cause to be executed mortgages and liens without limit as to the amount upon the property and franchise of the corporation.

With the consent in writing, and pursuant to a vote of the holders of a majority of the capital stock issued and outstanding, the directors shall have the authority to dispose in any manner of the whole property of this corporation.

The bylaws shall determine whether and to what extent the accounts and books of this corporation, or any of them, shall be open to the inspection of the shareholders; and no shareholder shall have any right of inspecting any account or book or document of this corporation, except as conferred by the law or the bylaws, or by resolution of the shareholders.

The shareholders and directors shall have power to hold their meetings and keep the books, documents and papers of the corporation outside of the State of Delaware, at such places as may be from time to time designated by the bylaws or by resolution of the shareholders or directors, except as otherwise required by the laws of Delaware.

It is the intention that the objects, purposes, and powers specified in the third paragraph hereof shall, except where otherwise specified in said paragraph, be nowise limited or restricted by reference to or inference from the terms of any other clause or paragraph in this certificate of incorporation, but that the objects, purposes, and powers specified in the third paragraph and in each of the clauses or paragraphs of this charter shall be regarded as independent objects, purposes and powers.

EIGHTH: Directors of the corporation shall not be liable to either the corporation or its shareholders for monetary damages for a breach of fiduciary duties unless the breach involves: (1) a director's duty of loyalty to the corporation or its shareholders; (2) acts or omissions not in good faith or which involve intentional misconduct or a knowing violation of law; (3) liability for unlawful payments of dividends or unlawful stock

SAMPLE

purchases or redemption by the corporation; or (4) a transaction from which the director derived an improper personal benefit.

I, THE UNDERSIGNED, for the purpose of forming a corporation under the laws of the State of Delaware, do make, file, and record this certificate and do certify that the facts herein are true; and I have accordingly hereunto set my hand.

DATED AT: _____

State of _____

County of _____
(leave blank unless you are incorporator)

_John Doe_____
(signature of person or officer of corporation named in fifth article)
(leave blank if using The Company Corporation)

CERTIFICATE OF INCORPORATION
of

_____

FIRST: The name of this corporation is _____

_____

SECOND: Its registered office in the State of Delaware is to be located at _____
_____ in the City of _____ County of _____ .
The registered agent in charge thereof is _____ at _____ .

THIRD: The nature of the business and the objects and purposes to be transacted, promoted, and carried on are to do any or all the things herein mentioned as fully and to the same extent as natural persons might or could do, and in any part of the world, viz:

"The purpose of the corporation is to engage in any lawful act or activity for which corporations may be organized under the General Corporation Law of Delaware."

FOURTH: The amount of the total authorized capital stock of this corporation is _____
_____ shares of _____ par value.

FIFTH: The name and mailing address of the incorporator is as follows:

NAME: ADDRESS:

_____   _____

                                     _____

SIXTH: The powers of the incorporator are to terminate upon filing of the certificate of incorporation, and the name(s) and mailing address(es) of persons who are to serve as director(s) until the first annual meeting of shareholders or until their successors are elected and qualify are as follows:

Name and address of director(s)

[fill in name(s)
and address(es)]

SEVENTH: The directors shall have power to make and to alter or amend the bylaws; to fix the amount to be reserved as working capital; and to authorize and cause to be executed mortgages and liens without limit as to the amount upon the property and franchise of the corporation.

With the consent in writing, and pursuant to a vote of the holders of a majority of the capital stock issued and outstanding, the directors shall have the authority to dispose in any manner of the whole property of this corporation.

The bylaws shall determine whether and to what extent the accounts and books of this corporation, or any of them, shall be open to the inspection of the shareholders; and no shareholder shall have any right of inspecting any account or book or document of this corporation, except as conferred by the law or the bylaws, or by resolution of the shareholders.

The shareholders and directors shall have power to hold their meetings and keep the books, documents and papers of the corporation outside of the State of Delaware, at such places as may be from time to time designated by the bylaws or by resolution of the shareholders or directors, except as otherwise required by the laws of Delaware.

It is the intention that the objects, purposes, and powers specified in the third paragraph hereof shall, except where otherwise specified in said paragraph, be nowise limited or restricted by reference to or inference from the terms of any other clause or paragraph in this certificate of incorporation, but that the objects, purposes, and powers specified in the third paragraph and in each of the clauses or paragraphs of this charter shall be regarded as independent objects, purposes, and powers.

EIGHTH: Directors of the corporation shall not be liable to either the corporation or its shareholders for monetary damages for a breach of fiduciary duties unless the breach involves: (1) a director's duty of loyalty to the corporation or its shareholders; (2) acts or omissions not in good faith or which involve intentional misconduct or a knowing violation of law; (3) liability for unlawful payments of dividends or unlawful stock

purchases or redemption by the corporation; or (4) a transaction from which the director derived an improper personal benefit.

I, THE UNDERSIGNED, for the purpose of forming a corporation under the laws of the State of Delaware, do make, file, and record this certificate and do certify that the facts herein are true; and I have accordingly hereunto set my hand.

DATED AT: _____

State of _____

County of _____
(leave blank unless you are incorporator)

_____
(signature of person or officer of corporation named in fifth article)
(leave blank if using The Company Corporation)

CERTIFICATE OF INCORPORATION
of

_____

FIRST: The name of this corporation is _____

_____

SECOND: Its registered office in the State of Delaware is to be located at _____ _____ in the City of _____ County of _____ .
The registered agent in charge thereof is _____ at _____ .

THIRD: The nature of the business and the objects and purposes to be transacted, promoted, and carried on are to do any or all the things herein mentioned as fully and to the same extent as natural persons might or could do, and in any part of the world, viz:

"The purpose of the corporation is to engage in any lawful act or activity for which corporations may be organized under the General Corporation Law of Delaware."

FOURTH: The amount of the total authorized capital stock of this corporation is _____ _____ shares of _____ par value.

FIFTH: The name and mailing address of the incorporator is as follows:

NAME: ADDRESS:

_____   _____

                                         _____

SIXTH: The powers of the incorporator are to terminate upon filing of the certificate of incorporation, and the name(s) and mailing address(es) of persons who are to serve as director(s) until the first annual meeting of shareholders or until their successors are elected and qualify are as follows:

Name and address of director(s)

[fill in name(s)
and address(es)]

SEVENTH: The directors shall have power to make and to alter or amend the bylaws; to fix the amount to be reserved as working capital; and to authorize and cause to be executed mortgages and liens without limit as to the amount upon the property and franchise of the corporation.

With the consent in writing, and pursuant to a vote of the holders of a majority of the capital stock issued and outstanding, the directors shall have the authority to dispose in any manner of the whole property of this corporation.

The bylaws shall determine whether and to what extent the accounts and books of this corporation, or any of them, shall be open to the inspection of the shareholders; and no shareholder shall have any right of inspecting any account or book or document of this corporation, except as conferred by the law or the bylaws, or by resolution of the shareholders.

The shareholders and directors shall have power to hold their meetings and keep the books, documents and papers of the corporation outside of the State of Delaware, at such places as may be from time to time designated by the bylaws or by resolution of the shareholders or directors, except as otherwise required by the laws of Delaware.

It is the intention that the objects, purposes, and powers specified in the third paragraph hereof shall, except where otherwise specified in said paragraph, be nowise limited or restricted by reference to or inference from the terms of any other clause or paragraph in this certificate of incorporation, but that the objects, purposes, and powers specified in the third paragraph and in each of the clauses or paragraphs of this charter shall be regarded as independent objects, purposes, and powers.

EIGHTH: Directors of the corporation shall not be liable to either the corporation or its shareholders for monetary damages for a breach of fiduciary duties unless the breach involves: (1) a director's duty of loyalty to the corporation or its shareholders; (2) acts or omissions not in good faith or which involve intentional misconduct or a knowing violation of law; (3) liability for unlawful payments of dividends or unlawful stock

purchases or redemption by the corporation; or (4) a transaction from which the director derived an improper personal benefit.

       I, THE UNDERSIGNED, for the purpose of forming a corporation under the laws of the State of Delaware, do make, file, and record this certificate and do certify that the facts herein are true; and I have accordingly hereunto set my hand.

DATED AT: _____

State of _____

County of _____
           (leave blank unless you are incorporator)

                                   _____
                                   (signature of person or officer of corporation named in fifth article)
                                   (leave blank if using The Company Corporation)

A CLOSE CORPORATION

SECTION VI

A *close corporation* is a corporation whose certificate of incorporation contains the basic elements contained in a standard Delaware corporation and, in addition, provides the following:

1. All of the corporation's issued stock must be held by not more than a specified number of persons, and in no case shall the number of shareholders exceed 50.

2. All of the issued stock shall be subject to one or more restrictions on transfer. The most widely used restriction is one that obligates a shareholder to offer to the corporation or other holders of shares of the corporation a prior opportunity to be exercised within a reasonable time to acquire the restricted securities.

Sometimes other restrictions may be included in the certificate of incorporation that

1. obligate the corporation to purchase all shares owned by a shareholder pursuant to an agreement regarding the purchase and sale of restricted shares;

2. require the corporation or shareholders of the corporation to consent to any proposed transfer of the restricted shares; or

3. prohibit the transfer of restricted shares to designated persons or classes of persons if such designation is not unreasonable.

Any restriction on the transfer of shares of a corporation for the purpose of maintaining its status as an electing small business corporation under Subchapter S of the Internal Revenue Code is presumed to be for a reasonable purpose.

Another unique feature of a close corporation is that the certificate of incorporation may provide that the business of the corporation shall be managed by the shareholders. No directors need be elected, thus eliminating the formality of annual directors meetings. With this feature, the shareholders of the corporation have the powers and responsibilities that directors normally have.

A close corporation is not permitted to make a public offering of its shares within the meaning of Federal Securities statutes and regulations.

If a shareholder wishes to limit the number of other shareholders and also wants himself or herself and/or other shareholders to have the first opportunity to buy shares from a selling shareholder (known as rights of first refusal), a close corporation is the ideal form. This first option to buy shares of stock can be the key to preventing unwanted persons from becoming shareholders in a corporation.

An existing Delaware corporation can elect to be a close corporation if two-thirds of the shareholders vote in favor of it. If passed, an amendment to the certificate of incorporation is then filed with the Secretary of State in Dover, Delaware.

A close corporation may change its status to a regular or open corporation by filing a certificate of amendment with the Secretary of State.

The close corporation was created to allow individuals to operate a corporation in the same informal way they would operate a partnership. Formal meetings are not required and shareholders may act as officers and directors without formal elections. A businessperson who does not expect a business to grow to the extent that it will sell its shares to the public would be well advised to consider forming a close corporation that elects to be an S corporation. This choice means that not only will the corporation benefit from the single-tax status of a partnership but the business can be run in the same informal manner as a partnership.

Another major benefit of close corporation status is that the owners have the right to exclude anyone from becoming a shareholder and can exercise this option for any reason. A corporation with only two or three owners cannot survive unless those two or three persons can work together. The close corporation option ensures that if one "owner" chooses to sell his or her shares to a stranger, the remaining "owner" can stop that sale by demanding the right to acquire the selling shareholder's shares.

On the following pages is a specimen copy and blank certificates that can be completed should a person wish to form a close corporation. It contains the provisions referred to above.

As with other Delaware corporations, the certificate of incorporation can be filed using any address initially. However, it is preferable to have it filed through a registered agent because a Delaware mailing address is necessary.

CERTIFICATE OF INCORPORATION
OF

ABC CORPORATION

A CLOSE CORPORATION

FIRST: The name of this corporation is _____ (repeat proposed name here) _____

_____ ABC Corporation _____

SECOND: Its registered office in the State of Delaware is to be located at 1013 Centre Road in the City of Wilmington, County of New Castle . The registered agent in charge thereof is The Company Corporation at address _____ same as above _____ .

THIRD: The nature of the business and the objects and purposes proposed to be transacted, promoted, and carried on are to engage in any lawful act or activity for which corporations may be organized under the General Corporation Law of Delaware.

FOURTH: The amount of total authorized capital stock of the corporation is divided into: # of shares desired, e.g., 1500 shares of no-par value (unless desire to establish a par value).

FIFTH: The name and mailing address of the incorporator is.

(leave blank if using The Company Corporation as agent; otherwise your name and address)

SIXTH: The powers of the incorporator are to terminate upon filing of the certificate of incorporation, and the name(s) and mailing address(es) of the persons who are to serve as director(s) until the first annual meeting of shareholders or until their successors are elected are as follows:

John Doe, Main Street, Atlantis, CA

SEVENTH: All of the corporation's issued stock, exclusive of treasury shares, shall be held of record by not more than fifty (50) persons.

EIGHTH: All of the issued stock of all classes shall be subject to the following restriction on transfer permitted by Section 202 of the General Corporation Law.

Each shareholder shall offer to the corporation or to other shareholders of the corporation a thirty (30)-day "first refusal" option to purchase the shareholder's stock should the shareholder elect to sell his or her stock.

NINTH: The corporation shall make no offering of any of its stock of any class that would constitute a "public offering" within the meaning of the United States Securities Act of 1933 as it may be amended from time to time.

TENTH: Directors of the corporation shall not be liable to either the corporation or its shareholders for monetary damages for a breach of fiduciary duties unless the breach involves: (1) a director's duty of loyalty to the corporation or its shareholders; (2) acts or omissions not in good faith or which involve intentional misconduct or a knowing violation of law; (3) liability for unlawful payments of dividends or unlawful stock purchases or redemption by the corporation; or (4) a transaction from which the director derived an improper personal benefit.

I, THE UNDERSIGNED, for the purpose of forming a corporation under the laws of the State of Delaware, do make, file, and record this certificate, and do certify that the facts herein stated are true; and I have accordingly hereunto set my hand.

DATED AT: _____

John Doe

(signature of person or officer of corporation named in fifth article)
(leave blank if using The Company Corporation)

SAMPLE

CERTIFICATE OF INCORPORATION
of

_____

A CLOSE CORPORATION

FIRST: The name of this corporation is _____

_____

SECOND: Its registered office in the State of Delaware is to be located at _____ in the City of _____ County of _____. The registered agent in charge thereof is _____ at _____ .

THIRD: The nature of the business and the objects and purposes proposed to be transacted, promoted, and carried on are to engage in any lawful act or activity for which corporations may be organized under the General Corporation Law of Delaware.

FOURTH: The amount of total authorized capital stock of the corporation is divided into:

_____ shares of _____

FIFTH: The name and mailing address of the incorporator is:

SIXTH: The powers of the incorporator are to terminate upon filing of the certificate of incorporation, and the name(s) and mailing address(es) of the persons who are to serve as director(s) until the first annual meeting of shareholders or until their successors are elected are as follows:

SEVENTH: All of the corporation's issued stock, exclusive of treasury shares, shall be held of record by not more than fifty (50) persons.

EIGHTH: All of the issued stock of all classes shall be subject to the following restriction on transfer permitted by Section 202 of the General Corporation Law.

Each shareholder shall offer to the corporation or to other shareholders of the corporation a thrty (30)-day "first refusal" option to purchase the shareholder's stock should the shareholder elect to sell his or her stock.

NINTH: The corporation shall make no offering of any of its stock of any class that would constitute a "public offering" within the meaning of the United States Securities Act of 1933, as it may be amended from time to time.

TENTH: Directors of the corporation shall not be liable to either the corporation or its shareholders for monetary damages for a breach of fiduciary duties unless the breach involves: (1) a director's duty of loyalty to the corporation or its shareholders; (2) acts or omissions not in good faith or which involve intentional misconduct or a knowing violation of law; (3) liability for unlawful payments of dividends or unlawful stock purchases or redemption by the corporation; or (4) a transaction from which the director derived an improper personal benefit.

I, THE UNDERSIGNED, for the purpose of forming a corporation under the laws of the State of Delaware, do make, file, and record this certificate, and do certify that the facts herein stated are true; and I have accordingly hereunto set my hand.

DATED AT: _____

_____
(signature of person or officer of corporation named in fifth article)
(leave blank if using The Company Corporation)

CERTIFICATE OF INCORPORATION
of

_____

A CLOSE CORPORATION

FIRST: The name of this corporation is _____

_____

SECOND: Its registered office in the State of Delaware is to be located at _____ in the City of _____ County of _____. The registered agent in charge thereof is _____ at _____ .

THIRD: The nature of the business and the objects and purposes proposed to be transacted, promoted, and carried on are to engage in any lawful act or activity for which corporations may be organized under the General Corporation Law of Delaware.

FOURTH: The amount of total authorized capital stock of the corporation is divided into:

_____ shares of _____

FIFTH: The name and mailing address of the incorporator is:

SIXTH: The powers of the incorporator are to terminate upon filing of the certificate of incorporation, and the name(s) and mailing address(es) of the persons who are to serve as director(s) until the first annual meeting of shareholders or until their successors are elected are as follows:

SEVENTH: All of the corporation's issued stock, exclusive of treasury shares, shall be held of record by not more than fifty (50) persons.

EIGHTH: All of the issued stock of all classes shall be subject to the following restriction on transfer permitted by Section 202 of the General Corporation Law.

Each shareholder shall offer to the corporation or to other shareholders of the corporation a thirty (30)-day "first refusal" option to purchase the shareholder's stock should the shareholder elect to sell his or her stock.

NINTH: The corporation shall make no offering of any of its stock of any class that would constitute a "public offering" within the meaning of the United States Securities Act of 1933, as it may be amended from time to time.

TENTH: Directors of the corporation shall not be liable to either the corporation or its shareholders for monetary damages for a breach of fiduciary duties unless the breach involves: (1) a director's duty of loyalty to the corporation or its shareholders; (2) acts or omissions not in good faith or which involve intentional misconduct or a knowing violation of law; (3) liability for unlawful payments of dividends or unlawful stock purchases or redemption by the corporation; or (4) a transaction from which the director derived an improper personal benefit.

I, THE UNDERSIGNED, for the purpose of forming a corporation under the laws of the State of Delaware, do make, file, and record this certificate, and do certify that the facts herein stated are true; and I have accordingly hereunto set my hand.

DATED AT: _____

_____
(signature of person or officer of corporation named in fifth article)
(leave blank if using The Company Corporation)

REGISTERED AGENTS

SECTION VII

In Delaware more than 30 companies provide registered agent services to corporations. Some of these companies are listed later in this section. One of the main functions of these companies is to provide a street address for corporations, because all corporations formed in Delaware are required to have a mailing address in the state. The service companies that can provide this (and other services) are known as registered agents.

Annual fees charged by registered agents for providing a Delaware address range from $75 to $250 per year. One of the largest agents is comprised of several companies and charges $170 per year. If an attorney's services are used, there are additional fees of $300 to $3,000. Registered agents generally charge an additional fee of $60 to $300 for the initial formation of a corporation.

One company, The Company Corporation, charges only $45* per calendar year during the first year for its annual registered agent service. This modest fee is less than that charged by others. This fee increases to $125 for subsequent years.

The Company Corporation charges *no initial fee* for the formation of the corporation. No legal fees are necessary because the clients complete the forms themselves. No counseling service is provided or needed if the person who is forming the corporation completes the forms.

Service is provided in a highly confidential and speedy manner. Upon receipt, the corporation forms are filed with the Secretary of State the same day.

Potential savings for using The Company Corporation for the initial formation of the corporation are up to $3,000 in legal fees, and up to $250 on an annual basis.

The Company Corporation operates differently than other registered agents. It operates on a volume basis and advertises for its customers on a direct basis. Its fees are substantially less than its competitors. All middleman fees are eliminated.

The Company Corporation does provide services to customers referred by attorneys, but does not require such referral.

All that is required is that a certificate of incorporation be completed by the customer and sent to The Company Corporation. The certificate is then forwarded to the appropriate places.

No legal advice or counseling is provided by The Company Corporation. Only administerial functions are provided. State statutes prohibit nonattorneys from reviewing the form itself or giving legal advice on how to prepare forms. However, if the form is complete (instructions are contained in this book), *none is necessary.* If for any reason the certificate of incorporation is not accepted by the Secretary of State in Dover, Delaware, it is returned without comment by The Company Corporation along with any of the Secretary of State's comments.

In addition to providing a permanent street address in Delaware, The Company Corporation, unlike any other registered agent, provides the following services at no cost to its customers:

Initial Service:

1. Act as registered agent and provide a service of process address in Delaware. The Company Corporation provides a mailing address for receiving and forwarding all legal documents, not general mail delivery. General mail forwarding can be arranged for an additional fee.

Prices and fees are subject to change without notice.

2. Furnish the incorporator. (Certificate of incorporation can be completed but unsigned if desired.)

3. File the certificate of incorporation with the Division of Corporation in Dover, Delaware, via computer.

4. File a copy of the certificate of incorporation with the Recorder of Deeds' office.

5. Prepare checks for payment of initial recording fees to the State of Delaware.

6. Reserve corporate name and file documents the same day request is received from customer.

7. Prepare printed stock certificates, corporate seal, and forms for minutes and bylaws if the client desires the option.

8. Supply the appropriate forms for qualifying the Delaware corporation in any other state in the United States for an additional fee.

Continuing Services:

9. Provide an application for federal identification number.

10. Provide an application for S-status filings with the IRS.

11. Process qualifications in other states and act as registered agent in qualified states.

12. Act as registered agent and provide a service of process address in Delaware.

13. Forward the corporation's annual report form from the Secretary of State, Dover, Delaware. Once each year the Delaware Secretary of State sends an annual report form to the Delaware mailing address of every corporation chartered in the state. The Company Corporation forwards this to its customers. It is completed by the customer and sent back to the Secretary of State, Dover, Delaware, for filing. If you prefer, The Company Corporation can process and handle all paperwork for you through our Tax-on-Time™ service at a modest fee.

14. Assist in locating facilities for annual meetings if the client wishes to have them and/or hold them in Delaware.

15. Receive legal documents served on the corporation in Delaware, including lawsuits, and forward these to the business address of the corporation.

16. Other products and services that The Company Corporation makes available to its customers, including books and manuals, trademark searches, domain name registrations, web presence programs, mail forwarding, shelf corporations, and express service.

17. Small Business Toolkit™, a program of products and services The Company Corporation makes available to help the smart, bottom-line oriented entrepreneur in every stage of the small business life cycle. These include health and dental insurance, merchant credit card service, long distance service, 24-hour legal assistance, stationery and office supplies, payroll processing, office equipment leasing, plus many other best-price goods and services. For more information about The Company Corporation's continuing services contact them at:

> 1013 Centre Road
> Wilmington, DE 19805
> Phone: 800-818-6082
> Fax: 302-636-5454
> www.incorporate.com/tnp

In addition, The Company Corporation will furnish upon request the Delaware fee schedule for filing forms with the state. These include, but are not limited to, forms for increases in the number of shares of stock, new classes of stock, amending certificates of incorporation, dissolutions, and the like.

Initial Fee $60–$300 for filing corporate documents. Legal Fees $300–$3,000 (most of these companies require that clients be referred by a lawyer). Annual Fee $75–$250.

American Guaranty & Trust Co.
220 Continental Drive
Newark, DE 19713

Capital Trust Co. of Delaware
1013 Centre Rd.
Wilmington, DE 19805

Corporate Systems Inc.
101 North Fairfield Dr.
Dover, DE 19801

Corporation Guarantee & Trust Co.
11th Floor, Rodney Square North
11th & Market Streets
Wilmington, DE 19801

Corporation Trust Co. (The)
1209 Orange Street
Wilmington, DE 19801

Delaware Corporation Organizers, Inc.
1201 North Market Street, 18th Floor
Wilmington, DE 19899

Delaware Registration Trust Co.
900 Market Street
Wilmington, DE 19801

Delaware Registry, Ltd.
3511 Silveside Road, Suite 105
Wilmington, DE 19810

Incorporating Services, Ltd.
15 East North Street
Dover, DE 19901

Incorporators of Delaware
48 The Green
Dover, DE 19901

National Corporate Research, Ltd.
9 East Loockerman Street
Dover, DE 19901

Prentice-Hall Corp. System, Inc. (The)
1013 Centre Road
Wilmington, DE 19805

Registered Agents, Ltd.
1220 North Market Street
Wilmington, DE 19801

United Corporate Services, Inc.
15 East North Street
Dover, DE 19901

The CSC United States Corporation Co.
1013 Centre Road
Wilmington, DE 19805

THE COMPANY CORPORATION

SECTION VIII

Any registered agent listed in this book can assist in filing forms for incorporating and providing other services to corporations. The Company Corporation provides its services in a different manner and at a lower cost than any other company; also, it will assist you in incorporating in the State of Delaware or in any other state. If you want to incorporate in a state other than Delaware, call 800-818-6082 and ask for a complete set of forms and information for the state that interests you. Details will be furnished to all buyers of this book free of charge.

The Company Corporation charges a $45 service fee for initial administerial services in filing the certificate of incorporation with the State of Delaware, providing that The Company Corporation is appointed registered agent. Other registered agents charge up to $300 for initial incorporating services in addition to a lawyer's fee. The annual fee for engaging The Company Corporation is $45 during the first year with no legal fees. The fee increases to $125 in subsequent years.

The cost to incorporate in Delaware is as follows:

$50	covers state fee (Delaware)
24	recording fee (county)
45	service fee (The Company Corporation)
45	registered agent fee (first calendar year)
$164	minimum amount paid to The Company Corporation at the time of filing

Most certificates of incorporation run unnecessarily to four or more pages costing $42 or more just to file. The forms in this book, most on one page, cost only $9 per page plus a $6 document recording fee ($24 minimum) to file with the Recorder of Deeds. Copy used in the certificates of incorporation contained in this book has been reproduced from forms supplied by the Secretary of State, Dover, Delaware.

Minutes of the first meeting and bylaws may be torn out of this book and used for the new corporation. Stock certificates and corporate seals are available from stationery stores.

As an option to its customers, The Company Corporation makes available a corporate kit that contains:

1. A vinyl-covered record book to hold corporate records (with extra-large holes) size 12″ × 10″ × 1.5″ with the corporate name printed on a gold insert.
2. A metal corporate seal (in a pouch) imprinted with the corporate name 1⅝″ in diameter. This can be used on various documents.
3. Twenty lithographed stock certificates of one class of stock printed with the corporate name and capitalization. (If there is more than one class of stock, you may request the price.)
4. Preprinted minute and bylaw forms to fit into the record book (also available on diskette).
5. A stock/transfer ledger for keeping an accurate and complete record of your corporate stock, including stock transfers.

The total minimum cost for utilizing The Company Corporation to file your Delaware corporation and to act as a registered agent in the State of Delaware is $164. With the above optional and useful material, the additional cost is $75, plus tax if applicable, making a total of $239. Details and costs for incorporating in other states are available upon request.

By popular request, The Company Corporation will provide the necessary forms and instructors to obtain a federal tax I.D. number and S status for each corporation for the nominal fee of $39.

Delaware & County Fee	*Incorporating Fee—Using The Company Corporation First Year's Registered Agent Fee*	*Total*
$74.00	$45.00	$164.00
	Optional Corporate Kit ($75.00)	75.00
	Apply for S Corporation Status and Federal I.D. Number (optional)	39.00
Total Payable to The Company Corporation—including kit		$278.00*

The Company Corporation cannot furnish personal counsel or advice or answer questions to inquiries that involve interpretations or opinions of law.

---

*All prices and fees subject to change without notice.

The Company Corporation

Incorporation Order Form

1. **Corporate Name:** (One of the following corporate endings is required—Inc., Company, Corporation, Incorporated, Corp., Co., Limited Liability Companies may use LLC)

   First Choice: _____

   Alternate : _____

2. **State in which you wish to be incorporated:** _____

   County: _____

3. **Type of Corporation:**

   ❑ General Corporation   ❑ Limited Liability Company   ❑ Professional

   ❑ Non Stock/Non-Profit (must provide corporate documents)

4. **Stock:** The corporation will be authorized to issue up to 1,500 shares of no par common stock unless you instruct otherwise

   Shares: _____   Par Value: _____

5. **Corporate Kits:**   ❑ Attache Kit ($99)   ❑ Deluxe Kit ($75)   ❑ Standard Kit ($60)

   Sales tax required for corporate kits and publications shipped to CA, CT, DC, FL, IL, MA, NJ, NY,PA, TX,WA.

Additional Services:	**Publications:**
❑ Express Formation Service ($60)	❑ Business Owners Guide to Accounting ($19.95) 189 pg
❑ Rapid Delivery ($16)	❑ Essential Limited Liability Company Handbook ($19.95) 262 pg
❑ Prepare Tax I.D. Application ($25)	❑ Essential Corporation Handbook ($29.95) 232 pg
❑ Prepare S Corporation Election ($25)	❑ The Successful Business Plan ($24.95) 320 pg

   Please check the Corporate Package you wish to order; see next page for description and prices

   ❑ Delaware Basic Package   ❑ Delaware Complete Package

   ❑ Non-Delaware Basic Package   ❑ Non-Delaware Complete Package

6. **Names of Directors:** (Only one director is required in most states. LLC's require two member names)

   Name: _____   Name : _____

   Address: _____   Address: _____

7. **Shipping Address for Articles and Kit:** (No P.O. Boxes)

   _____

   Phone: ( ) _____ Fax: ( ) _____ Email: _____

8. **Registered Agent:**

   _____

   Remember to add $45 if TCC is the registered agent or $50 if TCC is not the registered agent. (Registered Agent included in packages) Provide address if TCC is not Registered Agent

9. **Method of Payment:**

   ❑ Check/Money Order enclose   ❑ Western Union   ❑ MasterCard   ❑ Visa

   ❑ Discover   ❑ Amex

   Card #: _____ _Exp. Date: _____ __Total Amount: $ _____

   Name on Card: _____ _Authorized Signature: _____

THE COMPANY CORPORATION

1013 CENTRE ROAD   (800) 499-6315   WWW.INCORPORATE.COM/TNP

WILMINGTON, DE 19805 U.S.A.   FAX: (302) 636-5454   INFO@CORPORATE.COM

TNP199

Incorporation/LLC Prices by State

State	Corporation With Service Charge	Corporation State Fee Only	LLC With Service Charge	LLC State Fee Only
Alabama	$184	$85	$184	$85
Alaska	349	250	349	250
Arizona	344	245	344	245
Arkansas	149	50	149	50
California††	514	415	184*	85
Colorado	149	50	149	50
Connecticut	399	300	184	85
Delaware	119	74	139	70
District of Columbia	219	120	199	100
Florida	169	70	384	285
Georgia	299	200	314	215
Hawaii	249	150	279	180
Idaho	199	100	199	100
Illinois	219	120	499	400
Indiana	219	120	219	120
Iowa	149	50	149	50
Kansas	194	95	249	150
Kentucky	169	70	139	40
Louisiana	219	120	219	120
Maine	254	155	349	250
Maryland	169	70	179	80
Massachusetts	299	200	599	500
Michigan	189	90	189	90
Minnesota	234	135	234	135
Mississippi	149	50	149	50
Missouri	157	58	204	105
Montana	189	90	169	70
Nebraska†	309	210	374	275
Nevada	294	195	294	195
New Hampshire	214	115	184	85
New Jersey	229	130	209	110
New Mexico	199	100	149	50
New York	269	170	309**	210
North Carolina	224	125	224	125
North Dakota	234	135	234	135
Ohio	194	95	194	95
Oklahoma	149	50	199	100
Oregon	149	50	139	40
Pennsylvania†	349	250	199	100
Rhode Island	249	150	249	150
South Carolina	309	210	209	110
South Dakota	189	90	189	90
Tennessee	219	120	399	300
Texas	409	310	309	210
Utah	174	75	199	100
Vermont	174	75	174	75
Virginia	180	81	205	106
Washington	294	195	294	195
West Virginia	169	70	199	100
Wisconsin	214	115	299	130
Wyoming	199	100	199	100

The Company Corporation
800-818-6082

An additional $45.00 will be added to all fees for the first year's registered agent service. Subsequently, the charge is $125.00 per year for all states.

If The Company Corporation is not the registered agent, an additional $50.00 will be added to all prices. All prices include The Company Corporation's service fee.

> Our Tax-On-Time® service guarantees prompt filing of your annual report, and payment of fees and taxes (available to Delaware corporations only). Call us.

*When formed as a partnership, managed by company members of the franchise, tax is due in three months.

**Does not include publishing fees.

†Includes publishing fees.

‡California minimum franchise tax fee for corporations that plan on $1,000,000 or less in annual revenues.

All fees subject to change without notice.

Choose From Four Corporation Packages*

Basic Delaware Corporation/LLC Package
$289.00 (includes state filing fees)
$55.00 Savings!

- Prepare and file the Certificate of Incorporation for your corporation (for corporations with up to 1,500 shares of no par value stock).
- Provide registered agent representation for the first calendar year.
- Personalized Standard Corporate Kit including: seal, stock certificates and other important documents to simplify record keeping.
- Essential Corporation Handbook
- Express Service

Complete Delaware Corporation/LLC Package
$389.00 (includes state filing fees)
$70.00 Savings!

Includes everything in the *Basic Delaware Corporation Package*, plus:
- Application for federal tax identification number
- Application for Sub Chapter "S"
- E.A.R.N. membership
- Deluxe Corporate Kit

Basic Non-Delaware Corporation/LLC Package
$235.00 (includes state filing fees)
$59.00 Savings!

- Prepare and file the Certificate of Incorporation for your corporation (includes preliminary name check, in most states).
- Provide registered agent service for the first year.
- Personalized Standard Corporate Kit including: seal, stock certificates and other important documents to simplify record keeping.
- Essential Corporation Handbook
- Express Service

Complete Non-Delaware Corporation/LLC Package
$335.00 (plus state filing fees)
$74.00 Savings!

Includes everything in the *Basic Non-Delaware Corporation Package*, plus:
- Application for federal tax identification number
- Application for Sub Chapter "S"
- E.A.R.N. membership
- Deluxe Corporate Kit

*Please add $5.00 to package price if TCC is not appointed registered agent.

The Company Corporation

Incorporation Order Form

1. **Corporate Name:** (One of the following corporate endings is required—Inc., Company, Corporation, Incorporated, Corp., Co., Limited Liability Companies may use LLC)

   First Choice: _____

   Alternate : _____

2. **State in which you wish to be incorporated:** _____

   County: _____

3. **Type of Corporation:**

   ❑ General Corporation   ❑ Limited Liability Company   ❑ Professional

   ❑ Non Stock/Non-Profit (must provide corporate documents)

4. **Stock:** The corporation will be authorized to issue up to 1,500 shares of no par common stock unless you instruct otherwise

   Shares: _____   Par Value: _____

5. **Corporate Kits:**   ❑ Attache Kit ($99)   ❑ Deluxe Kit ($75)   ❑ Standard Kit ($60)

   Sales tax required for corporate kits and publications shipped to CA, CT, DC, FL, IL, MA, NJ, NY, PA, TX, WA.

   Additional Services:

   ❑ Express Formation Service ($60)

   ❑ Rapid Delivery ($16)

   ❑ Prepare Tax I.D. Application ($25)

   ❑ Prepare S Corporation Election ($25)

   Publications:

   ❑ Business Owners Guide to Accounting ($19.95) 189 pg

   ❑ Essential Limited Liability Company Handbook ($19.95) 262 pg

   ❑ Essential Corporation Handbook ($29.95) 232 pg

   ❑ The Successful Business Plan ($24.95) 320 pg

   Please check the Corporate Package you wish to order; see next page for description and prices

   ❑ Delaware Basic Package   ❑ Delaware Complete Package

   ❑ Non-Delaware Basic Package   ❑ Non-Delaware Complete Package

6. **Names of Directors:** (Only one director is required in most states. LLC's require two member names)

   Name: _____   Name : _____

   Address: _____   Address: _____

7. **Shipping Address for Articles and Kit:** (No P.O. Boxes)

   _____

   Phone: ( ) _____ Fax: ( ) _____ Email: _____

8. **Registered Agent:**

   _____

   Remember to add $45 if TCC is the registered agent or $50 if TCC is not the registered agent. (Registered Agent included in packages) Provide address if TCC is not Registered Agent

9. **Method of Payment:**

   ❑ Check/Money Order enclose   ❑ Western Union   ❑ MasterCard   ❑ Visa

   ❑ Discover   ❑ Amex

   Card #: _____ _Exp. Date: _____ _Total Amount: $ _____

   Name on Card: _____ _Authorized Signature: _____

THE COMPANY CORPORATION

1013 CENTRE ROAD

WILMINGTON, DE 19805 U.S.A.

(800) 499-6315

FAX: (302) 636-5454

WWW.INCORPORATE.COM/TNP

INFO@CORPORATE.COM

TNP199

Incorporation/LLC Prices by State

State	Corporation With Service Charge	Corporation State Fee Only	LLC With Service Charge	LLC State Fee Only
Alabama	$184	$85	$184	$85
Alaska	349	250	349	250
Arizona	344	245	344	245
Arkansas	149	50	149	50
California††	514	415	184*	85
Colorado	149	50	149	50
Connecticut	399	300	184	85
Delaware	119	74	139	70
District of Columbia	219	120	199	100
Florida	169	70	384	285
Georgia	299	200	314	215
Hawaii	249	150	279	180
Idaho	199	100	199	100
Illinois	219	120	499	400
Indiana	219	120	219	120
Iowa	149	50	149	50
Kansas	194	95	249	150
Kentucky	169	70	139	40
Louisiana	219	120	219	120
Maine	254	155	349	250
Maryland	169	70	179	80
Massachusetts	299	200	599	500
Michigan	189	90	189	90
Minnesota	234	135	234	135
Mississippi	149	50	149	50

State	Corporation With Service Charge	Corporation State Fee Only	LLC With Service Charge	LLC State Fee Only
Missouri	157	58	204	105
Montana	189	90	169	70
Nebraska†	309	210	374	275
Nevada	294	195	294	195
New Hampshire	214	115	184	85
New Jersey	229	130	209	110
New Mexico	199	100	149	50
New York	269	170	309**	210
North Carolina	224	125	224	125
North Dakota	234	135	234	135
Ohio	194	95	194	95
Oklahoma	149	50	199	100
Oregon	149	50	139	40
Pennsylvania†	349	250	199	100
Rhode Island	249	150	249	150
South Carolina	309	210	209	110
South Dakota	189	90	189	90
Tennessee	219	120	399	300
Texas	409	310	309	210
Utah	174	75	199	100
Vermont	174	75	174	75
Virginia	180	81	205	106
Washington	294	195	294	195
West Virginia	169	70	199	100
Wisconsin	214	115	299	130
Wyoming	199	100	199	100

An additional $45.00 will be added to all fees for the first year's registered agent service. Subsequently, the charge is $125.00 per year for all states.

If The Company Corporation is not the registered agent, an additional $50.00 will be added to all prices. All prices include The Company Corporation's service fee.

Our Tax-On-Time® service guarantees prompt filing of your annual report, and payment of fees and taxes (available to Delaware corporations only). Call us.

*When formed as a partnership, managed by company members of the franchise, tax is due in three months.

**Does not include publishing fees.

†Includes publishing fees.

‡California minimum franchise tax fee for corporations that plan on $1,000,000 or less in annual revenues.

All fees subject to change without notice.

Choose From Four Corporation Packages*

Basic Delaware Corporation/LLC Package

$289.00 (includes state filing fees)
$55.00 Savings!

- Prepare and file the Certificate of Incorporation for your corporation (for corporations with up to 1,500 shares of no par value stock).
- Provide registered agent representation for the first calendar year.
- Personalized Standard Corporate Kit including: seal, stock certificates and other important documents to simplify record keeping.
- Essential Corporation Handbook
- Express Service

Complete Delaware Corporation/LLC Package

$389.00 (includes state filing fees)
$70.00 Savings!

Includes everything in the *Basic Delaware Corporation Package,* plus:

- Application for federal tax identification number
- Application for Sub Chapter "S"
- E.A.R.N. membership
- Deluxe Corporate Kit

Basic Non-Delaware Corporation/LLC Package

$235.00 (includes state filing fees)
$59.00 Savings!

- Prepare and file the Certificate of Incorporation for your corporation (includes preliminary name check, in most states).
- Provide registered agent service for the first year.
- Personalized Standard Corporate Kit including: seal, stock certificates and other important documents to simplify record keeping.
- Essential Corporation Handbook
- Express Service

Complete Non-Delaware Corporation/ LLC Package

$335.00 (plus state filing fees)
$74.00 Savings!

Includes everything in the *Basic Non-Delaware Corporation Package,* plus:

- Application for federal tax identification number
- Application for Sub Chapter "S"
- E.A.R.N. membership
- Deluxe Corporate Kit

*Please add $5.00 to package price if TCC is not appointed registered agent.

PROTECT YOUR CORPORATION'S VALUABLE LEGAL STATUS *with an* EASY-TO-USE CORPORATE KIT

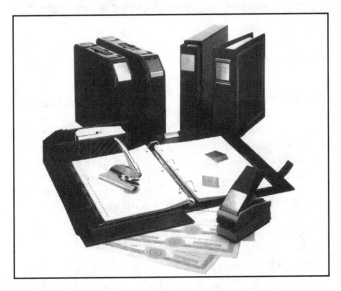

THE COMPLETE PERSONALIZED KIT INCLUDES:

1. Your personalized Corporate Binder with slipcase — protects your corporate records. Your corporate name will be printed on a gold inset on the spine of this handsome binder.

2. Your personalized corporate seal can be kept in a pouch inside your binder. Use your corporate seal for completion of legal documents such as leases and purchase agreements.

Your corporate name and year of incorporation will be permanently etched into the dies which create a raised impression on any paper. *(separately, seal is $25 for up to 45 characters.)*

3. For your permanent records: minutes & by-laws forms printed on three-hole paper for easy record-keeping. Complete forms included for any corporation.

4. 20 personalized stock certificates lithographed with your corporate name on each certificate. Printing also includes number of shares authorized by corporation. *(Additional stock certificates can be purchased. Minimum purchase is 20 @ $30.00 total, extras @ 35¢ each.)*

5. Celluloid tab index separators make it easy to turn to any section in your binder.

6. Stock/transfer ledger — to keep an accurate and complete record of your corporate stock, including stock transfers.

YOUR CHOICE *of* LUXURIOUS CORPORATE ORGANIZERS™

WE HAVE THREE DIFFERENT ORGANIZERS, STANDARD, DELUXE, AND THE ATTACHE ORGANIZER.

Each Corporate Organizer includes your personalized corporate seal,
20 stock certificates, stock transfer ledger, along with sample minutes and bylaws.

STANDARD CORPORATE KIT
$60

This handsome binder organizes the basic kit elements. Your corporate name is engraved on a brass plate on the spine. Makes record-keeping efficient and easy.

DELUXE CORPORATE KIT
$75

The Deluxe Organizer, our most popular, has a distinctive binder and matching slipcase, with your corporate name engraved on a brass plate.

ATTACHE ORGANIZER
$99

Our Attache Organizer is a superb blend of corporate design and function. Instead of a corporate seal, the Attache has a desktop corporate embosser, and comes in an attache carrying case to protect all your corporate essentials.

WE STRIVE FOR TOTAL CUSTOMER SATISFACTION!

If for any reason you are not totally satisfied with your kit,
call us, and we'll exchange the product or give you a full refund.

The Company Corporation cannot furnish personal counsel or advice or answer questions or inquiries that involve interpretations or opinions of law.

The Company Corporation

PROVIDING CORPORATE SERVICES
to BUSINESSES SINCE 1899.

© 1999 The Company Corporation

EXISTING CORPORATIONS THAT WISH TO CHANGE REGISTERED AGENTS

SECTION IX

In order for an existing Delaware corporation to obtain the advantages offered by The Company Corporation, only a simple form is necessary. If a person wishes to change agent to The Company Corporation, the total cost to that corporation the first year is $125.

A specimen of the Delaware form that makes it possible to change registered agents is on the next page.

If you wish to avail yourself of this low-cost service, write or call The Company Corporation for a copy of this form in duplicate. By mailing this form with a check for $125 (payable to The Company Corporation), the certification document will be forwarded to the Secretary of State's office in Dover, Delaware, for filing.

If the corporation has its present office in Kent or Sussex County, prepare an additional copy of the form and add $8 to the amount, making a total of $133.

CERTIFICATE OF CHANGE OF LOCATION OF REGISTERED
OFFICE AND REGISTERED AGENT
OF

_____

The board of directors of the _____,
a corporation of Delaware, on this _____ day of _____ A.D. _____ do hereby
resolve and order that the location of the registered office of this corporation within this State be, and the same
hereby is _____ , in the City of _____ ,
in the County of _____ .

The name of the registered agent therein and in charge thereof upon whom process against this corporation may be served is _____.

The _____ , a corporation of
Delaware, doth hereby certify that the foregoing is a true copy of a resolution adopted by the board of directors
at a meeting held as herein stated.

IN WITNESS WHEREOF, said corporation has caused this certificate to be signed by its President
and attested by its Secretary, and its corporate seal to be hereto affixed, the _____ day of
_____ A.D. _____ .

By _____

(SEAL)   President

ATTEST:

_____

Secretary

STATE FEE FOR QUALIFYING DELAWARE CORPORATIONS IN OTHER STATES

SECTION X

A Delaware corporation that has all or most of its activities in another state is required by law to register—"qualify"—the corporation in that state. Many Delaware corporations fail to register or qualify in other states, but a hazard in not doing so is usually a small fine and payment of a registration fee. Also, the unqualified Delaware corporation may not be able to use the courts of another state. Anyone can write to the Secretary of State in any state to determine its policy on "foreign" corporations that have not registered within that state.

On the following pages are the fees and taxes charged by each state for qualifying a Delaware corporation in another state as a foreign corporation (e.g., if a Minnesota resident has a business in Minnesota and forms a Delaware corporation, that resident is supposed to pay the home state a fee for qualifying a foreign corporation). The qualification procedure for foreign corporations is simple and can be accomplished at any time. A Delaware registered agent can file a copy of the certificate of incorporation with any particular state or states anytime during the life of the corporation. The Company Corporation provides this service to its customers at a processing cost of $90.

There are businesses that legally circumvent paying fees to their home state by establishing that they are "doing business" in Delaware and not in another state. Examples include corporations that receive and ship materials from Delaware, mail order businesses that use a Delaware office, corporations that own property in Delaware, and franchise or licensing companies that transact all contracts and orders in Delaware.

As to out-of-state residents who incorporate in Delaware, the Secretary of State's office in Dover, Delaware, does not notify any other state who the new Delaware corporation owners or shareholders are or in what state they have a business office.

The following chart lists the fees for qualifying a Delaware corporation in another state. The fees charged by the various states are, of course, subject to change. For the latest price list please contact an incorporation specialist at The Company Corporation at 800-818-6082 or visit their Web site at www.incorporate.com.

QUALIFICATION OF A DELAWARE CORPORATION
(One-Time Fee)

Each state's corporation department assesses fees to all corporations foreign to that state.

	For-Profit	Not-for-Profit
Alabama	$220	$ 75
Alaska	350	65
Arizona	175	175
Arkansas	300	300
California	900	30
Colorado	75	75
Connecticut	275	20
District of Columbia	150	50
Florida	70	85
Georgia	170	70
Hawaii	100	50
Idaho	100	30
Illinois	100*	50
Indiana	90	30
Iowa	100	25
Kansas	95	95
Kentucky	90	40
Louisiana	100	100
Maine	180	25
Maryland	50	50
Massachusetts	300	300
Michigan	60	20
Minnesota	200	50
Mississippi	525	125
Missouri	155	15
Montana	120	20
Nebraska	145	23
Nevada	125	35
New Hampshire	85	25
New Jersey	110	110
New Mexico	200	25
New York	225	135
North Carolina	250	100
North Dakota	135	50
Ohio	100	35
Oklahoma	300	300

	For-Profit	Not-for-Profit
Oregon	$440	$40
Pennsylvania	180	180
Rhode Island	165*	50
South Carolina	135	10
South Dakota	90	50
Tennessee	600	600
Texas	750	25
Utah	75	30
Vermont	100	50
Virginia	75*	75
Washington	175	30
West Virginia	360	31*
Wisconsin	100*	no fee
Wyoming	100	10

TOTAL APPROXIMATE QUALIFICATION FEES FOR ALL 50 STATES: $21,000

Either certified copies of certificates of incorporation (also called articles of incorporation) or certificates of good standing are required in most states. Additional copies of a validated certificate of incorporation can be obtained from the Secretary of State's office in Dover, Delaware. The cost is $21 for a certified copy of the certificate of incorporation and $20 for a certificate of good standing.

The Company Corporation will supply you with qualification forms for any state for a nominal fee.

It is always advisable to check with the individual state regarding current fee schedules and regulations.

These states require a certified copy of the corporation's certificate of incorporation and/or a certificate of good standing.

MINIMUM INCORPORATION FEE PAYABLE TO
CORPORATION DEPARTMENT
FOR DOMESTIC CORPORATIONS

SECTION XI

State fees are subject to change. For the latest price list please contact an incorporation specialist at The Company Corporation at 800-818-6082 or visit www.incorporate.com on the Web.

	For-Profit	Not-for-Profit
Alabama	$ 50	$ 45
Alaska	250	50
Arizona	60	40
Arkansas	50	50
California	900	30
Colorado	50	50
Connecticut	275	40
Delaware	70	70
District of Columbia	120	50
Florida	70	70
Georgia	60	60
Hawaii	100	50
Idaho	100	30
Illinois	100	50
Indiana	90	30
Iowa	50	20
Kansas	75	20
Kentucky	50	8
Louisiana	60	60
Maine	105	20
Maryland	40	40
Massachusetts	200	35
Michigan	60	20
Minnesota	135	70
Mississippi	50	50
Missouri	58	15
Montana	70	20
Nebraska	60	25
Nevada	125	25
New Hampshire	85	25
New Jersey	100	50
New Mexico	100	25

	For-Profit	Not-for-Profit
New York	$155	$ 75
North Carolina	125	50
North Dakota	90	40
Ohio	85	25
Oklahoma	50	25
Oregon	50	20
Pennsylvania	100	100
Rhode Island	150	35
South Carolina	235	25
South Dakota	40	20
Tennessee	100	100
Texas	300	25
Utah	75	30
Vermont	75	35
Virginia	75	75
Washington	175	30
West Virginia	192–320	10
Wisconsin	90	35
Wyoming	100	10

COMMON, PREFERRED, VOTING, AND NONVOTING STOCK

SECTION XII

A corporation may issue common or preferred stock. This stock is valued using its determined par value. Par value is simply the minimum the stock is worth at issue.

Stock in a corporation may also have conditions imposed upon it that permit shareholders either to have or not to have voting privileges. Voting or nonvoting stock is usually designated by class, such as class A voting stock and class B nonvoting stock.

Capital stock can also be issued with a stated value paid for in cash or by providing services to the corporation. However, under Delaware's corporate law, no capital is required by a Delaware corporation.

A Delaware corporation may file simple forms with the Secretary of State to add provisions for any of the above types of stock at any time after the corporation is formed.

The forms in this book are directed to a corporation with one class of stock. No-par common stock shares (with voting privileges) of up to 1,500 shares are used in the specimen forms. The filing fees, both initial and continuing, are lowest with this type of format. Also, this kind of approach to the type of stock is simple and services the needs of most small and medium-sized corporations.

On an annual basis, a franchise tax is based on the number of authorized shares of stock, irrespective of par value. It's an unnecessary expense to authorize more shares of stock than that necessary to meet the needs of the corporation. On 1,500 shares the annual tax is only $30. Examples of fees for more shares are $385 on 100,000 shares and $3,535 on 1,000,000 shares.

If, however, it is desirable to issue other classes of stock initially, this can be easily accomplished by adding language to this effect on the certificate of incorporation before it is filed with the state.

The state filing fees for the various types of stock may be obtained from the Secretary of State, Dover, Delaware, or a registered agent.

NO-PAR VERSUS PAR VALUE STOCK

SECTION XIII

Prior to the 1940s, it was customary for most corporations to issue *par value* stock. This meant that each share had a stated value on its face, such as $3, which supposedly represented the amount contributed by the shareholder. However, the value of a share of stock can fluctuate greatly, depending on the overall worth of the corporation, so the par value of the stock becomes misleading and essentially meaningless.

Consequently, another type of stock has become increasingly popular. It is called *no-par value* stock. In all respects but one, *no-par value* and *par value* stock are identical. Under the *no-par* method, a certificate of stock has no stated value but merely indicates the number of shares of *no-par value*. The actual value depends on what an investor is willing to pay, and this judgment is based on a number of factors, including the assets owned by the corporation and the assessment by investors of the corporation's potential profitability.

In addition, the initial filing fee and annual fees to the State of Delaware are lowest when the corporation issues 1,500 shares or less than $75,000 contributed capital. The minimum filing fee is only $15. The type of stock used as examples in this book is no-par. A corporation can convert its no-par value stock to par value stock merely by filing a simple form with the State of Delaware. This form can be forwarded to the Secretary of State by a registered agent, including The Company Corporation, for a nominal filing fee. On the whole, it's usually simpler and less costly to form a Delaware corporation and qualify it to do business in any state with its shares being no-par.

If a corporation becomes successful and authorizes more shares, as well as acquires substantial assets, there can be substantial annual savings in Delaware corporate franchise taxes from converting the no-par value stock to par value stock in certain circumstances, particularly when financing equipment.

To raise capital, a corporation can also issue bonds that are usually an interest-bearing instrument. A *bond* is a form of debt financing many corporations prefer over the sale of stock.

In business judgments involving decisions of this type, it is necessary to consider ideas of professionals such as authors, accountants, life insurance advisers, trust officers, lawyers, and other sources of information.

ONLY ONE OFFICER NEEDED

SECTION XIV

The Delaware corporation needs only one person to hold all the company offices. This same individual may also act as the incorporator and be the entire board of directors. One officer is the legal minimum.

On the other hand, one can have as many directors, officers, or vice presidents as desired. Many corporations find it helpful to invite to their boards of directors capable people who may make substantial contributions to building a successful corporation.

Delaware's current corporate law provides substantially greater flexibility than ever before in many areas, including a reduction in the number of officers from a minimum of three to one. Previously, a corporation had to have at least three officers—president, secretary, and treasurer. The only requirement now is one officer, which enables the corporation to have a person available to sign stock certificates and keep minutes of shareholder and directors' meetings when appropriate.

THE CORPORATE NAME

SECTION XV

The name selected for the new corporation when it is submitted to Delaware will be recorded as long as it is in proper form and no one else is using the same name or one that is too similar prior to the application of the new corporation. The name must contain the word *association, corporation, club, foundation, fund, company, incorporated, institute, society, union, syndicate,* or *limited.*

Delaware also permits words like the ones above in abbreviated form: *Co., Corp.* or *Ltd.* Corporate names must be distinguishable on the records of the state from the names of other corporations formed under the laws of Delaware.

The state provides a service whereby a corporate name can be reserved for a period of 30 days at a charge of $10. Any person can write or call the state directly to avail himself or herself of this service. The Company Corporation provides this service at no charge if appointed registered agent for the corporation. Other registered agents also provide this service, usually at low cost.

Certain property rights under the law accrue to the original owners of a business name or to a corporation that originates a name. These businesses may legally prevent a new firm from using a name that is the same or similar to theirs. If it is planned that the corporation will qualify as a foreign corporation (see Section X) in any state, the corporate name is registered in that state by the act of such a filing. Sometimes a name is available in Delaware but not in another state in which the corporation wishes to qualify. When this occurs, the corporate name may easily be changed. The filing cost is $100 and another $24 to the Recorder of Deeds for a total of $124. The form is available from the Secretary of State, Dover, Delaware. Your registered agent can also assist you at a modest cost.

POTENTIAL PROBLEMS WITH A CORPORATION'S NAME

The effect of a name change varies. Sometimes it just involves new stationery and notification to people with whom the corporation does business. In other cases a substantial cost can be incurred (e.g., when a large inventory of packaged goods bears the name). Some businesses use a name change to a marketing advantage. Many well-established corporations choose to change their name to create a different image or to reflect a different line of products or services than they had when the corporation was formed. It is wise to check the yellow pages of the telephone directory when first planning to use a name to see if similar ones exist.

To reduce the need for a name change, one can contact the corporation department in any state to determine if the name is available before filing the form.

When you know that an existing business uses a certain name, it is prudent not to select a name that is similar regardless of where that business is located. Theoretically, a name can be registered in all 50 states to avoid the possibility of a later name change. However, owners of corporations seldom go to this extent. Also, an unincorporated business somewhere in the United States may be using the same name that the corporation might use, and the right to the name could be challenged at some future time. Therefore, unless one were to search every business name in the nation on a regular basis, there is always the possibility of a need for a name change at some time during the life of a corporation.

OPERATING ANONYMOUSLY IF DESIRED

SECTION XVI

Many people who own Delaware corporations prefer to remain as anonymous as possible.

In Delaware, a corporation need not disclose who its shareholders are to the Secretary of State. If a person does not wish to disclose who the officer(s) and/or director(s) is/are, this may be accomplished in one of three ways.

1. *The first method is by having an acquaintance, friend, or relative of the founder(s) hold all the company offices.* This person does not have to be a shareholder in the corporation. (This person, however, should be advised that he or she could be liable in the event of a tax delinquency or for any illegal action by the founder.)

2. *The second way is to obtain and register a legal, fictitious corporate name.* A fictitious corporate name can be registered in a prothonotary's office in Delaware for $15. Other states have a similar procedure. Then this name can be used for corporate purposes, such as to sign checks and the like. A fictitious name may be registered where you reside with the Recorder of Deeds or a prothonotary's office (or its equivalent, such as a county clerk's office) or in Delaware.

3. *The third method is by the corporation's not filing its annual report with the Secretary of State.* This report is a simple form that is completed once each year. It basically indicates who the corporation's officers are, how many shares of stock have been authorized and other data on the corporation's assets. It lists officer(s), director(s), and number of shares. The state imposes a $50 annual fine on corporations that do not file this report. Many Delaware corporations have elected in the past to pay this annual fine rather than file the report, although the state frowns on this practice. Eventually, the state may revoke your good standing status.

The first and second methods are simpler and less costly, and therefore are recommended over the third for persons who wish to operate the corporation anonymously.

DEDUCTION OF CORPORATE STOCK
LOSS FROM PERSONAL INCOME

SECTION XVII

Section 1244 of the Internal Revenue Code allows a shareholder to deduct certain losses in investment of stock as *ordinary* income losses.

Section 1244 and IRS guidance materials state that if a shareholder in a corporation (a shareholder can be any individual or partnership, but not a corporation, estate, or trust) incurs a loss through sale of his or her stock or if the stock becomes worthless, he or she may deduct the loss up to $50,000 a year ($100,000 on a joint return) from personal income. Normally, a loss on a stock investment is subject to special capital loss limitations under the Internal Revenue Code. There are no disadvantages in qualifying the corporation under Section 1244 if the corporation is eligible, as most small ones are. The potential tax benefits are well worth it, and shareholders have nothing to lose. Also, more investors are attracted to purchasing stock in a corporation when made aware of the Section 1244 provision. Of course, a person should always be cautious in how and to whom stock in a corporation is offered so that federal or state securities laws are not violated. If you are not sure what constitutes a securities offering, contact your business attorney.

This legal arrangement of qualifying a corporation under Section 1244 can be put into effect upon the formation of the corporation by completing simple forms. Nothing has to be filed with the Internal Revenue Service. A copy of Section 1244 of the IRC is on the following pages.

NOTE: Every Subchapter S corporation (see Section XVIII) should qualify under Section 1244. Subchapter S and Section 1244 complement each other in the tax advantages they provide. Operating losses of an S corporation may be passed on to the shareholders currently, whereas a loss in value in the assets of a Section 1244 corporation can be taken as an ordinary loss on the sale and exchange of stock.

SECTION 1244. LOSSES ON SMALL BUSINESS STOCK.

(a) GENERAL RULE.—In the case of an individual, a loss on section 1244 stock issued to such individual or to a partnership which would (but for this section) be treated as a loss from the sale or exchange of a capital asset shall, to the extent provided in this section, be treated as an ordinary loss.

(b) MAXIMUM AMOUNT FOR ANY TAXABLE YEAR.—For any taxable year the aggregate amount treated by the taxpayers by reason of this section as an ordinary loss shall not exceed—

(1) $50,000 or

(2) $100,000 in the case of a husband and wife filing a joint return for such year under section 6013.

(c) SECTION 1244 STOCK DEFINED.—

(1) IN GENERAL.—For purposes of this section, the term "section 1244 stock" means common stock in a domestic corporation if—

(A) at the time such stock is issued, such corporation was a small business corporation,

(B) such stock was issued by such corporation for money or other property (other than stock and securities), and

(C) such corporation, during the period of its 5 most recent taxable years ending before the date and loss on such stock was sustained, derived more than 50 percent of its aggregate gross receipts from sources other than royalties, rents, dividends, interests, annuities, and sales or exchanges of stocks or securities.

(2) RULES FOR APPLICATION OF PARAGRAPH (1)(C).—

(A) Period taken into account with respect to new corporations.—For purposes of paragraph (1)(C), if the corporation has not been in existence for 5 taxable years ending before the date the loss on the stock was sustained, there shall be substituted for such 5-year period—

(i) the period of the corporation's taxable years ending before such date, or

(ii) if the corporation has not been in existence for 1 taxable year ending before such date, the period such corporation has been in existence before such date.

(B) Gross receipts from sales of securities.—For purposes of paragraph (1)(C), gross receipts from the sales or exchanges of stock or securities shall be taken into account only to the extent of gains therefrom.

(C) Nonapplication where deductions exceed gross income.—Paragraph (1)(C) shall not apply with respect to any corporation if, for the period taken into account for purposes of paragraph (1)(C), the amount of the deductions allowed by this chapter (other than by sections 172, 243, 244, and 245) exceeds the amount of gross income.

(3) SMALL BUSINESS CORPORATION DEFINED.—

(A) In general.—For purposes of this section, a corporation shall be treated as a small business corporation if the aggregate amount of money and other property received by the corporation for stock, as a contribution to capital, and as paid-in surplus, does not exceed $1,000,000. The determination under the preceding sentence shall be made as of the time of the issuance of the stock in question but shall include amounts received for such stock and for all stock theretofore issued.

(B) Amount taken into account with respect to property.—For purposes of subparagraph (A), the amount taken into account with respect to any property other than money shall be the amount equal to the adjusted basis to the corporation of such property for determining gain, reduced by any liability to which the property was subject or which was assumed by the corporation. The determination under the preceding sentence shall be made as of the time the property was received by the corporation.

(d) SPECIAL RULES.—

    (1) LIMITATIONS ON AMOUNT OF ORDINARY LOSS.—

        (A) Contributions of property having basis in excess of value.—If—

            (i) section 1244 stock was issued in exchange for property.

            (ii) the basis of such stock in the hands of the taxpayer is determined by reference to the basis in his hands of such property, and

            (iii) the adjusted basis (for determining loss) of such property immediately before the exchange exceeded its fair market value at such time, then in computing the amount of the loss on such stock for purposes of this section the basis of such stock shall be reduced by an amount equal to the excess described in clause (iii).

        (B) Increases in basis.—In computing the amount of the loss on stock for purposes of this section, any increase in the basis of such stock (through contributions to the capital of the corporation, or otherwise) shall be treated as allocable to stock which is not section 1244 stock.

    (2) RECAPITALIZATION, CHANGES IN NAME, ETC.—To the extent provided in regulations prescribed by the Secretary, common stock in a corporation, the basis of which (in the hands of a taxpayer) is determined in whole or in part by reference to the basis in his hands of stock in such corporation which meets the requirements of subsection (c)(1) (other than subparagraph (C) thereof), or which is received in a reorganization described in section 368(a)(1)(F) in exchange for stock which meets such requirements, shall be treated as meeting such requirements. For purposes of paragraphs (1)(C) and (3)(A) of subsection (c), a successor corporation in a reorganization described in section 368(a)(1)(F) shall be treated as the same corporation as its predecessor.

    (3) RELATIONSHIP TO NET OPERATING LOSS DEDUCTION.—For purposes of section 172 (relating to the net operating loss deduction), any amount of loss treated by reason of this section as an ordinary loss shall be treated as attributable to a trade or business of the taxpayer.

    (4) INDIVIDUAL DEFINED.—For purposes of this section, the term individual does not include a trust or estate.

(e) REGULATIONS.—The Secretary shall prescribe such regulations as may be necessary to carry out the purposes of this section.

S CORPORATION—BENEFITS OF CORPORATIONS TAXED AS A PROPRIETORSHIP OR PARTNERSHIP

SECTION XVIII

Forming an S corporation is the best of all worlds: it provides maximum liability protection (and other benefits of incorporation) with only a single tax at individual rates.

A corporation ordinarily pays tax on its profits at corporate rates. Tax is again owed—this time by shareholders—when dividends are paid.

Fortunately, this double taxation can easily be completely eliminated by electing "S" corporation status. As an S corporation, (named after its subchapter in the IRC) earnings are taxed only once. Rather than being taxed to the corporation, profits are included in your personal return and taxed at your individual rate.

If an S corporation has a loss for the year, the loss is passed directly to your tax return and thus reduces your personal tax bill. Losses of a regular C corporation must be retained in the business for a possible later offset against corporate earnings. Shareholders receive no immediate benefit.

S corporation tax breaks are available without loss of limited liability, easy transferability of stock, and other advantages available to a corporation.

A person may call any Internal Revenue office and obtain Form 2553.* This one-page form permits tax filing as an S corporation. Corporations eligible to elect this tax status must meet five simple requirements. The following is an excerpt from Form 2553:

Corporations eligible to elect.—The election may be made only if the corporation is a domestic corporation which meets all eight of the following requirements:

1. It is a domestic corporation.
2. It has no more than 75 shareholders. A husband and wife (and their estates) are treated as one shareholder for this requirement. All other persons are treated as separate shareholders.
3. It has only individuals, estates, or certain trusts as shareholders.
4. It has no nonresident alien shareholders.
5. It has only one class of stock (disregarding differences in voting rights). Generally, a corporation is treated as having only one class of stock if all outstanding shares of the corporation's stock confer identical rights to distribution and liquidation proceeds.
6. It is not one of the following ineligible corporations:
   a. A bank or thrift institution
   b. An insurance company subject to tax under the special rules of Subchapter L of the Internal Revenue Code
   c. A corporation that has elected to be treated as a possessions corporation under section 936
   d. A domestic international sales corporation (DISC) or former DISC.
7. It has a permitted tax year as required by section 1378 or makes a section 444 election to have a tax year other than a permitted tax year. Section 1378 defines a permitted tax

---

*The Company Corporation can provide you with the forms and instructions necessary to obtain S status for your corporation for the nominal fee of $25.

year as a tax year ending December 31, or any other tax year for which the corporation establishes a business purpose to the satisfaction of the IRS.

8. Each shareholder consents as explained in the instructions for Column K (See IRS Form 2553).

A complete set of forms for filing for S corporation status is included in this chapter or can be obtained from any IRS office or by calling IRS Toll-Free Tax Form Hotline (800-TAX-FORMS). These forms are relatively simple and can be completed without professional help. However, any good accountant or attorney can assist in completing this form if desired. The Company Corporation can provide assistance for a fee of $25.

Instructions for Form 2553

(Revised September 1997)

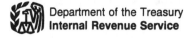
Department of the Treasury
Internal Revenue Service

Election by a Small Business Corporation

Section references are to the Internal Revenue Code unless otherwise noted.

General Instructions

Purpose.— To elect to be an S corporation, a corporation must file Form 2553. The election permits the income of the S corporation to be taxed to the shareholders of the corporation rather than to the corporation itself, except as noted below under **Taxes an S Corporation May Owe.**

Who May Elect.— A corporation may elect to be an S corporation only if it meets all of the following tests:

1. It is a domestic corporation.

2. It has no more than 75 shareholders. A husband and wife (and their estates) are treated as one shareholder for this requirement. All other persons are treated as separate shareholders.

3. Its only shareholders are individuals, estates, certain trusts described in section 1361(c)(2)(A), or, for tax years beginning after 1997, exempt organizations described in section 401(a) or 501(c)(3). Trustees of trusts that want to make the election under section 1361(e)(3) to be an electing small business trust should see Notice 97-12, 1997-3 I.R.B. 11.

Note: *See the instructions for Part III regarding qualified subchapter S trusts.*

4. It has no nonresident alien shareholders.

5. It has only one class of stock (disregarding differences in voting rights). Generally, a corporation is treated as having only one class of stock if all outstanding shares of the corporation's stock confer identical rights to distribution and liquidation proceeds. See Regulations section 1.1361-1(1) for more details.

6. It is not one of the following ineligible corporations:

a. A bank or thrift institution that uses the reserve method of accounting for bad debts under section 585;

b. An insurance company subject to tax under the rules of subchapter L of the Code;

c. A corporation that has elected to be treated as a possessions corporation under section 936; or

d. A domestic international sales corporation (DISC) or former DISC.

7. It has a permitted tax year as required by section 1378 or makes a section 444 election to have a tax year other than a permitted tax year. Section 1378 defines a permitted tax year as a tax year ending December 31, or any other tax year for which the corporation establishes a business purpose to the satisfaction of the IRS. See Part II for details on requesting a fiscal tax year based on a business purpose or on making a section 444 election.

8. Each shareholder consents as explained in the instructions for column K.

See sections 1361, 1362, and 1378 for additional information on the above tests.

An election can be made by a parent S corporation to treat the assets, liabilities, and items of income, deduction, and credit of an eligible wholly-owned subsidiary as those of the parent. For details, see Notice 97-4, 1997-2 I.R.B. 24.

Taxes an S Corporation May Owe.— An S corporation may owe income tax in the following instances:

1. If, at the end of any tax year, the corporation had accumulated earnings and profits, and its passive investment income under section 1362(d)(3) is more than 25% of its gross receipts, the corporation may owe tax on its excess net passive income.

2. A corporation with net recognized built-in gain (as defined in section 1374(d)(2)) may owe tax on its built-in gains.

3. A corporation that claimed investment credit before its first year as an S corporation will be liable for any investment credit recapture tax.

4. A corporation that used the LIFO inventory method for the year immediately preceding its first year as an S corporation may owe an additional tax due to LIFO recapture.

For more details on these taxes, see the Instructions for Form 1120S.

Where To File.— File this election with the Internal Revenue Service Center listed below.

If the corporation's principal business, office, or agency is located in	Use the following Internal Revenue Service Center address
New Jersey, New York (New York City and counties of Nassau, Rockland, Suffolk, and Westchester)	Holtsville, NY 00501
New York (all other counties), Connecticut, Maine, Massachusetts, New Hampshire, Rhode Island, Vermont	Andover, MA 05501
Florida, Georgia, South Carolina	Atlanta, GA 39901
Indiana, Kentucky, Michigan, Ohio, West Virginia	Cincinnati, OH 45999
Kansas, New Mexico, Oklahoma, Texas	Austin, TX 73301
Alaska, Arizona, California (counties of Alpine, Amador, Butte, Calaveras, Colusa, Contra Costa, Del Norte, El Dorado, Glenn, Humboldt, Lake, Lassen, Marin, Mendocino, Modoc, Napa, Nevada, Placer, Plumas, Sacramento, San Joaquin, Shasta, Sierra, Siskiyou, Solano, Sonoma, Sutter, Tehama, Trinity, Yolo, and Yuba), Colorado, Idaho, Montana, Nebraska, Nevada, North Dakota, Oregon, South Dakota, Utah, Washington, Wyoming	Ogden, UT 84201
California (all other counties), Hawaii	Fresno, CA 93888
Illinois, Iowa, Minnesota, Missouri, Wisconsin	Kansas City, MO 64999
Alabama, Arkansas, Louisiana, Mississippi, North Carolina, Tennessee	Memphis, TN 37501
Delaware, District of Columbia, Maryland, Pennsylvania, Virginia	Philadelphia, PA 19255

When To Make the Election.— Complete and file Form 2553 **(a)** at any time before the 16th day of the 3rd month of the tax year, if filed during the tax year the election is to take effect, or **(b)** at any time during the preceding tax year. An election made no later than 2 months and 15 days after the beginning of a tax year that is less than 2½ months long is treated as timely made for that tax year. An election made after the 15th day of the 3rd month but before the end of the tax year is effective for the next year. For example, if a calendar tax year

corporation makes the election in April 1998, it is effective for the corporation's 1999 calendar tax year.

However, an election made after the due date will be accepted as timely filed if the corporation can show that the failure to file on time was due to reasonable cause. To request relief for a late election, the corporation generally must request a private letter ruling and pay a user fee in accordance with Rev. Proc. 97-1, 1997-1 I.R.B. 11 (or its successor). But if the election is filed within 6 months of its due date and the original due date for filing the corporation's initial Form 1120S has not passed, the ruling and user fee requirements do not apply. To request relief in this case, write "FILED PURSUANT TO REV. PROC. 97-40" at the top of page 1 of Form 2553, attach a statement explaining the reason for failing to file the election on time, and file Form 2553 as otherwise instructed. See Rev. Proc. 97-40, 1997-33 I.R.B. 50, for more details.

See Regulations section 1.1362-6(b)(3)(iii) for how to obtain relief for an inadvertent invalid election if the corporation filed a timely election, but one or more shareholders did not file a timely consent.

Acceptance or Nonacceptance of Election.— The service center will notify the corporation if its election is accepted and when it will take effect. The corporation will also be notified if its election is not accepted. The corporation should generally receive a determination on its election within 60 days after it has filed Form 2553. If box Q1 in Part II is checked on page 2, the corporation will receive a ruling letter from the IRS in Washington, DC, that either approves or denies the selected tax year. When box Q1 is checked, it will generally take an additional 90 days for the Form 2553 to be accepted.

Do not file Form 1120S for any tax year before the year the election takes effect. If the corporation is now required to file **Form 1120,** U.S. Corporation Income Tax Return, or any other applicable tax return, continue filing it until the election takes effect.

Care should be exercised to ensure that the IRS receives the election. If the corporation is not notified of acceptance or nonacceptance of its election within 3 months of date of filing (date mailed), or within 6 months if box Q1 is checked, take follow-up action by corresponding with the service center where the corporation filed the election. If the IRS questions whether Form 2553 was filed, an acceptable proof of filing is **(a)** certified or registered mail receipt (timely filed) from the U.S. Postal Service or its equivalent from a designated private delivery service (see Notice 97-26, 1997-17 I.R.B. 6); **(b)** Form 2553 with accepted stamp; **(c)** Form 2553 with stamped IRS received date; or **(d)** IRS letter stating that Form 2553 has been accepted.

End of Election.— Once the election is made, it stays in effect until it is terminated. If the election is terminated in a tax year beginning after 1996, the corporation (or a successor corporation) can make another election on Form 2553 only with IRS consent for any tax year before the 5th tax year after the first tax year in which the termination took effect. See Regulations section 1.1362-5 for more details.

Cat. No. 49978N

Specific Instructions

Part I

Note: *All corporations must complete Part I.*

Name and Address of Corporation.— Enter the true corporate name as stated in the corporate charter or other legal document creating it. If the corporation's mailing address is the same as someone else's, such as a shareholder's, enter "c/o" and this person's name following the name of the corporation. Include the suite, room, or other unit number after the street address. If the Post Office does not deliver to the street address and the corporation has a P.O. box, show the box number instead of the street address. If the corporation changed its name or address after applying for its employer identification number, be sure to check the box in item G of Part I.

Item A. Employer Identification Number (EIN).— If the corporation has applied for an EIN but has not received it, enter "applied for." If the corporation does not have an EIN, it should apply for one on **Form SS-4,** Application for Employer Identification Number. You can order Form SS-4 by calling 1-800-TAX-FORM (1-800-829-3676).

Item D. Effective Date of Election.— Enter the beginning effective date (month, day, year) of the tax year requested for the S corporation. Generally, this will be the beginning date of the tax year for which the ending effective date is required to be shown in item I, Part I. For a new corporation (first year the corporation exists) it will generally be the date required to be shown in item H, Part I. The tax year of a new corporation starts on the date that it has shareholders, acquires assets, or begins doing business, whichever happens first. If the effective date for item D for a newly formed corporation is later than the date in item H, the corporation should file Form 1120 or Form 1120-A for the tax period between these dates.

Column K. Shareholders' Consent Statement.— Each shareholder who owns (or is deemed to own) stock at the time the election is made must consent to the election. If the election is made during the corporation's tax year for which it first takes effect, any person who held stock at any time during the part of that year that occurs before the election is made, must consent to the election, even though the person may have sold or transferred his or her stock before the election is made.

An election made during the first 2½ months of the tax year is effective for the following tax year if any person who held stock in the corporation during the part of the tax year before the election was made, and who did not hold stock at the time the election was made, did not consent to the election.

Each shareholder consents by signing and dating in column K or signing and dating a separate consent statement described below. The following special rules apply in determining who must sign the consent statement.

• If a husband and wife have a community interest in the stock or in the income from it, both must consent.

• Each tenant in common, joint tenant, and tenant by the entirety must consent.

• A minor's consent is made by the minor, legal representative of the minor or by a natural or adoptive parent of the minor if no legal representative has been appointed.

• The consent of an estate is made by the executor or administrator.

• The consent of an electing small business trust is made by the trustee.

• If the stock is owned by a trust (other than an electing small business trust), the deemed owner of the trust must consent. See section 1361(c)(2) for details regarding trusts that are permitted to be shareholders and rules for determining who is the deemed owner.

*Continuation sheet or separate consent statement.—*If you need a continuation sheet or use a separate consent statement, attach it to Form 2553. The separate consent statement must contain the name, address, and EIN of the corporation and the shareholder information requested in columns J through N of Part I. If you want, you may combine all the shareholders' consents in one statement.

Column L.— Enter the number of shares of stock each shareholder owns and the dates the stock was acquired. If the election is made during the corporation's tax year for which it first takes effect, do not list the shares of stock for those shareholders who sold or transferred all of their stock before the election was made. However, these shareholders must still consent to the election for it to be effective for the tax year.

Column M.— Enter the social security number of each shareholder who is an individual. Enter the EIN of each shareholder that is an estate, a qualified trust, or an exempt organization.

Column N.— Enter the month and day that each shareholder's tax year ends. If a shareholder is changing his or her tax year, enter the tax year the shareholder is changing to, and attach an explanation indicating the present tax year and the basis for the change (e.g., automatic revenue procedure or letter ruling request).

Signature.— Form 2553 must be signed by the president, treasurer, assistant treasurer, chief accounting officer, or other corporate officer (such as tax officer) authorized to sign.

Part II

Complete Part II if you selected a tax year ending on any date other than December 31 (other than a 52-53-week tax year ending with reference to the month of December).

Box P1.— Attach a statement showing separately for each month the amount of gross receipts for the most recent 47 months as required by section 4.03(3) of Rev. Proc. 87-32, 1987-2 C.B. 396. A corporation that does not have a 47-month period of gross receipts cannot establish a natural business year under section 4.01(1).

Box Q1.— For examples of an acceptable business purpose for requesting a fiscal tax year, see Rev. Rul. 87-57, 1987-2 C.B. 117.

In addition to a statement showing the business purpose for the requested fiscal year, you must attach the other information necessary to meet the ruling request requirements of Rev. Proc. 97-1 (or its successor). Also attach a statement that shows separately the amount of gross receipts from sales or services (and inventory costs, if applicable) for each of the 36 months preceding the effective date of the election to be an S corporation. If the corporation has been in existence for fewer than 36 months, submit figures for the period of existence.

If you check box Q1, you will be charged a $250 user fee (subject to change). Do not pay the fee when filing Form 2553. The service center will send Form 2553 to the IRS in Washington, DC, who, in turn, will notify the corporation that the fee is due.

Box Q2.— If the corporation makes a back-up section 444 election for which it is qualified, then the election will take effect in the event the business purpose request is not approved. In some cases, the tax year requested under the back-up section 444 election may be different than the tax year requested under business purpose. See **Form 8716,** Election To Have a Tax Year Other Than a Required Tax Year, for details on making a back-up section 444 election.

Boxes Q2 and R2.— If the corporation is not qualified to make the section 444 election after making the item Q2 back-up section 444 election or indicating its intention to make the election in item R1, and therefore it later files a calendar year return, it should write "Section 444 Election Not Made" in the top left corner of the first calendar year Form 1120S it files.

Part III

Certain qualified subchapter S trusts (QSSTs) may make the QSST election required by section 1361(d)(2) in Part III. Part III may be used to make the QSST election only if corporate stock has been transferred to the trust on or before the date on which the corporation makes its election to be an S corporation. However, a statement can be used instead of Part III to make the election.

Note: *Use Part III **only** if you make the election in Part I (i.e., Form 2553 cannot be filed with only Part III completed).*

The deemed owner of the QSST must also consent to the S corporation election in column K, page 1, of Form 2553. See section 1361(c)(2).

Paperwork Reduction Act Notice.— We ask for the information on this form to carry out the Internal Revenue laws of the United States. You are required to give us the information. We need it to ensure that you are complying with these laws and to allow us to figure and collect the right amount of tax.

You are not required to provide the information requested on a form that is subject to the Paperwork Reduction Act unless the form displays a valid OMB control number. Books or records relating to a form or its instructions must be retained as long as their contents may become material in the administration of any Internal Revenue law. Generally, tax returns and return information are confidential, as required by section 6103.

The time needed to complete and file this form will depend on individual circumstances. The estimated average time is:

Recordkeeping	6 hr., 28 min.
Learning about the law or the form	3 hr., 41 min.
Preparing, copying, assembling, and sending the form to the IRS	3 hr., 56 min.

If you have comments concerning the accuracy of these time estimates or suggestions for making this form simpler, we would be happy to hear from you. You can write to the Tax Forms Committee, Western Area Distribution Center, Rancho Cordova, CA 95743-0001. **DO NOT** send the form to this address. Instead, see **Where To File** on page 1.

Printed on recycled paper   *U.S. Government Printing Office: 1997 - 432-190/60241

Form **2553**

(Rev. September 1997)

Department of the Treasury
Internal Revenue Service

Election by a Small Business Corporation

(Under section 1362 of the Internal Revenue Code)

▶ For Paperwork Reduction Act Notice, see page 2 of instructions.

▶ See separate instructions.

OMB No. 1545-0146

Notes: 1. *This election to be an S corporation can be accepted only if all the tests are met under Who May Elect on page 1 of the instructions; all signatures in Parts I and III are originals (no photocopies); and the exact name and address of the corporation and other required form information are provided.*

2. *Do not file Form 1120S, U.S. Income Tax Return for an S Corporation, for any tax year before the year the election takes effect.*

3. *If the corporation was in existence before the effective date of this election, see Taxes an S Corporation May Owe on page 1 of the instructions.*

Part I	Election Information

	Name of corporation (see instructions)	**A** Employer identification number
Please Type or Print	Number, street, and room or suite no. (If a P.O. box, see instructions.)	**B** Date incorporated
	City or town, state, and ZIP code	**C** State of incorporation

D Election is to be effective for tax year beginning (month, day, year) . . . . ▶ / /

E Name and title of officer or legal representative who the IRS may call for more information

F Telephone number of officer, or legal representative

( )

G If the corporation changed its name or address after applying for the EIN shown in **A** above, check this box . . . . ▶ ☐

H If this election takes effect for the first tax year the corporation exists, enter month, day, and year of the **earliest** of the following: (1) date the corporation first had shareholders, (2) date the corporation first had assets, or (3) date the corporation began doing business . . . . ▶ / /

I Selected tax year: Annual return will be filed for tax year ending (month and day) ▶...............................

If the tax year ends on any date other than December 31, except for an automatic 52-53-week tax year ending with reference to the month of December, you **must** complete Part II on the back. If the date you enter is the ending date of an automatic 52-53-week tax year, write "52-53-week year" to the right of the date. See Temporary Regulations section 1.441-2T(e)(3).

J Name and address of each shareholder; shareholder's spouse having a community property interest in the corporation's stock; and each tenant in common, joint tenant, and tenant by the entirety. (A husband and wife (and their estates) are counted as one shareholder in determining the number of shareholders without regard to the manner in which the stock is owned.)	K Shareholders' Consent Statement. Under penalties of perjury, we declare that we consent to the election of the above-named corporation to be an S corporation under section 1362(a) and that we have examined this consent statement, including accompanying schedules and statements, and to the best of our knowledge and belief, it is true, correct, and complete. We understand our consent is binding and may not be withdrawn after the corporation has made a valid election. (Shareholders sign and date below.)		L Stock owned		M Social security number or employer identification number (see instructions)	N Share-holder's tax year ends (month and day)
	Signature	Date	Number of shares	Dates acquired		

Under penalties of perjury, I declare that I have examined this election, including accompanying schedules and statements, and to the best of my knowledge and belief, it is true, correct, and complete.

Signature of officer ▶   Title ▶   Date ▶

See Parts II and III on back.   Cat. No. 18629R   Form **2553** (Rev. 9-97)

Form 2553 (Rev. 9-97)

Part II   Selection of Fiscal Tax Year (All corporations using this part must complete item O and item P, Q, or R.)

O   Check the applicable box to indicate whether the corporation is:

   1. ☐ A new corporation adopting the tax year entered in item I, Part I.

   2. ☐ An existing corporation retaining the tax year entered in item I, Part I.

   3. ☐ An existing corporation changing to the tax year entered in item I, Part I.

P   Complete item P if the corporation is using the expeditious approval provisions of Rev. Proc. 87-32, 1987-2 C.B. 396, to request **(1)** a natural business year (as defined in section 4.01(1) of Rev. Proc. 87-32) or **(2)** a year that satisfies the ownership tax year test in section 4.01(2) of Rev. Proc. 87-32. Check the applicable box below to indicate the representation statement the corporation is making as required under section 4 of Rev. Proc. 87-32.

   1. Natural Business Year ▶ ☐ I represent that the corporation is retaining or changing to a tax year that coincides with its natural business year as defined in section 4.01(1) of Rev. Proc. 87-32 and as verified by its satisfaction of the requirements of section 4.02(1) of Rev. Proc. 87-32. In addition, if the corporation is changing to a natural business year as defined in section 4.01(1), I further represent that such tax year results in less deferral of income to the owners than the corporation's present tax year. I also represent that the corporation is not described in section 3.01(2) of Rev. Proc. 87-32. (See instructions for additional information that must be attached.)

   2. Ownership Tax Year ▶ ☐ I represent that shareholders holding more than half of the shares of the stock (as of the first day of the tax year to which the request relates) of the corporation have the same tax year or are concurrently changing to the tax year that the corporation adopts, retains, or changes to per item I, Part I. I also represent that the corporation is not described in section 3.01(2) of Rev. Proc. 87-32.

Note: *If you do not use item P and the corporation wants a fiscal tax year, complete either item Q or R below. Item Q is used to request a fiscal tax year based on a business purpose and to make a back-up section 444 election. Item R is used to make a regular section 444 election.*

Q   Business Purpose—To request a fiscal tax year based on a business purpose, you must check box Q1 and pay a user fee. See instructions for details. You may also check box Q2 and/or box Q3.

   1. Check here ▶ ☐ if the fiscal year entered in item I, Part I, is requested under the provisions of section 6.03 of Rev. Proc. 87-32. Attach to Form 2553 a statement showing the business purpose for the requested fiscal year. See instructions for additional information that must be attached.

   2. Check here ▶ ☐ to show that the corporation intends to make a back-up section 444 election in the event the corporation's business purpose request is not approved by the IRS. (See instructions for more information.)

   3. Check here ▶ ☐ to show that the corporation agrees to adopt or change to a tax year ending December 31 if necessary for the IRS to accept this election for S corporation status in the event (1) the corporation's business purpose request is not approved and the corporation makes a back-up section 444 election, but is ultimately not qualified to make a section 444 election, or (2) the corporation's business purpose request is not approved and the corporation did not make a back-up section 444 election.

R   Section 444 Election—To make a section 444 election, you must check box R1 and you may also check box R2.

   1. Check here ▶ ☐ to show the corporation will make, if qualified, a section 444 election to have the fiscal tax year shown in item I, Part I. To make the election, you must complete **Form 8716**, Election To Have a Tax Year Other Than a Required Tax Year, and either attach it to Form 2553 or file it separately.

   2. Check here ▶ ☐ to show that the corporation agrees to adopt or change to a tax year ending December 31 if necessary for the IRS to accept this election for S corporation status in the event the corporation is ultimately not qualified to make a section 444 election.

Part III   Qualified Subchapter S Trust (QSST) Election Under Section 1361(d)(2)*

Income beneficiary's name and address	Social security number
Trust's name and address	Employer identification number

Date on which stock of the corporation was transferred to the trust (month, day, year) . . . . ▶   /   /

In order for the trust named above to be a QSST and thus a qualifying shareholder of the S corporation for which this Form 2553 is filed, I hereby make the election under section 1361(d)(2). Under penalties of perjury, I certify that the trust meets the definitional requirements of section 1361(d)(3) and that all other information provided in Part III is true, correct, and complete.

Signature of income beneficiary or signature and title of legal representative or other qualified person making the election	Date

*Use Part III to make the QSST election only if stock of the corporation has been transferred to the trust on or before the date on which the corporation makes its election to be an S corporation. The QSST election must be made and filed separately if stock of the corporation is transferred to the trust after the date on which the corporation makes the S election.

✿ Printed on recycled paper   *U.S. Government Printing Office: 1997 - 432-190/60239

Form **SS-4**

(Rev. February 1998)

Department of the Treasury
Internal Revenue Service

Application for Employer Identification Number

(For use by employers, corporations, partnerships, trusts, estates, churches, government agencies, certain individuals, and others. See instructions.)

▶ Keep a copy for your records.

EIN

OMB No. 1545-0003

Please type or print clearly.

1 Name of applicant (legal name) (see instructions)

2 Trade name of business (if different from name on line 1)

3 Executor, trustee, "care of" name

4a Mailing address (street address) (room, apt., or suite no.)

5a Business address (if different from address on lines 4a and 4b)

4b City, state, and ZIP code

5b City, state, and ZIP code

6 County and state where principal business is located

7 Name of principal officer, general partner, grantor, owner, or trustor—SSN or ITIN may be required (see instructions) ▶

8a Type of entity (Check only one box.) (see instructions)

Caution: *If applicant is a limited liability company, see the instructions for line 8a.*

☐ Sole proprietor (SSN) _____
☐ Partnership
☐ REMIC
☐ State/local government
☐ Church or church-controlled organization
☐ Other nonprofit organization (specify) ▶ _____
☐ Other (specify) ▶

☐ Personal service corp.
☐ National Guard
☐ Farmers' cooperative

☐ Estate (SSN of decedent) _____
☐ Plan administrator (SSN) _____
☐ Other corporation (specify) ▶ _____
☐ Trust
☐ Federal government/military
(enter GEN if applicable) _____

8b If a corporation, name the state or foreign country (if applicable) where incorporated

State

Foreign country

9 Reason for applying (Check only one box.) (see instructions)
☐ Started new business (specify type) ▶ _____
_____
☐ Hired employees (Check the box and see line 12.)
☐ Created a pension plan (specify type) ▶

☐ Banking purpose (specify purpose) ▶ _____
☐ Changed type of organization (specify new type) ▶ _____
☐ Purchased going business
☐ Created a trust (specify type) ▶ _____
☐ Other (specify) ▶

10 Date business started or acquired (month, day, year) (see instructions)

11 Closing month of accounting year (see instructions)

12 First date wages or annuities were paid or will be paid (month, day, year). **Note:** *If applicant is a withholding agent, enter date income will first be paid to nonresident alien. (month, day, year)* . . . . ▶

13 Highest number of employees expected in the next 12 months. **Note:** *If the applicant does not expect to have any employees during the period, enter -0-. (see instructions)* . . . . ▶

Nonagricultural	Agricultural	Household

14 Principal activity (see instructions) ▶

15 Is the principal business activity manufacturing? . . . . ☐ Yes ☐ No
If "Yes," principal product and raw material used ▶

16 To whom are most of the products or services sold? Please check one box. ☐ Business (wholesale)
☐ Public (retail) ☐ Other (specify) ▶ ☐ N/A

17a Has the applicant ever applied for an employer identification number for this or any other business? . . . . ☐ Yes ☐ No
Note: *If "Yes," please complete lines 17b and 17c.*

17b If you checked "Yes" on line 17a, give applicant's legal name and trade name shown on prior application, if different from line 1 or 2 above.
Legal name ▶ Trade name ▶

17c Approximate date when and city and state where the application was filed. Enter previous employer identification number if known.

Approximate date when filed (mo., day, year)	City and state where filed	Previous EIN

Under penalties of perjury, I declare that I have examined this application, and to the best of my knowledge and belief, it is true, correct, and complete.

Business telephone number (include area code)

Fax telephone number (include area code)

Name and title (Please type or print clearly.) ▶

Signature ▶

Date ▶

Note: *Do not write below this line. For official use only.*

Please leave blank ▶	Geo.	Ind.	Class	Size	Reason for applying

For Paperwork Reduction Act Notice, see page 4.

Cat. No. 16055N

Form **SS-4** (Rev. 2-98)

General Instructions

Section references are to the Internal Revenue Code unless otherwise noted.

Purpose of Form

Use Form SS-4 to apply for an employer identification number (EIN). An EIN is a nine-digit number (for example, 12-3456789) assigned to sole proprietors, corporations, partnerships, estates, trusts, and other entities for tax filing and reporting purposes. The information you provide on this form will establish your business tax account.

Caution: *An EIN is for use in connection with your business activities only. Do **NOT** use your EIN in place of your social security number (SSN).*

Who Must File

You must file this form if you have not been assigned an EIN before and:

● You pay wages to one or more employees including household employees.

● You are required to have an EIN to use on any return, statement, or other document, even if you are not an employer.

● You are a withholding agent required to withhold taxes on income, other than wages, paid to a nonresident alien (individual, corporation, partnership, etc.). A withholding agent may be an agent, broker, fiduciary, manager, tenant, or spouse, and is required to file **Form 1042,** Annual Withholding Tax Return for U.S. Source Income of Foreign Persons.

● You file **Schedule C,** Profit or Loss From Business, **Schedule C-EZ,** Net Profit From Business, or **Schedule F,** Profit or Loss From Farming, of **Form 1040,** U.S. Individual Income Tax Return, **and** have a Keogh plan or are required to file excise, employment, or alcohol, tobacco, or firearms returns.

The following must use EINs even if they do not have any employees:

● State and local agencies who serve as tax reporting agents for public assistance recipients, under Rev. Proc. 80-4, 1980-1 C.B. 581, should obtain a separate EIN for this reporting. See **Household employer** on page 3.

● Trusts, except the following:

    1. Certain grantor-owned trusts. (See the **Instructions for Form 1041.**)

    2. Individual Retirement Arrangement (IRA) trusts, unless the trust has to file **Form 990-T,** Exempt Organization Business Income Tax Return. (See the **Instructions for Form 990-T.**)

● Estates

● Partnerships

● REMICs (real estate mortgage investment conduits) (See the **Instructions for Form 1066,** U.S. Real Estate Mortgage Investment Conduit Income Tax Return.)

● Corporations

● Nonprofit organizations (churches, clubs, etc.)

● Farmers' cooperatives

● Plan administrators (A plan administrator is the person or group of persons specified as the administrator by the instrument under which the plan is operated.)

When To Apply for a New EIN

New Business. If you become the new owner of an existing business, **do not** use the EIN of the former owner. IF YOU ALREADY HAVE AN EIN, USE THAT NUMBER. If you do not have an EIN, apply for one on this form. If you become the "owner" of a corporation by acquiring its stock, use the corporation's EIN.

Changes in Organization or Ownership. If you already have an EIN, you may need to get a new one if either the organization or ownership of your business changes. If you incorporate a sole proprietorship or form a partnership, you must get a new EIN. However, **do not** apply for a new EIN if:

● You change only the name of your business,

● You elected on **Form 8832,** Entity Classification Election, to change the way the entity is taxed, or

● A partnership terminates because at least 50% of the total interests in partnership capital and profits were sold or exchanged within a 12-month period. (See Regulations section 301.6109-1(d)(2)(iii).) The EIN for the terminated partnership should continue to be used. This rule applies to terminations occurring after May 8, 1997. If the termination took place after May 8, 1996, and before May 9, 1997, a new EIN must be obtained for the new partnership unless the partnership and its partners are consistent in using the old EIN.

Note: *If you are electing to be an "S corporation," be sure you file **Form 2553,** Election by a Small Business Corporation.*

File Only One Form SS-4. File only one Form SS-4, regardless of the number of businesses operated or trade names under which a business operates. However, each corporation in an affiliated group must file a separate application.

EIN Applied for, But Not Received. If you do not have an EIN by the time a return is due, write "Applied for" and the date you applied in the space shown for the number. **Do not** show your social security number (SSN) as an EIN on returns.

If you do not have an EIN by the time a tax deposit is due, send your payment to the Internal Revenue Service Center for your filing area. (See **Where To Apply** below.) Make your check or money order payable to Internal Revenue Service and show your name (as shown on Form SS-4), address, type of tax, period covered, and date you applied for an EIN. Send an explanation with the deposit.

For more information about EINs, see **Pub. 583,** Starting a Business and Keeping Records, and **Pub. 1635,** Understanding your EIN.

How To Apply

You can apply for an EIN either by mail or by telephone. You can get an EIN immediately by calling the Tele-TIN number for the service center for your state, or you can send the completed Form SS-4 directly to the service center to receive your EIN by mail.

Application by Tele-TIN. Under the Tele-TIN program, you can receive your EIN by telephone and use it immediately to file a return or make a payment. To receive an EIN by telephone, complete Form SS-4, then call the Tele-TIN number listed for your state under **Where To Apply.** The person making the call must be authorized to sign the form. (See **Signature** on page 4.)

An IRS representative will use the information from the Form SS-4 to establish your account and assign you an EIN. Write the number you are given on the upper right corner of the form and sign and date it.

*Mail or fax (facsimile) the signed SS-4 **within 24 hours** to the Tele-TIN Unit at the service center address for your state. The IRS representative will give you the fax number. The fax numbers are also listed in Pub. 1635.*

Taxpayer representatives can receive their client's EIN by telephone if they first send a fax of a completed **Form 2848,** Power of Attorney and Declaration of Representative, or **Form 8821,** Tax Information Authorization, to the Tele-TIN unit. The Form 2848 or Form 8821 will be used solely to release the EIN to the representative authorized on the form.

Application by Mail. Complete Form SS-4 at least 4 to 5 weeks before you will need an EIN. Sign and date the application and mail it to the service center address for your state. You will receive your EIN in the mail in approximately 4 weeks.

Where To Apply

The Tele-TIN numbers listed below will involve a long-distance charge to callers outside of the local calling area and can be used only to apply for an EIN. THE NUMBERS MAY CHANGE WITHOUT NOTICE. Call 1-800-829-1040 to verify a number or to ask about the status of an application by mail.

If your principal business, office or agency, or legal residence in the case of an individual, is located in:	Call the Tele-TIN number shown or file with the Internal Revenue Service Center at:
Florida, Georgia, South Carolina	Attn: Entity Control Atlanta, GA 39901 770-455-2360
New Jersey, New York City and counties of Nassau, Rockland, Suffolk, and Westchester	Attn: Entity Control Holtsville, NY 00501 516-447-4955
New York (all other counties), Connecticut, Maine, Massachusetts, New Hampshire, Rhode Island, Vermont	Attn: Entity Control Andover, MA 05501 978-474-9717
Illinois, Iowa, Minnesota, Missouri, Wisconsin	Attn: Entity Control Stop 6800 2306 E. Bannister Rd. Kansas City, MO 64999 816-926-5999
Delaware, District of Columbia, Maryland, Pennsylvania, Virginia	Attn: Entity Control Philadelphia, PA 19255 215-516-6999
Indiana, Kentucky, Michigan, Ohio, West Virginia	Attn: Entity Control Cincinnati, OH 45999 606-292-5467

Kansas, New Mexico, Oklahoma, Texas	Attn: Entity Control Austin, TX 73301 512-460-7843
Alaska, Arizona, California (counties of Alpine, Amador, Butte, Calaveras, Colusa, Contra Costa, Del Norte, El Dorado, Glenn, Humboldt, Lake, Lassen, Marin, Mendocino, Modoc, Napa, Nevada, Placer, Plumas, Sacramento, San Joaquin, Shasta, Sierra, Siskiyou, Solano, Sonoma, Sutter, Tehama, Trinity, Yolo, and Yuba), Colorado, Idaho, Montana, Nebraska, Nevada, North Dakota, Oregon, South Dakota, Utah, Washington, Wyoming	Attn: Entity Control Mail Stop 6271 P.O. Box 9941 Ogden, UT 84201 801-620-7645
California (all other counties), Hawaii	Attn: Entity Control Fresno, CA 93888 209-452-4010
Alabama, Arkansas, Louisiana, Mississippi, North Carolina, Tennessee	Attn: Entity Control Memphis, TN 37501 901-546-3920
If you have no legal residence, principal place of business, or principal office or agency in any state	Attn: Entity Control Philadelphia, PA 19255 215-516-6999

Specific Instructions

The instructions that follow are for those items that are not self-explanatory. Enter N/A (nonapplicable) on the lines that do not apply.

Line 1. Enter the legal name of the entity applying for the EIN exactly as it appears on the social security card, charter, or other applicable legal document.

Individuals. Enter your first name, middle initial, and last name. If you are a sole proprietor, enter your individual name, not your business name. Enter your business name on line 2. Do not use abbreviations or nicknames on line 1.

Trusts. Enter the name of the trust.

Estate of a decedent. Enter the name of the estate.

Partnerships. Enter the legal name of the partnership as it appears in the partnership agreement. **Do not** list the names of the partners on line 1. See the specific instructions for line 7.

Corporations. Enter the corporate name as it appears in the corporation charter or other legal document creating it.

Plan administrators. Enter the name of the plan administrator. A plan administrator who already has an EIN should use that number.

Line 2. Enter the trade name of the business if different from the legal name. The trade name is the "doing business as" name.

Note: *Use the full legal name on line 1 on all tax returns filed for the entity. However, if you enter a trade name on line 2 and choose to use the trade name instead of the legal name, enter the trade name on all returns you file. To prevent processing delays and errors, always use either the legal name only or the trade name only on all tax returns.*

Line 3. Trusts enter the name of the trustee. Estates enter the name of the executor, administrator, or other fiduciary. If the entity applying has a designated person to receive tax information, enter that person's name as the "care of" person. Print or type the first name, middle initial, and last name.

Line 7. Enter the first name, middle initial, last name, and SSN of a principal officer if the business is a corporation; of a general partner if a partnership; of the owner of a single member entity that is disregarded as an entity separate from its owner; or of a grantor, owner, or trustor if a trust. If the person in question is an alien individual with a previously assigned individual taxpayer identification number (ITIN), enter the ITIN in the space provided, instead of an SSN. You are not required to enter an SSN or ITIN if the reason you are applying for an EIN is to make an entity classification election (see Regulations section 301.7701-1 through 301.7701-3), and you are a nonresident alien with no effectively connected income from sources within the United States.

Line 8a. Check the box that best describes the type of entity applying for the EIN. If you are an alien individual with an ITIN previously assigned to you, enter the ITIN in place of a requested SSN.

Caution: *This is not an election for a tax classification of an entity. See "Limited liability company" below.*

If not specifically mentioned, check the "Other" box, enter the type of entity and the type of return that will be filed (for example, common trust fund, Form 1065). Do not enter N/A. If you are an alien individual applying for an EIN, see the **Line 7** instructions above.

Sole proprietor. Check this box if you file Schedule C, C-EZ, or F (Form 1040) and have a Keogh plan, or are required to file excise, employment, or alcohol, tobacco, or firearms returns, or are a payer of gambling

winnings. Enter your SSN (or ITIN) in the space provided. If you are a nonresident alien with no effectively connected income from sources within the United States, you do not need to enter an SSN or ITIN.

REMIC. Check this box if the entity has elected to be treated as a real estate mortgage investment conduit (REMIC). See the **Instructions for Form 1066** for more information.

Other nonprofit organization. Check this box if the nonprofit organization is other than a church or church-controlled organization and specify the type of nonprofit organization (for example, an educational organization).

If the organization also seeks tax-exempt status, you must file either **Package 1023,** Application for Recognition of Exemption, or **Package 1024,** Application for Recognition of Exemption Under Section 501(a). Get **Pub. 557,** Tax Exempt Status for Your Organization, for more information.

Group exemption number (GEN). If the organization is covered by a group exemption letter, enter the four-digit GEN. (Do not confuse the GEN with the nine-digit EIN.) If you do not know the GEN, contact the parent organization. Get Pub. 557 for more information about group exemption numbers.

Withholding agent. If you are a withholding agent required to file Form 1042, check the "Other" box and enter "Withholding agent."

Personal service corporation. Check this box if the entity is a personal service corporation. An entity is a personal service corporation for a tax year only if:

● The principal activity of the entity during the testing period (prior tax year) for the tax year is the performance of personal services substantially by employee-owners, and

● The employee-owners own at least 10% of the fair market value of the outstanding stock in the entity on the last day of the testing period.

Personal services include performance of services in such fields as health, law, accounting, or consulting. For more information about personal service corporations, see the **Instructions for Form 1120,** U.S. Corporation Income Tax Return, and **Pub. 542,** Corporations.

Limited liability company (LLC). See the definition of limited liability company in the **Instructions for Form 1065.** An LLC with two or more members can be a partnership or an association taxable as a corporation. An LLC with a single owner can be an association taxable as a corporation or an entity disregarded as an entity separate from its owner. See Form 8832 for more details.

● If the entity is classified as a partnership for Federal income tax purposes, check the "partnership" box.

● If the entity is classified as a corporation for Federal income tax purposes, mark the "Other corporation" box and write "limited liability co." in the space provided.

● If the entity is disregarded as an entity separate from its owner, check the "Other" box and write in "disregarded entity" in the space provided.

Plan administrator. If the plan administrator is an individual, enter the plan administrator's SSN in the space provided.

Other corporation. This box is for any corporation other than a personal service corporation. If you check this box, enter the type of corporation (such as insurance company) in the space provided.

Household employer. If you are an individual, check the "Other" box and enter "Household employer" and your SSN. If you are a state or local agency serving as a tax reporting agent for public assistance recipients who become household employers, check the "Other" box and enter "Household employer agent." If you are a trust that qualifies as a household employer, you do not need a separate EIN for reporting tax information relating to household employees; use the EIN of the trust.

QSSS. For a qualified subchapter S subsidiary (QSSS) check the "Other" box and specify "QSSS."

Line 9. Check only **one** box. Do not enter N/A.

Started new business. Check this box if you are starting a new business that requires an EIN. If you check this box, enter the type of business being started. **Do not** apply if you already have an EIN and are only adding another place of business.

Hired employees. Check this box if the existing business is requesting an EIN because it has hired or is hiring employees and is therefore required to file employment tax returns. **Do not** apply if you already have an EIN and are only hiring employees. For information on the applicable employment taxes for family members, see **Circular E,** Employer's Tax Guide (Publication 15).

Created a pension plan. Check this box if you have created a pension plan and need this number for reporting purposes. Also, enter the type of plan created.

Note: *Check this box if you are applying for a trust EIN when a new pension plan is established.*

Banking purpose. Check this box if you are requesting an EIN for banking purposes only, and enter the banking purpose (for example, a bowling league for depositing dues or an investment club for dividend and interest reporting).

Changed type of organization. Check this box if the business is changing its type of organization, for example, if the business was a sole proprietorship and has been incorporated or has become a partnership. If you check this box, specify in the space provided the type of change made, for example, "from sole proprietorship to partnership."

Purchased going business. Check this box if you purchased an existing business. **Do not** use the former owner's EIN. **Do not** apply for a new EIN if you already have one. Use your own EIN.

Created a trust. Check this box if you created a trust, and enter the type of trust created. For example, indicate if the trust is a nonexempt charitable trust or a split-interest trust.

Note: *Do not check this box if you are applying for a trust EIN when a new pension plan is established. Check "Created a pension plan."*

Exception. Do not file this form for certain grantor-type trusts. The trustee does not need an EIN for the trust if the trustee furnishes the name and TIN of the grantor/owner and the address of the trust to all payors. See the Instructions for Form 1041 for more information.

Other (specify). Check this box if you are requesting an EIN for any reason other than those for which there are checkboxes, and enter the reason.

Line 10. If you are starting a new business, enter the starting date of the business. If the business you acquired is already operating, enter the date you acquired the business. Trusts should enter the date the trust was legally created. Estates should enter the date of death of the decedent whose name appears on line 1 or the date when the estate was legally funded.

Line 11. Enter the last month of your accounting year or tax year. An accounting or tax year is usually 12 consecutive months, either a calendar year or a fiscal year (including a period of 52 or 53 weeks). A calendar year is 12 consecutive months ending on December 31. A fiscal year is either 12 consecutive months ending on the last day of any month other than December or a 52-53 week year. For more information on accounting periods, see **Pub. 538**, Accounting Periods and Methods.

Individuals. Your tax year generally will be a calendar year.

Partnerships. Partnerships generally must adopt one of the following tax years:
● The tax year of the majority of its partners,
● The tax year common to all of its principal partners,
● The tax year that results in the least aggregate deferral of income, or
● In certain cases, some other tax year.
See the **Instructions for Form 1065,** U.S. Partnership Return of Income, for more information.

REMIC. REMICs must have a calendar year as their tax year.

Personal service corporations. A personal service corporation generally must adopt a calendar year unless:
● It can establish a business purpose for having a different tax year, or
● It elects under section 444 to have a tax year other than a calendar year.

Trusts. Generally, a trust must adopt a calendar year except for the following:
● Tax-exempt trusts,
● Charitable trusts, and
● Grantor-owned trusts.

Line 12. If the business has or will have employees, enter the date on which the business began or will begin to pay wages. If the business does not plan to have employees, enter N/A.

Withholding agent. Enter the date you began or will begin to pay income to a nonresident alien. This also applies to individuals who are required to file Form 1042 to report alimony paid to a nonresident alien.

Line 13. For a definition of agricultural labor (farmwork), see **Circular A,** Agricultural Employer's Tax Guide (Publication 51).

Line 14. Generally, enter the exact type of business being operated (for example, advertising agency, farm, food or beverage establishment, labor union, real estate agency, steam laundry, rental of coin-operated vending machine, or investment club). Also state if the business will involve the sale or distribution of alcoholic beverages.

Governmental. Enter the type of organization (state, county, school district, municipality, etc.).

Nonprofit organization (other than governmental). Enter whether organized for religious, educational, or humane purposes, and the principal activity (for example, religious organization—hospital, charitable).

Mining and quarrying. Specify the process and the principal product (for example, mining bituminous coal, contract drilling for oil, or quarrying dimension stone).

Contract construction. Specify whether general contracting or special trade contracting. Also, show the type of work normally performed (for example, general contractor for residential buildings or electrical subcontractor).

Food or beverage establishments. Specify the type of establishment and state whether you employ workers who receive tips (for example, lounge—yes).

Trade. Specify the type of sales and the principal line of goods sold (for example, wholesale dairy products, manufacturer's representative for mining machinery, or retail hardware).

Manufacturing. Specify the type of establishment operated (for example, sawmill or vegetable cannery).

Signature. The application must be signed by (a) the individual, if the applicant is an individual, (b) the president, vice president, or other principal officer, if the applicant is a corporation, (c) a responsible and duly authorized member or officer having knowledge of its affairs, if the applicant is a partnership or other unincorporated organization, or (d) the fiduciary, if the applicant is a trust or an estate.

How To Get Forms and Publications

Phone. You can order forms, instructions, and publications by phone. Just call 1-800-TAX-FORM (1-800-829-3676). You should receive your order or notification of its status within 7 to 15 workdays.

Personal computer. With your personal computer and modem, you can get the forms and information you need using:
● IRS's Internet Web Site at **www.irs.ustreas.gov**
● Telnet at **iris.irs.ustreas.gov**
● File Transfer Protocol at **ftp.irs.ustreas.gov**

You can also dial direct (by modem) to the Internal Revenue Information Services (IRIS) at 703-321-8020. IRIS is an on-line information service on FedWorld.

For small businesses, return preparers, or others who may frequently need tax forms or publications, a CD-ROM containing over 2,000 tax products (including many prior year forms) can be purchased from the Government Printing Office.

CD-ROM. To order the CD-ROM call the Superintendent of Documents at 202-512-1800 or connect to **www.access.gpo.gov/su_docs**

Privacy Act and Paperwork Reduction Act Notice. We ask for the information on this form to carry out the Internal Revenue laws of the United States. We need it to comply with section 6109 and the regulations thereunder which generally require the inclusion of an employer identification number (EIN) on certain returns, statements, or other documents filed with the Internal Revenue Service. Information on this form may be used to determine which Federal tax returns you are required to file and to provide you with related forms and publications. We disclose this form to the Social Security Administration for their use in determining compliance with applicable laws. We will be unable to issue an EIN to you unless you provide all of the requested information which applies to your entity.

You are not required to provide the information requested on a form that is subject to the Paperwork Reduction Act unless the form displays a valid OMB control number. Books or records relating to a form or its instructions must be retained as long as their contents may become material in the administration of any Internal Revenue law. Generally, tax returns and return information are confidential, as required by section 6103.

The time needed to complete and file this form will vary depending on individual circumstances. The estimated average time is:

Recordkeeping	7 min.
Learning about the law or the form	19 min.
Preparing the form	45 min.
Copying, assembling, and sending the form to the IRS . .	20 min.

If you have comments concerning the accuracy of these time estimates or suggestions for making this form simpler, we would be happy to hear from you. You can write to the Tax Forms Committee, Western Area Distribution Center, Rancho Cordova, CA 95743-0001. **Do not** send this form to this address. Instead, see **Where To Apply** on page 2.

Printed on recycled paper   *U.S. Government Printing Office: 1998 - 432-190/60379

NONPROFIT CORPORATIONS

SECTION XIX

A nonprofit corporation is a special type of corporation formed for charitable or other purposes that are not profit seeking. It has many of the features of standard corporations with the major exception being its tax status.

The number of nonprofit corporations in the United States is remarkable, running into the hundreds of thousands. In some states like Ohio and New York, over one-third of all corporations chartered are nonprofit. While there are critics of the growing phenomenon of the nonprofit corporation, over 50 percent of the property in some towns and cities is tax-exempt. Real property of certain organizations is wholly exempt from real property taxation (e.g., churches, colleges). However, as long as the minimal requirements of the IRS are met, it is legal under existing law, and the nonprofit corporation is likely to keep expanding and growing.

For the most part nonprofit corporations do not issue stock. Instead, membership certificates are often used. The form for a nonstock, nonprofit corporation that is recommended for use is on the following page. It can be completed in the same way as the earlier certificates in this book and either mailed directly to the appropriate Secretary of State or through a registered agent.

Some individuals utilize nonprofit corporations as a tax shelter. Many corporate situations lend themselves to this tax-exempt status. These endeavors can provide desirable tax advantages to the owner(s) of a corporation that may qualify for a government grant to do research, educational experiments, and the like.

A corporation can often qualify for tax-exempt status and still pay its officers' salaries and expenses. The Internal Revenue Service may question these salaries and expenses on a tax audit, however, if they are excessive.

Other situations lending themselves to nonprofit status are religious, fraternal, and civic clubs. Neighborhood associations, too, often incorporate as nonprofit corporations, primarily to gain personal liability protection for their members. Sometimes a person or group creates a nonprofit foundation for charitable purposes, such as medical research.

Often a person's will can be worded to leave such assets as stockholdings or insurance proceeds (by insurance contract) to a nonprofit corporation that the person organized while living.

Because personal contributions to many nonprofit corporations are tax deductible, many tax-exempt corporations use this incentive to obtain substantial funds that can run into the millions of dollars for their operations. Many fundraising firms help nonprofit corporations with fundraising.

Owners of a nonprofit corporation should contact an Internal Revenue Service office and obtain forms to qualify for tax-exempt status. See IRS Publication 557 (800-TAX-FORMS).

Nonstock   Nonprofit

CERTIFICATE OF INCORPORATION
of

<u>Associated Charities, Inc.</u>

FIRST: The name of this corporation is <u>Associated Charities, Inc.</u>

SECOND. Its registered office in the State of Delaware is to be located at <u>1018 Centre Road</u>, in the City of <u>Wilmington</u>, County of <u>New Castle</u>. The registered agent in charge therefore is <u>The Company Corporation</u> at <u>the same address</u>.

THIRD: The nature of the business and the objects and purposes proposed to be transacted, promoted, and carried on are to do any and all the things herein mentioned, as fully and to the same extent as natural persons might or could do, and in any part of the world, viz:

This is a nonstock, nonprofit corporation. The purpose of the corporation is to engage in any lawful act or activity for which nonprofit corporations may be organized under the General Corporation Law of Delaware.

The corporation is organized exclusively for charitable, religious, educational, and scientific purposes, including, for such purposes, the making of distributions to organizations that qualify as exempt organizations under Section 501(c)(3) of the Internal Revenue Code of 1954 (or the corresponding provision of any future United States Internal Revenue law), to wit:

(In this space you may wish to include a statement describing the purpose and objectives of the corporation in more specific terms.)

FOURTH: The corporation shall not have any capital stock and the conditions of membership shall be stated in the bylaws.

FIFTH: The name and mailing address of the incorporator is: (leave blank if using The Company Corporation as your registered agent.)

SIXTH: The powers of the incorporator are to terminate upon filing of the certificate of incorporation, and the name(s) and mailing address(es) of the persons who are to serve as director(s) until their successors are elected are as follows:

Kathy Smith, 621 North Street, Anytown, Anystate 00000

SEVENTH: The activities and affairs of the corporation shall be managed by a board of directors. The number of directors which shall constitute the whole board shall be such as from time to time shall be fixed by, or in the manner provided in, the bylaws, but in no case shall the number be less than one. The directors need not be members of the corporation unless so required by the bylaws or by statute. The board of directors shall be elected by the members at the annual meeting of the corporation to be held on such date as the bylaws may provide, and shall hold office until their successors are respectively elected and qualified. The bylaws shall specify the number of directors necessary to constitute a quorum. The board of directors may, by resolution or resolutions passed by a majority of the whole board, designate one or more committees which, to the extent provided in said resolution or resolutions or in the bylaws of the corporation, shall have and may exercise all the powers of the board of directors in the management of the activities and affairs of the corporation. They may further have power to authorize the seal of the corporation to be affixed to all papers which may require it; and such committee or committees shall have such name or names as may be stated in the bylaws of the corporation or as may be determined from time to time by resolution adopted by the board of directors. The directors of the corporation may, if the bylaws so provide, be classified as to term of office. The corporation may elect such officers, as the bylaws may specify, subject to the provisions of the statute, who shall have titles and exercise such duties as the bylaws may provide. The board of directors is expressly authorized to make, alter, or repeal the bylaws of this corporation. This corporation may in its bylaws confer powers upon its board of directors in addition to the foregoing, and in addition to the powers and authorities expressly

SAMPLE

conferred upon them by statute. This is true, provided that the board of directors shall not exercise any power of authority conferred herein or by statute upon the members.

EIGHTH: Meetings of members may be held without the State of Delaware, if the bylaws so provide. The books of the corporation may be kept (subject to any provisions contained in the statutes) outside the State of Delaware at such place or places as may be from time to time designated by the board of directors.

NINTH: No part of the net earnings of the corporation shall inure to the benefit of, or be distributable to, its members, directors, officers or other private persons, except that the corporation shall be authorized and empowered to pay reasonable compensation for services rendered and to make payments and distributions in furtherance of the purposes set forth in article three hereof. No part of the activities of the corporation shall consist of the carrying on of propaganda, or otherwise attempting to intervene in (including the publishing or distribution of statements) any of these articles. The corporation shall not carry on any other activities not permitted to be carried on (a) by a corporation exempt from federal income tax under Section 501(c)(3) of the Internal Revenue Code of 1954 (or the corresponding provision of any future United States Internal Revenue law) or (b) by a corporation, contributions to which are deductible under Section 170(c)(2) of the Internal Revenue Code of 1954 (or the corresponding provision of any future United States Internal Revenue law).

TENTH: Upon the dissolution of the corporation, the board of directors shall, after paying or making provisions for the payment of all of the liabilities of the corporation, dispose of all of the assets of the corporation exclusively for the purpose of the corporation in such manner, or to such organization or organizations and operated exclusively for charitable, educational, religious, or scientific purposes as shall at the time qualify as an exempt organization under Section 501(c)(3) of the Internal Revenue Code of 1954 (or the corresponding provision of any future United States Law) as the board of directors shall determine. Any such assets not so disposed of shall be disposed of by the Court of Common Pleas of the county in which the principal office of the corporation is then located, exclusively for such purposes or to such organization or organizations, as said Court shall determine, which are organized and operated exclusively for such designated purposes.

ELEVENTH: The corporation reserves the right to amend, alter, change, or repeal any provision contained in this certificate of incorporation, in the manner now or hereafter prescribed by the statute, and all rights conferred upon members herein are granted subject to their reservation.

TWELFTH: Directors of the corporation shall not be liable to either the corporation or its members for monetary damages for a breach of fiduciary duties unless the breach involves: (1) a director's duty of loyalty to the corporation or its members; (2) acts or omissions not in good faith or which involve intentional misconduct or a knowing violation of law; (3) a transaction from which the director derived an improper personal benefit.

I, THE UNDERSIGNED, being each of the incorporators hereinbefore named, for the purpose of forming a nonprofit corporation pursuant to Chapter 1 of Title 8 of the Delaware Code, do make this certificate, hereby declaring and certifying that the facts herein stated are true, and accordingly have hereunto set my hand this

__14th__ day of __June__ A.D. _____ .

John Doe
(Signature of Incorporator. Leave blank if
The Company Corporation is your registered agent.)

Nonstock   Nonprofit

CERTIFICATE OF INCORPORATION
of

_____

FIRST: The name of this corporation is _____

SECOND: Its registered office in the State of Delaware is to be located at _____
_____ in the City of _____ , County of
_____ . The registered agent in charge thereof is _____
at _____ address.

THIRD: The nature of the business and the objects and purposes proposed to be transacted, promoted, and carried on are to do any and all the things herein mentioned, as fully and to the same extent as natural persons might or could do, and in any part of the world, viz:

This is a nonstock, nonprofit corporation. The purpose of the corporation is to engage in any lawful act or activity for which nonprofit corporations may be organized under the General Corporation Law of Delaware.

The corporation is organized exclusively for charitable, religious, educational, and scientific purposes, including, for such purposes, the making of distributions to organizations that qualify as exempt organizations under Section 501(c)(3) of the Internal Revenue Code of 1954 (or the corresponding provision of any future United States Internal Revenue law), to wit:

FOURTH: The corporation shall not have any capital stock and the conditions of membership shall be stated in the bylaws.

FIFTH: The name and mailing address of the incorporator is:

SIXTH: The powers of the incorporator are to terminate upon filing of the certificate of incorporation, and the name(s) and mailing address(es) of the persons who are to serve as director(s) until their successors are elected are as follows:

SEVENTH: The activities and affairs of the corporation shall be managed by a board of directors. The number of directors which shall constitute the whole board shall be such as from time to time shall be fixed by, or in the manner provided in, the bylaws, but in no case shall the number be less than one. The directors need not be members of the corporation unless so required by the bylaws or by statute. The board of directors shall be elected by the members at the annual meeting of the corporation to be held on such date as the bylaws may provide, and shall hold office until their successors are respectively elected and qualified. The bylaws shall specify the number of directors necessary to constitute a quorum. The board of directors may, by resolution or resolutions passed by a majority of the whole board, designate one or more committees which, to the extent provided in said resolution or resolutions or in the bylaws of the corporation, shall have and may exercise all the powers of the board of directors in the management of the activities and affairs of the corporation. They may further have power to authorize the seal of the corporation to be affixed to all papers which may require it; and such committee or committees shall have such name or names as may be stated in the bylaws of the corporation or as may be determined from time to time by resolution adopted by the board of directors. The directors of the corporation may, if the bylaws so provide, be classified as to term of office. The corporation may elect such officers, as the bylaws may specify, subject to the provisions of the statute, who shall have titles and exercise such duties as the bylaws may provide. The board of directors is expressly authorized to make, alter, or repeal the bylaws of this corporation. This corporation may in its bylaws confer powers upon its board of directors in addition to the foregoing, and in addition to the powers and authorities expressly conferred upon them by statute. This is true, provided that the board of directors shall not exercise any power of authority conferred herein or by statute upon the members.

EIGHTH: Meetings of members may be held without the State of Delaware, if the bylaws so provide. The books of the corporation may be kept (subject to any provisions contained in the statutes) outside the State of Delaware at such place or places as may be from time to time designated by the board of directors.

NINTH: No part of the net earnings of the corporation shall inure to the benefit of, or be distributable to, its members, directors, officers, or other private persons, except that the corporation shall be authorized and empowered to pay reasonable compensation for services rendered and to make payments and distributions in furtherance of the purposes set forth in article three hereof. No part of the activities of the corporation shall consist of the carrying on of propaganda, or otherwise attempting to intervene in (including the publishing or distribution of statements) any of these articles, the corporation shall not carry on any other activities not permitted to be carried on (a) by a corporation exempt from federal income tax under Section 501(c)(3) of the Internal Revenue Code of 1954 (or the corresponding provision of any future United States Internal Revenue law) or (b) by a corporation, contributions to which are deductible under Section 170(c)(2) of the Internal Revenue Code of 1954 (or the corresponding provision of any future United States Internal Revenue law).

TENTH: Upon the dissolution of the corporation, the board of directors shall, after paying or making provisions for the payment of all of the liabilities of the corporation, dispose of all of the assets of the corporation exclusively for the purpose of the corporation in such manner, or to such organization or organizations and operated exclusively for charitable, educational, religious, or scientific purposes as shall at the time qualify as an exempt organization under Section 501(c)(3) of the Internal Revenue Code of 1954 (or the corresponding provision of any future United States law) as the board of directors shall determine. Any such assets not so disposed of shall be disposed of by the Court of Common Pleas of the county in which the principal office of the corporation is then located, exclusively for such purposes or to such organization or organizations, as said Court shall determine, which are organized and operated exclusively for such designated purposes.

ELEVENTH: The corporation reserves the right to amend, alter, change, or repeal any provision contained in this certificate of incorporation, in the manner now or hereafter prescribed by the statute, and all rights conferred upon members herein are granted subject to their reservation.

TWELFTH: Directors of the corporation shall not be liable to either the corporation or its members for monetary damages for a breach of fiduciary duties unless the breach involves: (1) a director's duty of loyalty to the corporation or its members; (2) acts or omissions not in good faith or which involve intentional misconduct or a knowing violation of law; (3) a transaction from which the director derived an improper personal benefit.

I, THE UNDERSIGNED, being each of the incorporators hereinbefore named, for the purpose of forming a nonprofit corporation pursuant to Chapter 1 of Title 8 of the Delaware Code, do make this certificate, hereby declaring and certifying that the facts herein stated are true, and accordingly have hereunto set my hand this

_____ day of _____ A.D. _____ .

_____

(Signature of Incorporator. Leave blank if
The Company Corporation is your registered agent.)

Nonstock   Nonprofit

CERTIFICATE OF INCORPORATION
of

_____

FIRST: The name of this corporation is _____

SECOND: Its registered office in the State of Delaware is to be located at _____
_____ in the City of _____ , County of
_____ . The registered agent in charge thereof is _____
at _____ address.

THIRD: The nature of the business and the objects and purposes proposed to be transacted, promoted, and carried on are to do any and all the things herein mentioned, as fully and to the same extent as natural persons might or could do, and in any part of the world, viz:

This is a nonstock, nonprofit corporation. The purpose of the corporation is to engage in any lawful act or activity for which nonprofit corporations may be organized under the General Corporation Law of Delaware.

The corporation is organized exclusively for charitable, religious, educational, and scientific purposes, including, for such purposes, the making of distributions to organizations that qualify as exempt organizations under Section 501(c)(3) of the Internal Revenue Code of 1954 (or the corresponding provision of any future United States Internal Revenue law), to wit:

FOURTH: The corporation shall not have any capital stock and the conditions of membership shall be stated in the bylaws.

FIFTH: The name and mailing address of the incorporator is:

SIXTH: The powers of the incorporator are to terminate upon filing of the certificate of incorporation, and the name(s) and mailing address(es) of the persons who are to serve as director(s) until their successors are elected are as follows:

SEVENTH: The activities and affairs of the corporation shall be managed by a board of directors. The number of directors which shall constitute the whole board shall be such as from time to time shall be fixed by, or in the manner provided in, the bylaws, but in no case shall the number be less than one. The directors need not be members of the corporation unless so required by the bylaws or by statute. The board of directors shall be elected by the members at the annual meeting of the corporation to be held on such date as the bylaws may provide, and shall hold office until their successors are respectively elected and qualified. The bylaws shall specify the number of directors necessary to constitute a quorum. The board of directors may, by resolution or resolutions passed by a majority of the whole board, designate one or more committees which, to the extent provided in said resolution or resolutions or in the bylaws of the corporation, shall have and may exercise all the powers of the board of directors in the management of the activities and affairs of the corporation. They may further have power to authorize the seal of the corporation to be affixed to all papers which may require it; and such committee or committees shall have such name or names as may be stated in the bylaws of the corporation or as may be determined from time to time by resolution adopted by the board of directors. The directors of the corporation may, if the bylaws so provide, be classified as to term of office. The corporation may elect such officers, as the bylaws may specify, subject to the provisions of the statute, who shall have titles and exercise such duties as the bylaws may provide. The board of directors is expressly authorized to make, alter, or repeal the bylaws of this corporation. This corporation may in its bylaws confer powers upon its board of directors in addition to the foregoing, and in addition to the powers and authorities expressly conferred upon them by statute. This is true, provided that the board of directors shall not exercise any power of authority conferred herein or by statute upon the members.

EIGHTH: Meetings of members may be held without the State of Delaware, if the bylaws so provide. The books of the corporation may be kept (subject to any provisions contained in the statutes) outside the State of Delaware at such place or places as may be from time to time designated by the board of directors.

NINTH: No part of the net earnings of the corporation shall inure to the benefit of, or be distributable to, its members, directors, officers, or other private persons, except that the corporation shall be authorized and empowered to pay reasonable compensation for services rendered and to make payments and distributions in furtherance of the purposes set forth in article three hereof. No part of the activities of the corporation shall consist of the carrying on of propaganda, or otherwise attempting to intervene in (including the publishing or distribution of statements) any of these articles, the corporation shall not carry on any other activities not permitted to be carried on (a) by a corporation exempt from federal income tax under Section 501(c)(3) of the Internal Revenue Code of 1954 (or the corresponding provision of any future United States Internal Revenue law) or (b) by a corporation, contributions to which are deductible under Section 170(c)(2) of the Internal Revenue Code of 1954 (or the corresponding provision of any future United States Internal Revenue law).

TENTH: Upon the dissolution of the corporation, the board of directors shall, after paying or making provisions for the payment of all of the liabilities of the corporation, dispose of all of the assets of the corporation exclusively for the purpose of the corporation in such manner, or to such organization or organizations and operated exclusively for charitable, educational, religious, or scientific purposes as shall at the time qualify as an exempt organization under Section 501(c)(3) of the Internal Revenue Code of 1954 (or the corresponding provision of any future United States law) as the board of directors shall determine. Any such assets not so disposed of shall be disposed of by the Court of Common Pleas of the county in which the principal office of the corporation is then located, exclusively for such purposes or to such organization or organizations, as said Court shall determine, which are organized and operated exclusively for such designated purposes.

ELEVENTH: The corporation reserves the right to amend, alter, change, or repeal any provision contained in this certificate of incorporation, in the manner now or hereafter prescribed by the statute, and all rights conferred upon members herein are granted subject to their reservation.

TWELFTH: Directors of the corporation shall not be liable to either the corporation or its members for monetary damages for a breach of fiduciary duties unless the breach involves: (1) a director's duty of loyalty to the corporation or its members; (2) acts or omissions not in good faith or which involve intentional misconduct or a knowing violation of law; (3) a transaction from which the director derived an improper personal benefit.

I, THE UNDERSIGNED, being each of the incorporators hereinbefore named, for the purpose of forming a nonprofit corporation pursuant to Chapter 1 of Title 8 of the Delaware Code, do make this certificate, hereby declaring and certifying that the facts herein stated are true, and accordingly have hereunto set my hand this

_____ day of _____ A.D. _____ .

_____

(Signature of Incorporator. Leave blank if
The Company Corporation is your registered agent.)

PROFESSIONAL CORPORATIONS

SECTION XX

Professionals in some areas of the United States may be able to take advantage of the benefits of Delaware corporate laws.

The same form used for a business corporation is also usable by a professional. Professionals should add the initials "P.A." (Professional Association) or "P.C." (Professional Corporation) to the corporate title on the certificate of incorporation (e.g., Jones & Smith, P.A.). Such abbreviations as *Inc.* do not appear.

However, such professionals as physicians, dentists, architects, attorneys, and the like are treated differently under the law than are business corporations because of the nature of professionals' activities.

In order to assure that corporation status for a professional for tax purposes is not disallowed, the corporation that is engaged in the business of providing a professional service must

1. be owned by professionals in the same field and within the same professional practice (within the same office);

2. make provision by agreement to leave stock to other professionals in the same profession and within the same practice, and have a purchase agreement in the event of death with the same provision;

3. not engage in any other business or activity or in an investment of any kind with a professional in the same practice other than that of providing the primary professional service; and

4. make certain that the professional relationship between the person furnishing the professional service and the person receiving it does not eliminate the personal liability of the professional for misconduct or negligence.

NOTE: Because corporate laws vary greatly from state to state with regard to professionals, it is advisable for the professional to write the Secretary of State and that professional's regulation board in the state where he or she practices to obtain information about any other provisions that should be included in the records of this type of Delaware corporation.

Some states have licensing requirements (particularly for attorneys and physicians) that do not permit a professional corporation to be formed out of state so that a Delaware professional corporation is possible only for professionals licensed in Delaware. To be completely safe, a professional should request an opinion in writing from a state's licensing department before proceeding with the formation of a Delaware corporation.

FOR ADDITIONAL INFORMATION

SECTION XXI

To obtain a complete copy of Delaware's corporation laws, contact The Company Corporation (1013 Centre Road, Wilmington, Delaware 19805, 800-818-6082). This publication outlines the entire corporation law. The writing is cumbersome, but it is well indexed and contains various kinds of helpful information.

If you wish to make an interesting comparison between the advantages of Delaware's corporation laws and those of any other state, you may write the Secretary of State, c/o the corporation department of any state, and request information on obtaining a copy of that state's corporation laws.

CORPORATIONS FORMED IN STATES OTHER THAN DELAWARE

SECTION XXII

An existing corporation formed in any state other than Delaware may wish to register to do business in Delaware.

A specimen foreign corporation certificate is on the next page. An official of the foreign corporation (i.e., a corporation in a state other than Delaware) may complete the form. A registered agent in Delaware must be appointed. (The Company Corporation will forward the form to the Secretary of State and act as registered agent for an annual fee of $125.) The registered agent then files the form with the Secretary of State, Dover, Delaware. The state tax and fees covering the registration of a foreign corporation are $150. This method applies best when a non-Delaware corporation merely wants to register to do business in Delaware. However, there is a way to obtain all the benefits of Delaware corporate law that this one does not accomplish and that is being favored by more and more corporations, including large as well as one-person or family corporations. The objective of the following method is for an existing corporation to obtain the advantages of Delaware's corporate laws.

Under this second method, when a new Delaware corporation is formed, the non-Delaware corporation is merged into this new one. The minimum Delaware fee for a merger is approximately $189, if both corporations have simple formats and no more stock is issued by the surviving Delaware corporation.

An agreement by the two corporations outlining the terms of their merger that specifies the number of shares of the old corporation to be exchanged for the number of shares of the new corporation is helpful. This agreement becomes part of the new corporation's records. After the agreement is completed, a registered agent can assist in filing the forms with the state.

To take advantage of Delaware law, in almost all cases it pays to form a new Delaware corporation and merge the old one into the new one.

FOREIGN CORPORATION CERTIFICATE

THE UNDERSIGNED, a corporation duly organized and existing under the laws of the State of
_____ , in accordance with the provisions of Section 371 of Title 8 of the Delaware
Code, does hereby certify:

FIRST: That _____ is a corporation
duly organized and existing under the laws of the State of _____ and is filing herewith
a certificate evidencing its corporate existence.

SECOND: That the name and address of its registered agent in said State of Delaware upon whom
service of process may be had is _____

_____

THIRD: That the assets of said corporation are $ _____ and that the liabilities
thereof are $ _____ ; and that the assets and liabilities indicated are as of a date within six
months prior to the filing date of this certificate.

FOURTH: That the business which it proposes to do in the State of Delaware is as follows:

FIFTH: That the business which it proposes to do in the State of Delaware is a business it is authorized
to do in the jurisdiction of its incorporation.

IN WITNESS WHEREOF, said corporation has caused this certificate to be signed on its behalf and
its corporate seal affixed this _____ day of _____ , _____ .

(CORPORATE SEAL)

_____

_____
President

FOREIGN CORPORATION CERTIFICATE

THE UNDERSIGNED, a corporation duly organized and existing under the laws of the State of _____ , in accordance with the provisions of Section 371 of Title 8 of the Delaware Code, does hereby certify:

FIRST: That _____ is a corporation duly organized and existing under the laws of the State of _____ and is filing herewith a certificate evidencing its corporate existence.

SECOND: That the name and address of its registered agent in said State of Delaware upon whom service of process may be had is _____

_____

THIRD: That the assets of said corporation are $ _____ and that the liabilities thereof are $ _____ ; and that the assets and liabilities indicated are as of a date within six months prior to the filing date of this certificate.

FOURTH: That the business which it proposes to do in the State of Delaware is as follows:

FIFTH: That the business which it proposes to do in the State of Delaware is a business it is authorized to do in the jurisdiction of its incorporation.

IN WITNESS WHEREOF, said corporation has caused this certificate to be signed on its behalf and its corporate seal affixed this _____ day of _____ , _____ .

(CORPORATE SEAL)

_____

_____
President

MINUTES, BYLAWS, ARTICLES OF INCORPORATION, STANDARD FORMS, REVIEW

SECTION XXIII

All of the forms necessary to launch a new corporation are featured on the following pages. For those who are incorporating but not utilizing the services of a registered agent, this book contains blank forms that may be removed and used. Simply fill in the blanks on these forms. The only items that are desirable for a corporation to have that are not included in this book are the corporate seal and stock certificates. You can purchase these through a stationery or office supply store or through The Company Corporation as a complete bound set of corporate forms.

A Delaware corporation without the services of a registered agent is formed as follows:

1. Arrange to obtain a Delaware mailing address if practical.

2. File a certificate of incorporation with the Secretary of State in Dover, Delaware.

3. When the certificate is returned from the Secretary of State, file a copy with the Recorder of Deeds' office, using the Delaware mailing address.

4. Instead of using the forms supplied by a registered agent, tear out the forms on the following pages.

5. Fill in the blanks on those forms with appropriate information. Keep these forms with the corporate records. From time to time, keep a record of any meeting the directors have by using these forms and filling in the blanks.

6. If desirable, buy stock certificates (either printed or unprinted) from a stationery or office supply store.

7. Acquire a corporate seal, which can be purchased at a stationery or office supply store.

Listed below are the forms on the following pages:

A. *Statement by Incorporator(s) of Action Taken in Lieu of Organization Meeting.* This form may be used in all cases and for all types of corporations. Signatures are the same as they appear on the certificate of incorporation.

B. *Minutes of the First Meeting of the Board of Directors.* Complete and use only if there is more than one director. This form is not needed if the corporation is a close corporation.

C. *Waiver of Notice of the First Meeting of the Board of Directors.* Complete and use only if there is more than one director.

D. *Organization Minutes of the Sole Director.* Complete and use only if there is just one director and one person holds all offices. This form is not needed if the corporation is a close corporation.

E. *Bylaws and Articles of Incorporation.* Complete and use in all cases and keep with the corporate records.

NOTE: Do not send any of the following forms to your registered agent. Keep them with your corporate records.

STATEMENT BY INCORPORATOR(S) OF ACTION TAKEN
IN LIEU OF ORGANIZATION MEETING OF

_____

The undersigned being the incorporator(s) of the corporation makes the following statement of action taken to organize the corporation in lieu of an organization meeting.

Bylaws regulating the conduct of the business and affairs of the corporation were adopted and appended to this statement.

The following persons were appointed directors of the corporation until the first annual meeting of the shareholders or until their successors shall be elected or appointed and shall qualify:

The directors were authorized and directed to issue from time to time the shares of capital stock of the corporation, now or hereafter authorized, wholly or partly for cash, or labor done, or services performed, or for personal property, or real property or leases thereof, received for the use and lawful purposes of the corporation, or for any consideration permitted by law, as in the discretion of the directors may seem for the best interests of the corporation.

_____

_____

_____

The following are to be appended to this statement:

Copy of the Certificate of Incorporation

Bylaws

The STATEMENT BY INCORPORATOR(S) OF ACTION TAKEN IN LIEU OF ORGANIZATION MEETING, together with a copy of the bylaws, which were adopted in said statement, was then presented to the meeting by the secretary.

RESOLVED, that the STATEMENT BY INCORPORATOR(S) OF ACTION TAKEN IN LIEU OF ORGANIZATION MEETING, dated _____ , which has been presented to this meeting, be and hereby is in all respects approved, ratified, and confirmed, and further;

RESOLVED, that the bylaws in the form adopted by the incorporator(s) in the aforementioned statement be and hereby are adopted as and for the bylaws of this corporation.

The secretary then presented and read to the meeting a copy of the certificate of incorporation of the corporation and reported that on the day of _____ , the original thereof was duly filed in the office of the Secretary of State and that a certified copy thereof was recorded on _____ , in the office of the Recorder of the County of _____ .

Upon motion duly made, seconded, and carried, said report was adopted, and the secretary was directed to append to these minutes a certified copy of the certificate of incorporation.

The chairman presented and read, article by article, the proposed bylaws for the conduct and regulation of the business and affairs of the corporation.

Upon motion duly made, seconded, and carried, they were adopted and in all respects, ratified, confirmed, and approved, as and for the bylaws of the corporation. The secretary was directed to cause them to be inserted in the minute book.

The secretary submitted to the meeting a seal proposed for use as the corporate seal of the corporation. Upon motion duly made, seconded, and carried, it was

RESOLVED, that the seal now presented at this meeting, an impression of which is directed to be made in the margin of the minute book, be and the same hereby is adopted as the seal of the corporation.

The chair requested that the secretary of the corporation be authorized to procure the necessary books and that the treasurer of the corporation be authorized to pay all expenses and to reimburse all persons for expenses made in connection with the organization of this corporation. After discussion, on motion duly made, seconded, and unanimously carried, it was

RESOLVED, that the secretary of this corporation be and hereby is authorized and directed to procure all corporate books, books of account, and share certificate books required by the statutes of the State of Delaware or necessary or appropriate in connection with the business of this corporation; and it was further

RESOLVED, that the treasurer of this corporation be and hereby is authorized to pay all charges and expenses incident to or arising out of the organization of this corporation and to reimburse any person who has made any disbursements therefor.

The secretary then presented to the meeting a proposed form of certificates for fully paid and nonassessable shares of stock of this corporation. The chairman directed that the specimen copy of such form of certificate be annexed to the minutes of the meeting. Upon motion duly made, seconded, and unanimously carried it was

RESOLVED, that the form of certificate for fully paid and nonassessable shares of stock of this corporation submitted to this meeting, be and hereby is adopted as the certificate to represent fully paid and nonassessable shares of stock and that a specimen of such certificate be annexed to the minutes of the meeting.

MINUTES OF THE FIRST MEETING OF
THE BOARD OF DIRECTORS OF

_____

The first meeting of directors was held at _____
on the _____ day of _____ , at _____ o'clock ____M.

The following were present:

being a quorum and all the directors of the corporation.

One of the directors called the meeting to order. Upon motion duly made, seconded, and carried,
_____ was duly elected chairman of the meeting, and
_____ was duly elected secretary thereof. They accepted their
respective offices and proceeded with the discharge of their duties.

A written waiver of notice of this meeting signed by the directors was submitted, read by the secretary, and ordered appended to these minutes.

The chairman stated that the election of officers was then in order.

The following were duly nominated and, note having been taken, were unanimously elected officers of the corporation to serve for one year and until their successors are elected and qualified:

President: _____

Vice President:_____

Secretary: _____

Treasurer:_____

The president and secretary thereupon assumed their respective offices in place and stead of the temporary chairman and the temporary secretary.

WAIVER OF NOTICE OF THE FIRST MEETING OF
THE BOARD OF DIRECTORS OF

_____

      We, the undersigned, being all the directors of the above corporation, hereby agree and consent that the first meeting of the board be held on the date and at the time and place stated below for the purpose of electing officers and the transaction thereat of all such other business as may lawfully come before said meeting and hereby waive all notice of the meeting and of any adjournment thereof.

Place of meeting: _____

Date of meeting: _____

Time of meeting: _____

_____
Director

_____
Director

_____
Director

Dated: _____

ORGANIZATION MINUTES OF THE SOLE DIRECTOR OF

_____

The undersigned, being the sole director of the corporation, organized under the General Corporation Law of Delaware, took the following action to organize the corporation and in furtherance of its business objectives on the date and at the place set forth below:

A certified copy of the certificate of incorporation filed in the office of the Secretary of State on _____ , and recorded in the office of the Recorder of the County of _____ on _____ , was appended to these minutes.

The office of the corporation was fixed at _____ in the City of _____ , State of _____.

Bylaws regulating the conduct of the business and affairs of the corporation were adopted and appended to these minutes.

It was decided to issue from time to time all of the authorized shares of the capital stock of the corporation, now or hereafter authorized, wholly or partly for cash, for labor done, or services performed, or for personal property, or real property or leases thereof, received for the use and lawful purposes of the corporation, or for any consideration permitted by law as in the discretion of the director may seem for the best interest of the corporation.

The following were appointed officers of the corporation to serve for one year and until their successors were appointed or elected and qualified:

President: _____   Secretary: _____

Vice President: _____   Treasurer: _____

Each officer thereupon assumed the duties of his or her office.

A written proposal from _____ addressed to the corporation and dated _____ pertaining to the issuance of the shares of the corporation was appended to the minutes.

The following action was taken upon said proposal:

RESOLVED, that said proposal or offer be and the same hereby is approved and accepted and that in accordance with the terms thereof, the corporation issue to the offeror(s) or nominee(s) _____ _____ fully paid and nonassessable shares of this corporation, and it is

RESOLVED, that upon the delivery to the corporation of said assets and the execution and delivery of such proper instruments as may be necessary to transfer and convey the same to the corporation, the officers of this corporation are authorized and directed to execute and deliver the certificates for such shares as are required to be issued and delivered on acceptance of said proposal in accordance with the foregoing.

BYLAWS AND ARTICLES OF INCORPORATION OF

_____

ARTICLE I—OFFICES

SECTION 1. REGISTERED OFFICE.—The registered office shall be established and maintained at _____ in the County of _____ in the State of Delaware.

SECTION 2. OTHER OFFICES.—The corporation may have other offices, either within or without the State of Delaware, at such place or places as the Board of Directors may from time to time appoint or the business of the corporation may require.

ARTICLE II—MEETING OF SHAREHOLDERS

SECTION 1. ANNUAL MEETINGS.—Annual meetings of shareholders for the election of directors and for such other business as may be stated in the notice of the meeting, shall be held at such place, either within or without the State of Delaware, and at such time and date as the Board of Directors, by resolution, shall determine and as set forth in the notice of the meeting. In the event the Board of Directors fails to so determine the time, date, and place of the meeting, the annual meeting of shareholders shall be held at the registered office of the corporation in Delaware on _____ .

If the date of the annual meeting shall fall upon a legal holiday, the meeting shall be held on the next succeeding business day. At each annual meeting, the shareholders entitled to vote shall elect a Board of Directors and may transact such other corporate business as shall be stated in the notice of the meeting.

SECTION 2. OTHER MEETINGS.—Meetings of shareholders for any purpose other than the election of directors may be held at such time and place, within or without the State of Delaware, as shall be stated in the notice of the meeting.

SECTION 3. VOTING.—Each shareholder entitled to vote in accordance with the terms and provisions of the certificate of incorporation and these bylaws shall be entitled to one vote, in person or by proxy, for each share of stock entitled to vote held by such shareholder, but no proxy shall be voted after three years from its date unless such proxy provides for a longer period. Upon the demand of any shareholder, the vote for directors and upon any question before the meeting shall be by ballot. All elections for directors shall be decided by plurality vote; all other questions shall be decided by majority vote except as otherwise provided by the certificate of incorporation or/and laws of the State of Delaware.

SECTION 4. SHAREHOLDER LIST.—The officer who has charge of the stock ledger of the corporation shall at least ten days before each meeting of shareholders prepare a complete alphabetically addressed list of the shareholders entitled to vote at the ensuing election, with the number of shares held by each. Said list shall be open to the examination of any shareholder, for any purpose germane to the meeting, during ordinary business hours, for a period of at least ten days prior to the meeting, either at a place within the city where the meeting is to be held, which place shall be specified in the notice of the meeting, or, if not specified, at the place where the meeting is to be held. The list shall be available for inspection at the meeting.

SECTION 5. QUORUM.—Except as otherwise required by law, by the certificate of incorporation or by these bylaws, the presence, in person or by proxy, of shareholders holding a majority of the stock of the corporation entitled to vote shall constitute a meeting, a majority in interest of the shareholders entitled to vote thereat, present in person or by proxy, shall have power to adjourn the meeting from time to time, without notice other than announcement at the meeting, until the requisite amount of stock entitled to vote shall be present. At any such adjourned meeting at which the requisite amount of stock entitled to vote shall be represented, any business may be transacted which might have been transacted at the meeting as originally noticed; but only those shareholders entitled to vote at the meeting as originally noticed shall be entitled to vote at any adjournment or adjournments thereof.

SECTION 6. SPECIAL MEETING.—Special meeting of the shareholders, for any purpose, unless otherwise prescribed by statute or by the certificate of incorporation, may be called by the president and shall be called by the president or secretary at the request in writing of a majority of the directors or shareholders entitled to vote. Such request shall state the purpose of the proposed meeting.

SECTION 7. NOTICE OF MEETINGS.—Written notice, stating the place, date, and time of the meeting and the general nature of the business to be considered, shall be given to each shareholder entitled to vote thereat at his or her address as it appears on the records of the corporation, not less than ten nor more than fifty days before the date of the meeting.

SECTION 8. BUSINESS TRANSACTED.—No business other than that stated in the notice shall be transacted at any meeting without the unanimous consent of all the shareholders entitled to vote thereat.

SECTION 9. ACTION WITHOUT MEETING.—Except as otherwise provided by the certificate of incorporation, whenever the vote of shareholders at a meeting is required or permitted to be taken in connection with any corporate action by any provisions of the statutes or the certificate of incorporation or of these bylaws, the meeting and vote of shareholders may be dispensed with if all the shareholders who would have been entitled to vote upon the action if such meeting were held shall consent in writing to such corporate action being taken.

ARTICLE III—DIRECTORS

SECTION 1. NUMBER AND TERM.—The number of directors shall be _____ . The directors shall be elected at the annual meeting of shareholders and each director shall be elected to serve until his or her successor shall be elected and shall qualify. The number of directors may not be less than three except that where all the shares of the corporation are owned beneficially and of record by either one or two shareholders, the number of directors may be less than three but not less than the number of shareholders.

SECTION 2. RESIGNATIONS.—Any director, member of a committee, or other officer may resign at any time. Such resignation shall be made in writing and shall take effect at the time specified therein, and if no time be specified, at the time of its receipt by the president or secretary. The acceptance of a resignation shall not be necessary to make it effective.

SECTION 3. VACANCIES.—If the office of any director, member of a committee or other officer becomes vacant, the remaining directors in office, though less than a quorum by a majority vote, may appoint any qualified person to fill such vacancy, who shall hold office for the unexpired term and until his or her successor shall be duly chosen.

SECTION 4. REMOVAL.—Any director or directors may be removed either for or without cause at any time by the affirmative vote of the holders of majority of all the shares of stock outstanding and entitled to vote at a special meeting of the shareholders called for the purpose, and the vacancies thus created may be filled at the meeting held for the purpose of removal by the affirmative vote of a majority in interest of the shareholders entitled to vote.

SECTION 5. INCREASE OF NUMBER.—The number of directors may be increased by amendment of these bylaws by the affirmative vote of a majority of the directors, though less than a quorum, or by the affirmative vote of a majority in interest of the shareholders, at the annual meeting or at a special meeting called for that purpose, and by like vote the additional directors may be chosen at such meeting to hold office until the next annual election and until their successors are elected and qualify.

SECTION 6. COMPENSATION.—Directors shall not receive any stated salary for their services as directors or as members of committees, but by resolution of the board a fixed fee and expenses of attendance may be allowed for attendance at each meeting. Nothing contained in these bylaws shall be construed to preclude any director from serving the corporation in any other capacity as an officer, agent, or otherwise, and receiving compensation thereof.

SECTION 7. ACTION WITHOUT MEETING.—Any action required or permitted to be taken at any meeting of the Board of Directors, or of any directors' committee, may be taken without a meeting if prior to such action a written consent thereto is signed by all members of the board, or of such committee as the case may be, and such written consent is filed with the minutes of proceedings of the board or committee.

ARTICLE IV—OFFICERS

SECTION 1. OFFICERS.—The officers of the corporation shall consist of a president, a treasurer, and a secretary, and shall be elected by the Board of Directors and shall hold office until their successors are elected and qualified. In addition, the Board of Directors may elect a chair, one or more vice presidents and such assistant secretaries and assistant treasurers as it may deem proper. None of the officers of the corporation need be directors. The officers shall be elected at the first meeting of the Board of Directors after each annual meeting. More than two offices may be held by the same person.

SECTION 2. OTHER OFFICERS AND AGENTS.—The Board of Directors may appoint such officers and agents as it may deem advisable, who shall hold their offices for such terms and shall exercise such power and perform such duties as shall be determined from time to time by the Board of Directors.

SECTION 3. CHAIR.—The chair of the Board of Directors, if one be elected, shall preside at all meetings of the Board of Directors, and shall have and perform such other duties as from time to time may be assigned by the Board of Directors.

SECTION 4. PRESIDENT.—The president shall be the chief executive officer of the corporation and shall have the general powers and duties of supervision and management usually vested in the office of president of a corporation. He or she shall preside at all meetings of the shareholders if present thereat, and in the absence or nonelection of the chair of the Board of Directors, at all meetings of the Board of Directors, and shall have general supervision, direction and control of the business of the corporation. Except as the Board of Directors shall authorize the execution thereof in some other manner, the president shall execute bonds, mortgages, and other contracts in behalf of the corporation, and shall cause the seal to be affixed to any instrument requiring it, and when so affixed the seal shall be attested by the signature of the secretary or the treasurer or an assistant secretary or an assistant treasurer.

SECTION 5. VICE PRESIDENT.—Each vice president shall have such powers and shall perform such duties as shall be assigned by the directors.

SECTION 6. TREASURER.—The treasurer shall have the custody of the corporate funds and securities and shall keep full and accurate account of receipts and disbursements in books belonging to the corporation. He or she shall deposit all moneys and other valuables in the name and to the credit of the corporation in such depositories as may be designated by the Board of Directors.

The treasurer shall disburse the funds of the corporation as may be ordered by the Board of Directors or the president, taking proper vouchers for such disbursements. He or she shall render to the president and Board of Directors at the regular meetings of the Board of Directors, or whenever they may request it, an account of all his or her transactions as treasurer and of the financial condition of the corporation. If required by the Board of Directors, the treasurer shall give the corporation a bond for the faithful discharge of his or her duties in such amount and with such surety as the board shall prescribe.

SECTION 7. SECRETARY.—The secretary shall give, or cause to be given, notice of all meetings of shareholders and directors, and all other notices required by law or by these bylaws, and in case of his or her absence or refusal or neglect to do so, any such notice may be given by any person thereunto directed by the president, or by the directors, or shareholders, upon whose requisition the meeting is called as provided in these bylaws. The secretary shall record all the proceedings of the meetings of the corporation and of directors in a book to be kept for that purpose and shall affix the seal to all instruments requiring it, when authorized by the directors or the president, and attest the same.

SECTION 8. ASSISTANT TREASURERS & ASSISTANT SECRETARIES.—Assistant treasurers and assistant secretaries, if any, shall be elected and shall have such powers and shall perform such duties as shall be assigned to them, respectively, by the directors.

ARTICLE V

SECTION 1. CERTIFICATE OF STOCK.—Every holder of stock in the corporation shall be entitled to have a certificate signed by, or in the name of the corporation by, the chair or vice chair of the Board of Directors, or the president or a vice president and the treasurer or an assistant treasurer, or the secretary of the corporation, certifying the number of shares owned by him or her in the corporation. If the corporation shall be authorized to issue more than one class of stock or more than one series of any class, the designations, preferences and relative, participating, optional or other special rights of each class of stock or series thereof, and the qualifications, limitations, or restrictions of such preferences and/or rights shall be set forth in full or summarized on the face or back of the certificate that the corporation shall issue to represent such class or series of stock, provided that, except as otherwise provided in the General Corporation Law of Delaware in lieu of the foregoing requirements, there may be set forth on the face or back of the certificate that the corporation shall issue to represent such class or series of stock, a statement that the corporation will furnish without charge to each shareholder who so requests the powers, designations, preferences and relative, participating, optional or other special rights of each class of stock or series thereof and the qualifications, limitations or restrictions of such preferences and/or rights. Where a certificate is countersigned (1) by a transfer agent other than the corporation or its employee, or (2) by a registrar other than the corporation or its employee, the signatures of such officers may be facsimiles.

SECTION 2. LOST CERTIFICATES.—New certificates of stock may be issued in the place of any certificate therefore issued by the corporation, alleged to have been lost or destroyed, and the directors may, in their discretion, require the owner of the lost or destroyed certificate or his or her legal representatives to give the corporation a bond, in such sum as they may direct, not exceeding double the value of the stock, to indemnify the corporation against it on account of alleged loss of any such new certificate.

SECTION 3. TRANSFER OF SHARES.—The shares of stock of the corporation shall be transferable only upon its books by the holders thereof in person or by their duly authorized attorneys or legal representatives, and upon such transfer the old certificates shall be surrendered to the corporation by the delivery thereof to the person in charge of the stock and transfer books and ledgers, or to such other persons as the directors may designate, by whom they shall be canceled, and new certificates shall thereupon be issued. A record shall be made of each transfer and whenever a transfer shall be made for collateral security, and not absolutely, it shall be so expressed in the entry of the transfer.

SECTION 4. SHAREHOLDERS RECORD DATE.—In order that the corporation may determine the shareholders entitled to notice of or to vote at any meeting of shareholders or any adjournment thereof, or to express consent to corporate action in writing without a meeting, or entitled to receive payment of any dividend or other distribution or allotment of any rights, or entitled to exercise any rights in respect of any change, conversion, or exchange of stock, or for the purpose of any other lawful action, the Board of Directors may fix, in advance, a record date, which shall not be more than sixty nor less than ten days before the day of such meeting, nor more than sixty days prior to any other action. A determination of shareholders of record entitled to notice of or to vote at a meeting of shareholders shall apply to any adjournment of the meeting provided, however, that the Board of Directors may fix a new record date for the adjourned meeting.

SECTION 5. DIVIDENDS.—Subject to the provisions of the certificate of incorporation, the Board of Directors may, out of funds legally available therefore at any regular or special meeting, declare dividends upon the capital stock of the corporation as and when they deem expedient. Before declaring any dividends there may be set apart out of any funds of the corporation available for dividends, such sum or sums as the directors from time to time in their discretion deem proper working capital or as a reserve fund to meet contingencies or for equalizing dividends or for such other purposes as the directors shall deem conducive to the interests of the corporation.

SECTION 6. SEAL.—The corporate seal shall be circular in form and shall contain the name of the corporation, the year of its creation and the words "CORPORATE SEAL DELAWARE." Said seal may be used by causing it or a facsimile thereof to be impressed or affixed or otherwise reproduced.

SECTION 7. FISCAL YEAR.—The fiscal year of the corporation shall be determined by resolution of the Board of Directors.

SECTION 8. CHECKS.—All checks, drafts, or other orders for the payment of money, notes, or other evidences of indebtedness issued in the name of the corporation shall be signed by officer or officers, agent or agents of the corporation, and in such manner as shall be determined from time to time by resolution of the Board of Directors.

SECTION 9. NOTICE AND WAIVER OF NOTICE.—Whenever any notice is required by these bylaws to be given, personal notice is not meant unless expressly stated, and any notice so required shall be deemed to be sufficient if given by depositing the same in the United States mail, postage prepaid, addressed to the person entitled thereto at his or her address as it appears on the records of the corporation, and such notice shall be deemed to have been given on the day of such mailing. Shareholders not entitled to vote shall not be entitled to receive notice of any meetings except as otherwise provided by statute.

Whenever any notice whatever is required to be given under the provisions of any law, or under the provisions of the certificate of incorporation of the corporation or these bylaws, a waiver thereof in writing signed by the person or persons entitled to said notice, whether before or after the time stated therein, shall be deemed proper notice.

ARTICLE VI—AMENDMENTS

These bylaws may be altered and repealed, and bylaws may be made at any annual meeting of the shareholders or at any special meeting thereof if notice thereof is contained in the notice of such special meeting by the affirmative vote of a majority of the stock issued and outstanding or entitled to vote thereat, or by the regular meeting of the Board of Directors, if notice thereof is contained in the notice of such special meeting.

WHAT TO DO WHEN AN EXISTING, ESTABLISHED BUSINESS INCORPORATES

SECTION XXIV

There are some steps involved to transfer the financial records of a nonincorporated business to a corporation.

Below is a guideline to follow when a proprietorship or general partnership becomes a corporation:

1. Arrange to form the corporation. Select a registered agent if necessary.

2. New books and records should be prepared to reflect the new corporate status and the corporation name.

   a. Decide whether to transfer accounts receivable to the corporation. If accounts receivable are transferred to the corporation, notify customers of the change. This is optional.

   b. Decide whether to transfer accounts payable to the corporation. Again, notify creditors if the change is made.

   c. Decide whether to transfer capital assets to the corporation.

   d. Decide whether to transfer inventory to corporation records.

   e. Decide on the ending date of the corporate year to be used for income-tax-reporting purposes.

   f. Decide whether to notify all company associates and businesses dealt with as well as customers of the new corporate status. This can be done with sales-producing advertising and often at no cost. Newspaper editors will usually provide publicity of this change on the financial page. The owner(s) of the corporation should type and send an announcement to the financial editor of the newspaper where the company's office is located.

3. Order new letterheads reflecting the corporate name.

4. Open a bank account in the name of the corporation.

5. Transfer insurance policies to the corporation.

6. Arrange for any leases or other documents to be changed to reflect the corporation status.

7. Arrange to redo with the new corporation any employment contracts that exist with the old company.

8. If your unincorporated business will transfer its assets to the new corporation, you may have to comply with your state's bulk sales laws. Your attorney can assist you in determining whether the bulk sales law applies.

It would be helpful to consult with an accountant and, if there are complications with agreements, with an attorney on handling the above details.

A few of the companies that have already incorporated through this book—
From all 50 states and countries throughout the world

Name	Type of Business
AIDA Group Travel Coordinators & Travel Agents, Inc.	Group and individual travel to the general public
Airspeed Refinishing, Inc.	Custom painting of aircraft and other vehicles
Alaska Book Company	Book sales
Allied Auto International, Ltd.	Services and delivery of foreign vehicles to U.S.
Amazing Diets, Inc.	Publishers
American Armed Forces Association	Fraternal servicemen's organization
The American Society of Child Advocates	Nonprofit society to promote children's rights
Arundel Pool Management, Inc.	Management, opening, closing, and maintenance of swimming pools
Balancing Act Corp.	Manufacture of weighing scales
The Balloon Company	Operate a balloon for hire
Better Builders & Remodelers, Inc.	Building and remodeling of residential and commercial buildings
Better Business Maintenance Co.	Janitorial and maintenance services
Bost Farms, Inc.	Farming
Calphil Corp.	Import/export
Chronos, Inc.	Financial planning
Cicero Cheese Manufacturing Corp.	Manufacture of cheese
Cindex, Inc.	Computer technical services
Covered Bridge Craft Barn and Garden Centre, Inc.	Retail and wholesale sales of crafts, antiques, and plants through garden center
Creative Products, Inc.	Marketing organization
Criminal Justice Associates, Inc.	Consultations to criminal justice schools and agencies
The Cron Corp.	Printing, publishing, and management services
Cultural Commercial Exchange, Inc.	Cultural/commercial centers and festival sponsorship
Dakota Nomad, Inc.	Bicycle and cross-country ski retail sales and manufacture of accessories
Denticare of Delaware, Inc.	Prepaid dental healthcare plan
Dexterity Unlimited, Inc.	Retail and wholesale sales and production of handcrafted items
Different Drummer, Inc.	Yacht charter
The Dinky Rink, Inc.	Roller skating
Doug's Aircraft Interiors, Inc.	Aircraft upholstery and accessories
Electron Optics Corp.	Manufacture of surveillance equipment
Energy Independence Now, Inc.	Alternative energy sources
Eunitron, Inc.	Provide investment advisory service (publish a market letter)
European Overseas American, Inc.	Banking abroad, merchant banking
Excelsior International Corp.	Import/export
Fallbrook Ranchers, Inc.	Avocado and josoba nut ranching
Family Name Researchers, Inc.	Researching of surnames, family trees, genealogy, production of armorial bearings, etc.
Finance Corporation for Credit & Commerce	Financial and investment services
Flash Clinic, Inc.	Service and repair of electronic flash equipment
Garon Enterprises, Inc.	Numismatics
Golconda Feed & Grain, Inc.	Agricultural products
Green Cargo, Inc.	Diversified sales of plants and accessories
Group Two, Inc.	Educational seminars
The Growing Concern, Inc.	Greenhouses, solar systems
Guardian Protective Coatings, Inc.	Applications and sales of protective coatings
Honey Creek Farm, Inc.	Livestock farming
Hypertension Clinic, Inc.	Medical and health care, and teaching
Imperial Adhesives, Ltd.	Light manufacturing
Infinity's Child, Inc.	Decorating glass
Institute for Neuropsychopharmacologic Research, Inc.	Scientific research

Name	Type of Business
International Development Service Corp.	Export/import trade
International Geophysics, Inc.	Geophysical sales and services
Jetair, Inc.	Dealers in aircraft, flight instruction, and general aviation services
K & B Sink Tops, Inc.	Manufacture sink and countertops
The Lighthouse Repertory Theatre, Inc.	Theatrical productions
Mafia, Inc.	Bumper stickers
Mountain Sales, Inc.	Redwood table sales (handmade)
Music Makers Unlimited, Inc.	Musical services, band and orchestra
Nova Hang Gliders, Inc.	Sales and service of hang gliders and accessories
OMV Corp.	Real estate
Old Worlds Antiques Corp.	Wholesale and retail antiques
PeTaxi, Inc.	Rescue, receiving, air-shipping of pets, pet sitting, escort service for housepets
Pickwick Enterprises Corp.	Fish and chips shop
Pineville Medical Clinic, Inc.	Health and medical service
Plane, Inc.	Transportation
Psychynotics Foundation	Research and teaching of hypnosis, mind control metaphysics, psychic phenomena
R and B Logging, Inc.	Timber logging
Rainsong Institute	Advocacy of efficient energy use
Red Dawn Productions, Inc.	Film production
Reel Creations, Inc.	Music
Regina Careers, Ltd.	Self-training courses for home study
Scientific Resumes, Inc.	Polygraph testing
Seaboard Resources, Inc.	Management consulting and trading
Sign of the Times Corp.	Silk-screened garments
Simmons Industries, Inc.	Design, development, manufacture, and sales of poultry processing and related equipment and supplies
Snowcrest Corp.	Horsebreeding and training
Sponsler-Nitrogen-Service, Inc.	Retail—fertilizer, chemicals and apply same
Stock Shot Corp.	Marketing curling and skiing equipment
Tectonics International, Inc.	Architecture, engineering, construction, development, and management services in U.S. and abroad
Texmark Corp.	Act as holding company for retail and wholesale operations of liquor and supermarkets, brewing industry
The Thomas Talin Company	Fragrance
Thor-Bred Health Food Corp.	Health food for thoroughbred horses and other animals
To Have and To Hold Shops, Inc.	Misses sportswear
Transcontinental International, Inc.	Coal and energy products, sales and production
Transprocess Manufacturing Marketing Support Corp.	Business, tax and economy advice
Undersea Life Sciences Corp.	Consulting services for diving/hyperbaric-related industries
Union-Euro-Market, Inc.	Investments
Virginia Pork Corp.	Commercial swine production
Whitehouse Foods, Inc.	Retail grocery store
Woodcat Investments, Inc.	Investments
World Amateur Backgammon Championships, Inc.	Promotion of backgammon and other tournaments
World Backgammon Federation, Inc.	Sanctioning body for backgammon tournaments and official players and promoters organization
World Business Investment, Inc.	Real estate investment, sales, and business opportunities
World Cycle, Inc.	Motorcycle repair and sales
Xanthippe Corp.	Investments
Zoii, Inc.	Natural clothing and crafts

APPENDIX:
State-Specific Articles of Incorporation

If you determine that you should incorporate your business in a state other than Delaware, this Section provides you with current, fill-in-the-blank form articles of incorporation, as well as filing information, fees, and filing addresses for most states. Because filing fees change from time to time, it is best to contact your particular state to be sure the fees haven't been raised recently.

On the following pages are forms for these states:

Alaska	Louisiana	Oklahoma
Arizona	Maine	Oregon
Arkansas	Massachusetts	Pennsylvania
California	Michigan	Rhode Island
Colorado	Minnesota	South Dakota
Connecticut	Mississippi	Tennessee
District of Columbia	Missouri	Texas
Florida	Nevada	Vermont
Georgia	New Jersey	Virginia
Hawaii	New Mexico	Washington
Idaho	New York	West Virginia
Illinois	North Carolina	Wisconsin
Iowa	North Dakota	Wyoming
Kansas	Ohio	

Where necessary, photocopy forms before filling them in so that they can be filed in duplicate or triplicate as required.

IF YOU DESIRE ADVICE IN COMPLETING YOUR ARTICLES OF INCORPORATION, WE ADVISE THAT YOU SEEK PRIVATE LEGAL COUNSEL.

The enclosed forms set out the MINIMUM statutory requirements for Articles of Incorporation.

Articles of Incorporation may contain optional provisions explained under Optional Provisions in the instruction sheet.

INFORMATION AND INSTRUCTIONS TO FILE ARTICLES OF INCORPORATION UNDER THE ALASKA CORPORATIONS CODE

One or more natural persons at least 18 years of age may act as incorporators of a corporation by signing, verifying, and delivering to the Corporations Section an original and an exact copy of the Articles of Incorporation. The submitted documents must be dark, legible print and on paper which is no larger than 8-½ by 11 inches. "Computer printed material is not acceptable." The articles should contain a statement that they are being filed under the provisions of the Alaska Corporations Code (Alaska Statute (AS) 10.06).

ARTICLES OF INCORPORATION

Effective July 1, 1989, AS 10.06.208 provides that the following shall be included in the Articles of Incorporation:

1. the name of the corporation;

    (The name must contain "Corporation," "Company," "Incorporated," "Limited," or an abbreviation of these words.)

2. the purpose for which the corporation is organized may be stated as any lawful business allowed by the Alaska Corporations Code, and/or a more specific purpose. In addition, the Standard Industrial Code(s) (SIC) which most closely describes the business activities of the corporation must be stated. The SIC may be determined from the attached Standard Industrial Classification Code listing;

3. if the corporation is authorized to issue only one class of shares, the total number of shares that the corporation is authorized to issue;

4. If the corporation is authorized to issue more than one class of shares, or if a class of shares is to have two or more series,

    (A) the total number of shares of each class the corporation is authorized to issue, and the total number of shares of each series that the corporation is authorized to issue or of which the board is authorized to fix the number of shares;

    (B) the designation of each class, the designation of each series or that the board may determine the designation of any series;

    (C) the rights, preferences, privileges, and restrictions granted to or imposed on the respective classes or series of shares or the holders of the shares, or that the board, within any limits and restrictions stated, may determine or alter the rights, preferences, privileges, and restrictions granted to or imposed on a wholly unissued class of shares or a wholly unissued series of any class of shares, and

(D) if the number of shares of a series is authorized to be fixed by the board, the articles of incorporation may also authorize the board, within the limits and restrictions stated in the articles or stated in a resolution of the board originally fixing the number of shares constituting a series, to increase or decrease, but not below the number of shares of the series then outstanding, the number of shares of a series are decreased, the shares constituting the decrease shall resume the status they had before the adoption of the resolution originally fixing the number of shares of the series.

5. The physical address of its initial registered office and the name of its initial registered agent (a mailing address must also be given if different from the physical address);

6. The name and address of each alien affiliate or a statement that there are no alien affiliates (see Definitions).

FILING FEE: The filing fee for Articles of Incorporation is $250.00.

☞   **The Articles of Incorporation, statement of SIC code, and filing fee should be submitted for filing to:**

Corporations Section
P.O. Box 110808
Juneau, Alaska 99811-0808
Telephone: (907) 465-2530

PLEASE ALLOW A MINIMUM OF TWO WEEKS FOR PROCESSING.

The date of incorporation will be the date the documents are received in this office in statutory compliance, unless a future date is requested.

If the documents are not in statutory compliance, they will be returned for correction. A $5.00 reprocessing fee is due when the documents are resubmitted for filing.

Alaska Corporation Net Income Tax

Every corporation earning gross income from sources within the state, except for those corporations that are specifically exempted, must file a corporation net income tax return. A corporation may elect to file a consolidated Alaska return with its affiliates. The return must be filed and full payment must be made on or before the 15th day of the third month following the close of the tax year.

Form 04-611 is the prescribed form on which the Alaska Corporation Net Income Tax is to be reported for most corporations. However, those corporations engaged in oil and gas production or pipeline transportation must use Form 04-650. The forms may be obtained by contacting the **Alaska Department of Revenue, Income and Exise Audit Division, P.O. Box 110420, Juneau, Alaska 99811-0420, Telephone (907) 465-2320.**

ARTICLES OF INCORPORATION
(Domestic Business Corporation)

The undersigned natural person(s) of the age of 18 years or more, acting as incorporator(s) of a corporation under the Alaska Corporations Code (AS 10.06) adopt the following Articles of Incorporation:

PLEASE TYPE OR PRINT CLEARLY IN BLACK INK

ARTICLE I (See Number 1 of Instructions)

The name of the corporation is:

ARTICLE II (See Number 2 of Instructions)

The corporation is organized for the purpose of:

ARTICLE III (See Numbers 3 and 4 of Instructions)

The aggregate number of shares which the corporation shall have authority to issue is:

NO. OF SHARES	CLASS	SERIES	PAR VALUE (Optional)
NO. OF SHARES	CLASS	SERIES	PAR VALUE (Optional)
NO. OF SHARES	CLASS	SERIES	PAR VALUE (Optional)

08-400 (Rev. 12/96)
MM/dgl

(5)

ARTICLE IV (See Number 5 of Instructions)

1. **The name of the registered agent (only one registered agent may be given):**

   _____

2. **The physical (street) address of the registered agent's office:**

   No. and Street:_____

   City:_____, Alaska   Zip Code:_____

3. **Mailing (P.O. Box) address of the registered agent's office. If physical and mailing addresses are the same, please state "N/A."**

   P.O. Box_____

   City:_____, Alaska   Zip Code:_____

ARTICLE V (See Number 6 of Instructions)

The name and address of each alien affiliate is: (If none, please indicate "N/A."

Name: Complete Resident or Business Address:

_____   _____

                                             _____

                                             _____

                                             _____

Attach additional pages for continuation of previous article and/or additional articles. Please indicate which article you are continuing and/or insert any desired additional provisions authorized by the code by adding additional articles here (see optional provisions in the instructions). The PRINTED name and SIGNATURE of each incorporator:

Signed by the incorporator or incorporators this _____ day of _____, 19_____.

Name	**Complete Resident or Business Address:** (Optional)
_____	_____
_____	_____
_____	_____
_____	_____

THE SIGNATURE OF EACH INCORPORATOR MUST BE NOTARIZED.

_____ says on oath or affirms that he has read the foregoing (or attached) document and believes all statements made in the document are true.

SUBSCRIBED AND SWORN before me this _____ day of _____, 19_____.

_____
Notary Public

Seal

My Commission Expires:_____

STATEMENT OF STANDARD INDUSTRIAL CODE (SIC)

The SIC which most clearly describe the initial activities of the corporation are:

Primary:_____   Secondary:_____   Other:_____

PHOENIX OFFICE
1300 West Washington
Phoenix, AZ 85007-2929
Phone:(602) 542-3135
Toll Free:
1-800-345-5819
(AZ Residents Only)

ARIZONA CORPORATION COMMISSION

TUCSON OFFICE
400 West Congress
Tucson, AZ 85701-1347
Phone: (520) 628-6560
Toll Free:
1-800-345-5819
(AZ Residents Only)

GENERAL FILING INSTRUCTIONS
FOR
ARIZONA CORPORATIONS

ALL CORPORATIONS, DOMESTIC AND FOREIGN, MUST COMPLY WITH THE FOLLOWING AT THE TIME YOUR DOCUMENTS ARE DELIVERED FOR FILING.

1. **Make sure that the corporate name you are using has been checked with the Commission and is available for use by your corporation.** (Telephone approval is advisory only, but the name may be formally reserved for 120 days for a fee of $10.00. A foreign corporation may register its name for the same fee.) If you are a holder of a tradename that is identical or non-distinguishable from the proposed name, you will be asked to provide a copy of the tradename certificate or "received" copy of the tradename application. Call our office for details at: (602) 542-3135 in Phoenix or (520) 628-6560 in Tucson.

2. Deliver the original **and one (1) or more exact copies** of the Articles of Incorporation (for domestic corporations) OR Application for Authority (for foreign corporations) to the Commission. Your filed copy will be returned to you when all requirements have been satisfied. Notarization is not required.

3. Statutory Agent **must have a street address** (P.O. Box not accepted), and may be either an individual Arizona resident, a domestic corporation or limited iiability company, or foreign corporation or limited libility company authorized to transact business in Arizona.

4. The Certificate of Disclosure **must be signed** and dated within 30 days of delivery to this office by all incorporators of a new corporation, or by any duly authorized officer if a foreign corporation.

5. If the person executing the documents has a power of attorney authorizing him/her to do so, a copy of the **document granting authority must be received**.

6. **Pay the required (U.S.) fees**. Please make check payable to the Arizona Corporation Commission. **Expedited service is available for an additional $35.00 fee**.

	Regular	Expedited		Regular	Expedited
Arizona Business	$60.00	$95.00	Arizona Non-Profit	$40.00	$75.00
Foreign Business	$175.00	$210.00	Foreign Non-Profit	$175.00	$210.00

7. Advise the Commission in writing of the **fiscal year end date** adopted by the corporation.

8. AFTER FILING THE ARTICLES OR APPLICATION, THEY MUST BE PUBLISHED. Within sixty (60) days after filing with the Commission, there must be published in a newspaper of general circulation in the county of the known place of business in Arizona, three (3) consecutive publications of a copy of your APPROVED Articles of Incorporation or Application for Authority. Within ninety (90) days after filing, an Affidavit evidencing the publication must be filed with the Commission.

   FOREIGN CORPORATIONS PLEASE NOTE: Pursuant to Article XIV, §8. of the Arizona Constitution and A.R.S. §10-1503.B, all Applications For Authority must be accompanied by a certified copy of your CURRENT articles of incorporation (including all amendments) and a Certificate of Existence (Good Standing), both to be authenticated by the Secretary of State or other official having legal custody of the corporate records in your state, province or country under the laws of which you are incorporated.

ALL CORPORATE DOCUMENTS FILED WITH THE ARIZONA CORPORATION COMMISSION, INCLUDING THE ANNUAL STATEMENT OF FINANCIAL CONDITION, ARE PUBLIC RECORD. AS SUCH, ALL CORPORATE FILES ARE OPEN FOR PUBLIC INSPECTION.

CF:0033
Rev: 2/98

DO NOT PUBLISH
THIS SECTION

ARTICLE I
The corporate
name must
contain a
corporate
ending which
may be
"corporation,
"
"association,
" "company,"
"limited,"
"incorporated
" or an
abbreviation
of any of
these words.
If you are
the holder or
assignee of a
tradename or
trademark,
attach
Declaration
of Tradename
Holder form.

ARTICLE 3
The name cannot
imply that the
corporation is
organized for any
purpose other than the
initial business
indicated in this article.

ARTICLE 4
The total number of
authorized shares
cannot be "Zero" or
"Not Applicable."

ARTICLE 5
May be in care of the
statutory agent.

ARTICLE 6
The statutory agent
address cannot be a
P.O. Box. It must be a
physical address in
Arizona. The agent
must sign the Articles
or provide a consent to
acceptance of
appointment.

ARTICLES OF INCORPORATION

OF

_____

(An Arizona Business Corporation)

1. <u>Name</u>. The name of the Corporation is _____

_____.

2. <u>Purpose</u>.

The purpose for which this Corporation is organized is the transaction of any or all lawful business for which corporations may be incorporated under the laws of Arizona, as they may be amended from time to time.

3. <u>Initial Business</u>.

The Corporation initially intends to conduct the business of _____ ___ ___

_____

_____.

4. <u>Authorized Capital</u>.

The Corporation shall have authority to issue _____ shares of Common Stock.

5. <u>Known Place of Business</u>. (In Arizona)

The street address of the known place of business of the Corporation is:

_____

_____

_____.

6. <u>Statutory Agent</u>. (In Arizona)

The name and address of the statutory agent of the Corporation is:

_____

_____

_____.

7. Board of Directors

The initial board of directors shall consist of _____ director(s). The name(s) and address(es) of the person(s) who is(are) to serve as the director(s) until the first annual meeting of shareholders or until his(her)(their) successor(s) is(are) elected and qualifies is(are):

Name: _____   _____

Address: _____   _____

City, State, Zip: _____   _____

Name: _____   _____

Address: _____   _____

City, State, Zip: _____   _____

The number of persons to serve on the board of directors thereafter shall be fixed by the Bylaws.

8. Incorporators.

The name(s) and address(es) of the incorporator(s) is (are):

Name: _____   _____

Address: _____   _____

City, State, Zip: _____   _____

ARTICLE 8
A minimum of 1
incorporator is
required. All
incorporators must
sign both the Articles
of Incorporation and
the Certificate of
Disclosure.

All powers, duties and responsibilities of the incorporators shall cease at the time of delivery of these Articles of Incorporation to the Arizona Corporation Commission.

9. Indemnification of Officers, Directors, Employees and Agents.

The Corporation shall indemnify any person who incurs expenses or liabilities by reason of the fact he or she is or was an officer, director, employee or agent of the Corporation or is or was serving at the request of the Corporation as a director, officer, employee or agent of another Corporation, partnership, joint venture, trust or other enterprise. This indemnification shall be mandatory in all circumstances in which indemnification is permitted by law.

10. Limitation of Liability.

To the fullest extent permitted by the Arizona Revised Statutes, as the same exists or may hereafter be amended, a director of the Corporation shall not be liable to the Corporation or its stockholders for monetary damages for any action taken or any failure to take any action as a director. No repeal, amendment or modification of this article, whether direct or indirect, shall eliminate or reduce its effect with respect to any act or omission of a director of the Corporation occurring prior to such repeal, amendment or modification.

**DO NOT PUBLISH
THIS SECTION**

Phone and fax
numbers are optional

The agent may
consent to the
appointment by either
executing the consent,
attaching a cover
letter, or if paying by
check, executing the
check.

The Articles must be
accompanied by a
Certificate of
Disclosure, executed
within 30 days of
delivery to the
Commission, by all
incorporators.

EXECUTED this _____ day of _____, 19____ by all of the
incorporators.

Signed:_____   _____

_____   _____
[Print Name Here]   [Print Name Here]

PHONE _____   FAX _____

Acceptance of Appointment By Statutory Agent

The undersigned hereby acknowledges and accepts the appointment as statutory agent of the
above-named corporation effective this _____ day of _____, 19_____.

Signed _____

_____
[Print Name Here]

CF42 Rev.4/98

State of Arkansas
SECRETARY OF STATE

Sharon Priest
SECRETARY OF STATE

Dear Customer:

Enclosed you will find the Articles of Incorporation or Application Seeking Authorization to do Business in Arkansas which you have requested as well as a form entitled "Corporate Franchise Tax".

This informational form is a new REQUIREMENT and MUST ACCOMPANY your filing. The due date for this tax is June 1 in the calendar year following the year of incorporation or qualification and each June 1 thereafter.

DOMESTIC corporations must submit duplicate articles completed and signed, the tax information form and the filing fee of $50.00. FOREIGN corporations seeking authorization to do business in Arkansas must submit duplicate applications completed and signed, an original certificate of existence from the domestic state of incorporation dated within thirty days, the tax information form and the filing fee of $300.00. No application can be accepted without an Arkansas Registered Agent/Office.

Corporations wishing to file as a non-profit corporation or a cooperative association DO NOT USE these forms. Please call the Corporations Department, (501) 682-3409, for information regarding the filing of such entities.

In addition, another state agency may regulate the corporation you are filing and communication with this agency may be necessary. For general state information you may call (501) 682-3000. Below is a partial list of agencies you may wish to contact.

Alcohol Beverage Control	(501) 682-1105
Securities Department	324-9260
Arkansas Oil & Gas Commission	862-4965
Arkansas State Bank Department	324-9019
Contractors Licensing Board	372-4661
Arkansas Insurance Department	686-2900
Arkansas Industrial Development Commission	682-1121
Arkansas Manufactured Home Commission	324-9032

For General information on other taxes which may be applicable to your corporation you may wish to contact the Department of Finance and Administration at (501) 682-4775.

Forms to file amendments, dissolutions, withdrawals and changes in registered agent/office may be obtained by contacting the Corporations Department.

Sincerely,

Sharon Priest

Sharon Priest

State of Arkansas

Sharon Priest, Secretary of State

Corporations Division
State Capitol
Little Rock, Arkansas 72201-1094

Application for Certificate of Authority
(Please type or print)

Pursuant to the provisions of Arkansas Code of 1987 Annotated, the undersigned as the duly authorized and acting president, secretary, treasurer, superintendent or managing agent in the State of Arkansas, of the foreign corporation named below (the "corporation") for which this statement is submitted, under oath hereby state:

1a.   The name of the corporation is:_____.

1b.   Fictitious name to be used in Arkansas: _____

_____

(The corporation may use a fictitious name to transact business in Arkansas if its real name is unavailable and it delivers to the Secretary of State for filing a copy of the resolution of its board of directors certified by its secretary adopting a fictitious name.)

2.   The state, territory or foreign country under whose laws the corporation was incorporated is:

_____

3.   Date Incorporated _____ Period of Duration: _____

4.   The nature of the business of the corporation and the object or purposes to be transacted, promoted or carried on by it are:

_____

5.   The address of the general office or place of business of the corporation in Arkansas is designated to be:

_____
(Street Address)   (City)   (State)   (Zip)

6.   The name and address of the registered agent of the corporation upon whom *Service of Process* is authorized to be in Arkansas is:

_____
(Name)

_____
(Street Address)   (City)   (State)   (Zip)

7.   The address of the general office or principal place of business of the corporation is:

_____
(Street Address)   (City)   (State)   (Zip)

8.   The number and par value, if any, of shares of the corporation's capital stock owned or to be owned by residents of Arkansas:

_____

9.   Value of Assets in Arkansas $ _____.

Total value of all Assets (including Arkansas) $ _____.

10.   The foreign corporation shall deliver with the completed application a certificate of existence (or document of similar import) duly authorized by the Secretary of State or other official having custody of corporate records in the state or country under whose laws it is incorporated.

11.   A filing fee of $300.00 is submitted herewith in accordance with Act 958 of 1987.

Witness the hand and seal of the corporation executed under oath by the undersigned in behalf of the corporation on this the _____ day of _____ , 19 _____.

_____
(Name of Corporation)

_____
(Signature of Authorized Officer)

_____
(Title of Position Held by Authorized Officer)

Fee $300.00   F-01/Rev. 10-1-88

State of Arkansas

Sharon Priest, Secretary of State

Corporations Division
State Capitol
Little Rock, Arkansas 72201-1094

Application for Certificate of Authority
(Please type or print)

Pursuant to the provisions of Arkansas Code of 1987 Annotated, the undersigned as the duly authorized and acting president, secretary, treasurer, superintendent or managing agent in the State of Arkansas, of the foreign corporation named below *(the "corporation")* for which this statement is submitted, under oath hereby state:

1a. The name of the corporation is:_____ .

1b. Fictitious name to be used in Arkansas: _____

_____.

(The corporation may use a fictitious name to transact business in Arkansas if its real name is unavailable and it delivers to the Secretary of State for filing a copy of the resolution of its board of directors certified by its secretary adopting a fictitious name.)

2. The state, territory or foreign country under whose laws the corporation was incorporated is:

_____.

3. Date Incorporated _____Period of Duration: _____.

4. The nature of the business of the corporation and the object or purposes to be transacted, promoted or carried on by it are:

_____.

5. The address of the general office or place of business of the corporation in Arkansas is designated to be:

_____
(Street Address)   (City)   (State)   (Zip)

6. The name and address of the registered agent of the corporation upon whom *Service of Process* is authorized to be in Arkansas is:

_____.
(Name)

_____.
(Street Address)   (City)   (State)   (Zip)

7. The address of the general office or principal place of business of the corporation is:

_____.
(Street Address)   (City)   (State)   (Zip)

8. The number and par value, if any, of shares of the corporation's capital stock owned or to be owned by residents of Arkansas:

_____.

9. Value of Assets in Arkansas $ _____.

Total value of all Assets (including Arkansas) $ _____.

10. The foreign corporation shall deliver with the completed application a certificate of existence (or document of similar import) duly authorized by the Secretary of State or other official having custody of corporate records in the state or country under whose laws it is incorporated.

11. A filing fee of $300.00 is submitted herewith in accordance with Act 958 of 1987.

Witness the hand and seal of the corporation executed under oath by the undersigned in behalf of the corporation on this the _____day of _____, 19 _____.

_____
(Name of Corporation)

_____
(Signature of Authorized Officer)

_____
(Title of Position Held by Authorized Officer)

Fee $300.00   F-01/Rev. 10-1-88

Sharon Priest
SECRETARY OF STATE

State of Arkansas
SECRETARY OF STATE

CORPORATE FRANCHISE TAX

In order for this corporation to receive its annual corporate franchise tax reporting form, please complete and file with the office of the Secretary of State at the time of Incorporation or qualification.

_____

Corporate Name as Applied for in Arkansas

_____

Contact Person

_____

Street Address or Post Office Box

_____

City, State, ZIP

_____

Telephone Number

NOTE: This tax is due on or before June 1 of the year following incorporation or qualification in this state.

_____

Signature of Incorporator, Officer or Agent
for the Corporation

FT-11

ORGANIZATION OF CALIFORNIA STOCK CORPORATIONS

Business corporations authorized to issue stock, excluding such special organizations as cooperatives, credit unions, etc., are organized under the General Corporation Law, and particularly Title 1, Division 1, Chapter 2, California Corporations Code.

Sections 200-202, California Corporations Code, outline the minimum content requirements of Articles of Incorporation for stock corporations. The attached sample was drafted to meet those **minimum** statutory requirements. The sample may be used as a guide in preparing documents to be filed with the Secretary of State to incorporate. It is, however, suggested that you seek private counsel for advice regarding the proposed corporation's specific business needs which may require the inclusion of special permissive provisions.

THE FEE FOR FILING ARTICLES OF INCORPORATION ON BEHALF OF A STOCK CORPORATION IS $100.00. Additionally, the $600.00/$800.00 minimum annual franchise tax must be submitted with the Articles of Incorporation to enable filing. The minimum tax is $600.00 or $800.00. The Secretary of State's Office will accept either amount for filing. The applicant is responsible for determining the proper amount to submit to this office. For assistance in making this determination, the applicant may refer to California Revenue and Taxation Code Sections 23153 and 23221. The tax payment must be sent to the Secretary of State along with the Articles of Incorporation, and it may be included with the filing fee in a single remittance made payable to the California Secretary of State.

(Please review the attachment, FTB Pub. 1060, for information regarding additional taxes that must be paid.)

The Secretary of State will certify two copies of the filed Articles of Incorporation without charge, **provided that the copies are submitted to the Secretary of State with the original to be filed.** Any additional copies, submitted with the original, will be certified upon request and the prepayment of $8.00 per copy.

An additional $15.00 **special handling fee** is applicable for expedited processing of documents delivered in person, over the counter, to the Sacramento Headquarters Office or to any of the corporate branch offices which are located in Fresno, Los Angeles, San Diego and San Francisco. The $15.00 special handling fee must be remitted by separate check for each submittal as it will be **RETAINED WHETHER THE DOCUMENTS ARE FILED OR REJECTED.** The special handling fee does not apply to documents submitted by mail.

> **PLEASE NOTE:** CASH IS NOT ACCEPTED IN THE FRESNO BRANCH OFFICE, THE LOS ANGELES BRANCH OFFICE OR THE SAN DIEGO BRANCH OFFICE.

When forming a new corporation you may also wish to contact one or more of the following agencies for additional information:

♦ The Franchise Tax Board -for information regarding **franchise tax** requirements.

♦ The Board of Equalization - for information regarding **sales tax** and/or **use tax** liability.

♦ The Commissioner of Corporations - for information regarding **issuance** and **sale** of securities in California, Franchise Investment Law and/or Escrow Law requirements.

- The Department of Insurance - for information regarding **insurer** requirements

- The Commissioner of Financial Institutions - for information regarding the organization of **banks** and corporate name style requirements.

- The Department of Consumer Affairs - for information regarding **licensing** requirements.

- The Employment Development Department - for information regarding **disability unemployment insurance tax.**

- The Director of Industrial Relations, Division of Worker's Compensation - for information regarding **workman's compensation** requirements.

- The city and/or county clerk and/or recorder where the principal place of business is located - for information regarding business licenses, fictitious business names (if doing business under a name other than the corporate name), and for specific requirements regarding zoning, building permits, etc. based on the business activities of the corporation.

- The Internal Revenue Service (IRS) - for information regarding **federal employee identification numbers.**

The Secretary of State does not license corporations or business entities. For licensing requirements, please contact the city and/or county where the principal place of business is located and/or the state agency with jurisdiction over the business, e.g. Contractors' State License Board.

Samples are also available for the incorporation of California **professional** and **close** corporations and for the incorporation of various classifications of California nonprofit corporations.

Documents may be mailed or hand delivered for over the counter processing to the Sacramento Headquarters Office at:

Business Filings
1500 11th Street
Sacramento, CA 95814
Attention: Document Filing Support Unit
(916) 653-2318

OR

may be hand delivered for over the counter processing to any of the corporate branch offices which are located in:

- Fresno   (209) 243-2100
  2497 West Shaw, Suite 101
  Fresno, CA 93711

- Los Angeles   (213) 897-3062
  300 South Spring Street, Room 12513
  Los Angeles, CA 90013-1233

- San Diego   (619) 525-4113
  1350 Front Street, Suite 2060
  San Diego, CA 92101-3690

- San Francisco   (415) 439-6959
  235 Montgomery Street, Suite 725
  San Francisco, CA 94104

NOTE: When filing Articles of Incorporation in a corporate branch office it is necessary to submit duplicate original documents, plus any copies to be certified and returned. These offices do not process mailed in documents.

INSTRUCTIONS:

To incorporate you may prepare documents following the sample provided. Documents **must** be typed with letters in dark contrast to the paper. Documents submitted which would produce poor microfilm will be returned unfiled. Articles of Incorporation may be drafted to include all required provisions and any statutorily permissive provisions, including initial directors. The Secretary of State does not have samples containing permissive provisions.

Article I - is to be completed with the name of the corporation exactly as the name is to appear on the records of the Secretary of State.

Article II - has been taken directly from the California Corporations Code as is required by law and should not be modified when drafting documents.

Article III - is to be completed with the name and California street address, or physical location, of the agent for service of process (a post office box is not acceptable). The designated agent, individual or corporation, **must** agree to accept process on behalf of the corporation prior to designation. A proposed corporation cannot designate itself as agent for service of process. When designating another corporation as agent, the agent corporation **must** have on file, with the Secretary of State, a statement pursuant to Section 1505, California Corporations Code. When a corporate agent is used, the address of the designated corporation is not to be included in the articles.

Article IV - is to be completed with the total number of shares that the corporation will be authorized to issue.

> **NOTE:** Before shares of stock are sold or issued the corporation must comply with the Corporate Securities Law administered by the Commissioner of Corporations. For information regarding permits to issue shares please contact that agency.

The Articles of Incorporation must be originally signed by an incorporator unless directors are named in the articles. If directors are named in the articles, each person named must sign and acknowledge the document. The name(s) of the person(s) signing must be typed directly below the signature(s).

The original and at least two copies of the completed document are then mailed or hand delivered to the Secretary of State, together with the applicable fee. (If documents are to being hand delivered for filing in the Fresno, Los Angeles San Diego or San Francisco office, a duplicate original is also required.)

To expedite processing, Articles of Incorporation submitted by mail should be accompanied by a self-addressed envelope and a letter referencing the proposed corporate name as well as your own name, telephone number and return address.

ARTICLES OF INCORPORATION

I

The name of this corporation is _____ *(NAME OF CORPORATION)*.

II

The purpose of the corporation is to engage in any lawful act or activity for which a corporation may be organized under the **GENERAL CORPORATION LAW** of California other than the banking business, the trust company business or the practice of a profession permitted to be incorporated by the California Corporations Code.

III

The name and address in the State of California of this corporation's initial agent for service of process is:

Name _____

Address _____

City _____ State **CALIFORNIA** Zip _____

IV

This corporation is authorized to issue only one class of shares of stock; and the total number of shares which this corporation is authorized to issue is _____.

_____
(Signature of Incorporator)
(Typed Name of Incorporator), Incorporator

Please include a typed
self-addressed envelope

MUST BE TYPED
FILING FEE: $50.00
MUST SUBMIT TWO COPIES

Mail to: Secretary of State
Corporations Section
1560 Broadway, Suite 200
Denver, CO 80202
(303) 894-2251
Fax (303) 894-2242

For office use only   001

ARTICLES OF INCORPORATION

Corporation Name_____

Principal Business Address_____
(Include City, State, Zip)

Cumulative voting shares of stock is authorized. Yes ☐   No ☐

If duration is less than perpetual enter number of years _____

Preemptive rights are granted to shareholders.   Yes ☐   No ☐

Stock information: (If additional space is needed, continue on a separate sheet of paper.)

Stock Class_____Authorized Shares_____Par Value_____

Stock Class_____Authorized Shares_____Par Value_____

The name of the initial registered agent and the address of the registered office is:(If another corporation, use last name space)

Last Name_____First & Middle Name_____

Street Address_____
(Include City, State, Zip)
The undersigned consents to the appointment as the initial registered agent.

Signature of Registered Agent_____

These articles are to have a delayed effective date of: _____

Incorporators: Names and addresses: (If more than two, continue on a separate sheet of paper.

NAME   ADDRESS

_____   _____

_____   _____

Incorporators who are natural persons must be 18 years or more. The undersigned, acting as incorporator(s) of a corporation under the Colorado Business Corporation Act, adopt the above Articles of Incorporation.

Signature_____   Signature_____

Revised 7/95

CERTIFICATE OF INCORPORATION

STOCK CORPORATION

Office of the Secretary of the State

30 Trinity Street / P.O. Box 150470 / Hartford, CT 06115-04 / new 1-97

Space For Office Use Only

1. NAME OF CORPORATION:

2. TOTAL NUMBER OF AUTHORIZED SHARES: _____

If the corporation has more than one class of shares, it must designate each class and the number of shares authorized within each class below

Class	Number of shares per class

3. TERMS, LIMITATIONS, RELATIVE RIGHTS AND PREFERENCES OF EACH CLASS OF SHARES AND SERIES THEREOF PURSUANT TO CONN. GEN. STAT. SECTION 33-665:

Space For Office Use Only

4. APPOINTMENT OF REGISTERED AGENT

Print or type name of agent:	Business/initial registered office address:
	Residence address:

Acceptance of appointment

_____

Signature of agent

5. OTHER PROVISIONS:

6. EXECUTION

Dated this _____ day of _____, 19 _____

Certificate must be signed by each incorporator.

PRINT OR TYPE NAME OF INCORPORATOR(S)	SIGNATURE(S)	COMPLETE ADDRESS(ES)

INSTRUCTIONS FOR COMPLETION OF THE CERTIFICATE OF INCORPORATION
STOCK CORPORATION

(Instructions correspond with numbered entries on the form)

NAME OF CORPORATION: Please provide the name of the corporation. The name of the corporation must contain one of the following designations: "corporation", "incorporated", or "company", or the abbreviation "corp.", "inc." or "co.", or words or abbreviations of like import in another language. The name must also be **distinguishable** from other business names on the records of the Secretary of the State.

TOTAL NUMBER OF AUTHORIZED SHARES: Please provide the total number of shares the corporation is authorized to issue. Corporations must pay a minimum franchise tax of $150 dollars for authorizing up to 20,000 shares at the time of incorporation. If the number of shares authorized is greater than 20,000, the franchise tax is calculated based on a sliding scale set forth in section 33-618 as amended. If the corporation seeks authority to issue more than one class of shares, it must clearly designate each class in the block labeled Class and the corresponding number of authorized shares in each class in the block labeled Number of shares per class.

TERMS, LIMITATIONS, RELATIVE RIGHTS AND PREFERENCES OF EACH CLASS OF SHARES AND SERIES THEREOF PURSUANT TO CONN. GEN. STAT. SECTION 33-665: Please set forth all information required by section 33-665 as amended for each class of stock authorized in item number 2.

APPOINTMENT OF REGISTERED AGENT: The corporation may appoint either a natural person who is a resident of Connecticut, a Connecticut corporation or a foreign corporation which has a certificate of authority to transact business in Connecticut. Please note the following: if the agent being appointed is a natural person, that person's business address must be provided under the heading Business/initial registered office address and their residence address under the heading Residence address; if the agent appointed is a corporation, it must provide its principal office address under the Business/initial registered office address heading; the agent must sign accepting the appointment in the space provided; the signatory must state the capacity under which they sign if signing on behalf of a corporation; the corporation may not appoint itself as its registered agent and; all addresses must include a street number, street name, city, state, postal code.

OTHER INFORMATION: Please present in the space provided or on an attachment any information which a stock corporation is permitted but not required to provide.

EXECUTION: The document must be executed by one or more incorporators, each of whom must provide an address containing a street and number, city, state and a postal code. The execution constitutes legal statement under the penalties of false statement that the information provided in the document is true.

Government
of the
District of Columbia

DEPARTMENT OF CONSUMER AND REGULATORY AFFAIRS
BUSINESS REGULATION ADMINISTRATION
CORPORATIONS DIVISION
614 H STREET, N.W. ROOM 407
WASHINGTON, D.C. 20001

INSTRUCTION SHEET - ARTICLES OF INCORPORATION
FOR PROFIT AND NON-PROFIT CORPORATIONS

1. Articles must be typed on plain bond paper; do not use letterhead paper. Letter sized and legal paper are both acceptable.

2. Submit two (2) original signed sets of articles. (For non-profit corporations and cooperative associations, two (2) sets originally signed and notarized.) DO NOT SIGN ARTICLES THROUGH CARBON PAPER.

3. In articles, state the specific purposes the corporation will pursue. In the District of Columbia, general purposes (such as "any lawful purpose") are not acceptable.

4. The registered agent of the corporation must be either

(1) an individual person who **resides** in the District of Columbia (a business office does not qualify as residency), or

(2) **another** corporation which has the authority in Its own articles to act as a registered agent in the District of Columbia.

(3) Written consent from the registered agent must be attached to **articles.**

5. The registered office address can **never** be a post office box.

6. For other specific requirements of articles of incorporation, you should review the particular statue under which you are incorporating:

Business Corporations - D.C. Code, Title 29, Chapter 3
Non-Profit Corporations - D.C. Code, Title 29, Chapter 5
Professional Corporations - D.C. Code, Title 29, Chapter 6
Cooperative Associations - D.C. Code, Title 29, Chapter 11

All references are to the 1981 edition of the District of Columbia Code. Reading copies of the Code are available at all branches of the D.C. Library.

Fee Schedule for Articles of Incorporation

1. Business and Professional Corporations

Filing Fee......................$100.00
Initial License Fee..........(See Note Below)
TOTAL..........................Varies

The initial license fee varies with the amount of proposed authorized stock. The minimum initial license fee is $20.00, which covers up to $100,000 worth of authorized stock. For authorized stock in excess of $100,000, contact the Superintendent of Corporation's office for the correct fee computation. **THE MINIMUM TOTAL FEE FOR BUSINESS AND PROFESSIONAL CORPORATIONS IS $120.00**

2. Non-Profit Corporations

Filing Fee......................$30.00
Indexing........................$20.00
TOTAL........................$50.00

3. Cooperative Associations

Filing Fee....................... $5.00
Indexing........................ $1.00
TOTAL.......................... $6.00

4. Certified copies of articles are $25.00 per document. Certificates of Good Standing and Certificates of status are $10.00 each. Long form certificates are $20.00 each.

Non-Profit Fees
Certified Copy.....................$25.00
Long form certificates...........$20.00
Good Standing Certificate.....$20.00

MAKE ALL CHECKS PAYABLE TO "D.C. TREASURER"

For General Information Call:
Superintendent of Corporations - (202) 727-7278
Corporate Information and Name Availability - (202) 727-7283

Articles of Incorporation
for
District of Columbia

(For Profit Corporation)

1. The name of the corporation is: _____ (Must have corporate
designator such as Inc., or Corp., or Co.)

2. The registered office address of the corporation is _____
(Cannot be a post office box)

3. The registered agent at the above address is: _____

4. The purpose of the corporation is: _____ (i.e. provide
architectural landscaping, ownership of a restaurant, etc.)

5. The corporation is authorized to issue _____ shares. (Must be at least one)

6. The name of the Incorporator(s) are:

_____

Name   Address

_____

Name   Address

7. The name and phone number of a person to be contacted in there is a question about the filing
of these articles is: _____.
                    Name   Area Code and Phone

8. The period of duration for this corporation is perpetual.

I/We, the undersigned natural persons of the age of eighteen years of more acting as
incorporator(s) under the Business Corporation Act, adopt these Articles of Incorporation.

_____

Signature of Incorporator(s)

Date signed :

Government
of the
District of Columbia

**DEPARTMENT OF CONSUMER AND REGULATORY AFFAIRS
BUSINESS REGULATION ADMINISTRATION
CORPORATIONS DIVISION
614 H STREET, N.W. ROOM 407
WASHINGTON, D.C. 20001**

WRITTEN CONSENT TO ACT AS REGISTERED AGENT FOR A FOREIGN CORPORATION (FOR PROFIT)

TO:
The Superintendent of Corporations
Department of Consumer and Regulatory Affairs
Business Regulation Administration, Corporations Division
614 H Street, N.W. Room 407
Washington, D.C. 20001

(A) BY A DISTRICT OF COLUMBIA RESIDENT

PURSUANT TO THE DISTRICT OF COLUMBIA BUSINESS CORPORATION ACT AS AMENDED (D.C. CODE, 1981 EDITION, TITLE 29, SECTION 29-310(2))

I, _____
A Bona fide Resident of the District of Columbia Herein Consent to Act as a Registered Agent For.

_____
Name of Corporation

SIGNATURE OF REGISTERED AGENT _____

DATE:_____

(B) BY A LEGALLY AUTHORIZED CORPORATION

THE CORPORATION HEREIN NAMED IS:

_____

An Authorized Corporate Registered Agent in the District of Columbia, per Signatures of it's President/Vice-President and Secretary/Assistant Secretary, Herein Consents to Act as Registered Agent For:

_____
NAME OF CORPORATION

SIGNATURE:_____OF PRESIDENT OR VICE-PRESIDENT

ATTEST:_____OF SECRETARY OR ASSISTANT SECRETARY

DATE:_____

2/4/99

INSTRUCTIONS FOR A PROFIT CORPORATION

The following are instructions, a transmittal letter and sample articles of incorporation pursuant to Chapter 607 and 621 Florida Statutes (F.S.).

NOTE: THIS IS A BASIC FORM MEETING MINIMAL REQUIREMENTS FOR FILING ARTICLES OF INCORPORATION.

The Division of Corporations strongly recommends that corporate documents be reviewed by your legal counsel. The Division is a filing agency and as such does not render any legal, accounting, or tax advice.

This office does not provide you with corporate seals, minute books, or stock certificates. It is the responsibility of the corporation to secure these items once the corporation has been filed with this office.

Questions concerning S Corporations should be directed to the Internal Revenue Service by telephoning 1-800-829-1040. This is an IRS designation which is not determined by this office.

A preliminary search for name availability can be made on the Internet (www.dos.state.fl.us) or through Compuserve access to the Division's records. Preliminary name searches and name reservations are no longer available from the Division of Corporations. You are responsible for any name infringement that may result from your corporate name selection.

Pursuant to Chapter 607 or 621 F.S., the articles of incorporation **must** set forth the following:

Article I: The name of the corporation **must** include a corporate suffix such as Corporation, Corp., Incorporated, Inc., Company, or Co.

A Professional Association **must** contain the word "chartered" or "professional association" or "P.A.".

You **must** provide an English translation for all names not written in English.

Article II: The principal place of business and mailing address of the corporation.

Article III: The number of shares of stock that this corporation is authorized to have **must** be stated.

CR2E010(7/97)

Article IV: The name and Florida street address of the initial registered agent. The registered agent **must** sign in the space provided accepting the designation as registered agent.

Article V: The Incorporator **must** sign and type or print his/her name in the space provided.

Add a separate article if applicable or necessary for:

An Effective Date: An effective date may be added to the Articles of Incorporation, otherwise the date of receipt will be the file date. (An effective date can not be more than five (5) business days prior to the date of receipt or ninety (90) days after the date of filing).

Specific Purpose for a "Professional Corporation":   Add an "article" stating the specific purpose if you are using this form for a "professional corporation" see s. 621.03, F.S. A profit corporation's purpose is provided for in s. 607.0301, F.S. and it is not necessary to list it in the articles of incorporation.

****

The fee for filing a profit corporation is:
$35.00   Filing Fee
$35.00   Designation of Registered Agent
$52.50   Certified Copy (optional)
$ 8.75   Certificate of Status (optional)
(Make checks payable to Department of State)

Mailing Address: Street Address:
Department of State   Department of State
Division of Corporations   Division of Corporations
P.O. Box 6327   409 E. Gaines St.
Tallahassee, FL 32314   Tallahassee, FL 32399
(850) 487-6052   (850) 487-6052

ARTICLES OF INCORPORATION

The undersigned incorporator, for the purpose of forming a corporation under the Florida Business Corporation Act, hereby adopts the following Articles of Incorporation.

ARTICLE I   NAME
The name of the corporation shall be:

ARTICLE II   PRINCIPAL OFFICE
The principal place of business and mailing address of this corporation shall be:

ARTICLE III   SHARES
The number of shares of stock that this corporation is authorized to have outstanding at any one time is:

ARTICLE IV   INITIAL REGISTERED AGENT AND STREET ADDRESS
The name and Florida street address of the initial registered agent are:

ARTICLE V   INCORPORATOR
The **name and address** of the incorporator to these Articles of Incorporation are:

_____   _____
        Signature/Incorporator   **Date**

(An additional article must be added if an effective date is requested.)

Having been named as registered agent and to accept service of process for the above stated corporation at the place designated in this certificate, I hereby accept the appointment as registered agent and agree to act in this capacity. I further agree to comply with the provisions of all statutes relating to the proper and complete performance of my duties, and I am familiar with and accept the obligations of my position as registered agent

_____   _____
        Signature/Registered Agent   **Date**

TRANSMITTAL LETTER

Department of State
Division of Corporations
P. O. Box 6327
Tallahassee, FL 32314

SUBJECT: _____
(Proposed corporate name - must include suffix)

Enclosed is an original and one(1) copy of the articles of incorporation and a check for :

❏ $70.00   ❏ $78.75   ❏$122.50   ❏ $131.25
Filing Fee   Filing Fee   Filing Fee   Filing Fee,
                  & Certificate   & Certified Copy   Certified Copy
                                                       & Certificate

ADDITIONAL COPY REQUIRED

FROM: _____
Name (Printed or typed)

_____
Address

_____
City, State & Zip

_____
Daytime Telephone number

NOTE: Please provide the original and one copy of the articles.

LEWIS A. MASSEY
Secretary of State

OFFICE OF SECRETARY OF STATE
CORPORATIONS DIVISION
Suite 315, West Tower, 2 Martin Luther King Jr., Drive
Atlanta, Georgia 30334-1530
(404) 656-2817
Registered agent, officer, entity status information on the Internet
http://www.sos.state.ga.us

CATHY COX
Assistant Secretary of State -
Operations

WARREN H. RARY
Director

TRANSMITTAL INFORMATION
NEW GEORGIA PROFIT OR NONPROFIT CORPORATIONS

DO NOT WRITE IN SHADED AREA - SOS USE ONLY

DOCKET #		PENDING #		CONTROL #	
DOCKET CODE	DATE FILED		AMOUNT RECEIVED		CHECK/ RECEIPT #
TYPE CODE	EXAMINER		JURISDICTION (COUNTY) CODE		

NOTICE TO APPLICANT: PRINT PLAINLY OR TYPE REMAINDER OF THIS FORM.

1.

Corporate Name Reservation Number

Corporate Name

2.

Applicant/Attorney | Telephone Number

Address

City | State | Zip Code

3.

I understand that the information on this form will be entered in the Secretary of State business registration database. I certify that a Notice of Incorporation or Notice of Intent to Incorporate with a publishing fee of $40.00 has been or will be mailed or delivered to the authorized newspaper as required by law.

Mail or deliver to the Secretary of State, at the above address, the following:

1) This transmittal form
2) The original and one copy of the Articles of Incorporation
3) A filing fee of $60.00 payable to Secretary of State. Filing fees are NON-refundable.

NOTE: **DO NOT submit this form if you are changing the name of an existing corporation.**

_____
Authorized Signature

_____
Date

Registered agent, officer, entity status information on the Internet: http://www.sos.state.ga.us

FORM 227

Publication of Notice of Intent to Incorporate.

All corporations must publish a notice of intent to incorporate in the newspaper which is the official legal organ of the county where the initial registered office of the corporation is to be located, or in a newspaper of general circulation in such county and for which at least 60 percent of its subscriptions are paid. The Clerk of Superior Court can advise you as to the legal organ in your county. *The notice of intent to incorporate and a $40.00 publication fee should be forwarded directly to the newspaper no later than the next business day after filing articles of incorporation with the Secretary of State.*

The notice should be in the following format:

NOTICE OF INCORPORATION

Dear Publisher:

Please publish once a week for two consecutive weeks a notice in the following form:

Notice is given that articles of incorporation that will incorporate (Name of Corporation) have been delivered to the Secretary of State for filing in accordance with the Georgia Business Corporation Code (or Georgia Nonprofit Corporation Code). The initial registered office of the corporation is located at *(Address of Registered Office)* and its initial registered agent at such address is *(Name of Registered Agent)*.

Enclosed is (check, draft or money order) in the amount of $40.00 in payment of the cost of publishing this notice.

Sincerely,

(Authorized signature)

It should be noted that certain other specific wording might be required in the Articles of Incorporation if the nonprofit corporation wishes to apply to the Internal Revenue Service for tax-exempt status. Nonprofit corporations are not automatically tax-exempt by simply filing articles of incorporation. Professional legal and/or tax advice should be obtained on these matters. The Office of Secretary of State cannot advise you in this regard.

General Information.

Articles of Incorporation which do not include the minimum information described herein, including the Secretary of State filing fee, will be returned along with a notice that describes the deficiency. A filing that is not corrected within 60 days is deemed abandoned, thus requiring the applicant to start the process again, including payment of another filing fee. If corrected within 60 days, the initial date of receipt will be the date of incorporation, except when the deficiency is failure to include the filing fee.

Nonprofit corporations which will be soliciting or accepting contributions in Georgia should contact the Charitable Organizations section of the Office of Secretary of State at 802 West Tower, #2 Martin Luther King, Jr. Drive, Atlanta, GA 30334 to determine if additional registration is required by law.

*FEIN, Federal Employee Identification Number, may be obtained by calling the Internal Revenue Service at (404) 522-0050.

Corporate income and net worth tax information may be obtained by calling the Georgia Department of Revenue at (404) 656-4191.

Sales and use tax, withholding tax and other tax information may be obtained by calling the Centralized Taxpayer Registration Unit of the Georgia Department of Revenue at (404) 651-8651.

Workers compensation information may be obtained by calling (404) 656-3875.

Unemployment insurance information may be obtained by calling (404) 656-5590.

STATE OF HAWAII
DEPARTMENT OF COMMERCE AND CONSUMER AFFAIRS
Business Registration Division
1010 Richards Street
Mailing Address: P.O. Box 40, Honolulu, Hawaii 96810

INSTRUCTIONS FOR PREPARING AND FILING ARTICLES OF INCORPORATION
(Section 415-54, Hawaii Revised Statutes)

1. Articles of Incorporation must be typewritten or printed in **BLACK INK.**

2. Be sure all information has been entered on the form, and that the information is complete and **LEGIBLE.**

3. The Articles of Incorporation cannot have any attachments. If additional space is required, you must prepare your own articles.

4. Submit one original, executed copy and one true copy. We will return the true copy to you after the articles have been processed.

5. Certified Copies. This is **OPTIONAL.** If you want certified copies, submit the number of copies you want certified, together with the original articles and fees. Fee for certified copy is $10.00 per copy plus $0.25 per page.

6. Fees must be submitted with the document. Make checks payable to the DEPARTMENT OF COMMERCE AND CONSUMER AFFAIRS, for the exact amount. Filing fee is **NOT REFUNDABLE.** There is a $15.00 fee plus interest charge on all dishonored checks.

7. Date of incorporation will be the date that the Articles of Incorporation are filed in compliance with the Hawaii Business Corporation Act (Chapter 415).

Article I: State the exact corporate name. The name must contain the word "Corporation", "Incorporated", or "Limited", or the abbreviation of one of the words, "Corp.", "Inc.", or "Ltd."

Article II: State the **COMPLETE** street address (number, street, city, state, and zip code) of the initial or principal office of the corporation. If no specific street address is available, state the rural route number or post office box designated by the United States Postal Service.

Article III: State the number of shares the corporation shall have the authority to issue. The form provides for common stock only. If preferred shares are desired, you must prepare your own Articles of Incorporation.

Article IV: State the number of members of the initial Board of Directors. At least one member of the board must be a resident of the State of Hawaii. The directors of every corporation shall be one or more in number if the corporation has only one stockholder. If the corporation has two stockholders, the corporation shall have two or more directors. If the corporation has three or more stockholders, the corporation shall have three or more directors. State the names and complete residence street addresses of the initial directors of the corporation. If no specific street address is available, state the rural route number or post office box designated by the United States Postal Service.

Article V: State the names of the initial officers of the corporation next to the respective titles. Each corporation must have a President, Vice-President, Secretary and Treasurer. Also state the complete residence street address for each. If no specific street address is available, state the rural route number or post office box designated by the United States Postal Service.

Execution: The form must be signed and certified by at least one individual (incorporator). Signature must be in **BLACK INK.**

This material can be made available for individuals with special needs. Please call the Division Secretary, Business Registration Division, DCCA, at 586-2744, to submit your request.

D1-3-Instr.
Rev. 7/98

Nonrefundable Filing Fee - $100

Submit original and
One True Copy

State of Hawaii
DEPARTMENT OF COMMERCE AND CONSUMER AFFAIRS
Business Registration Division
1010 Richards Street
Mailing Address: P.O. Box 40, Honolulu, HI 96810

ARTICLES OF INCORPORATION
(Section 415-54, Hawaii Revised Statutes)

PLEASE TYPE OR PRINT LEGIBLY IN BLACK INK

The undersigned, for the purpose of forming a corporation under the laws of the State of Hawaii, do hereby make and execute these Articles of Incorporation:

I

The name of the corporation shall be:

_____

Note: The name must contain the word "Corporation," "Incorporated," or "Limited," or an abbreviation of one of the words.

II

The mailing address (must be a street address) of the initial or principal office of the corporation is:

_____

III

The aggregate number of common shares all of the same class which the corporation shall have authority to issue is

_____

D1-3
Rev. 7/98

B13 (Fee)
B23 (Certification)

IV

The initial Board of Directors shall consist of _____ members whose names and residence addresses are as follows:

Name   Residence Address

_____   _____

_____   _____

_____   _____

_____   _____

_____   _____

Note: At least one member of the board must be a resident of the State of Hawaii.

V

The officers of the corporation shall be a president, one or more vice presidents, a secretary and a treasurer, and such other officers and assistant officers as may be deemed necessary, who shall be appointed by the Board of Directors as shall be prescribed by the By-Laws.

The following individuals are the initial officers of the corporation:

Office Title   Name   Residence Address

President   _____   _____

Vice-President _____   _____

Secretary   _____   _____

Treasurer   _____   _____

_____   _____   _____

We certify that we have read the above statements and that the same are true and correct to the best of our knowledge and belief.

Signed this _____ day of _____, 19____.

_____   _____
(Type/Print Name of Incorporator)   (Type/Print Name of Incorporator)

_____   _____
(Signature of Incorporator)   (Signature of Incorporator)

Please sign in black ink.

-2-

200

ARTICLES OF INCORPORATION
(General Business)

To the Secretary of State of the State of Idaho
The undersigned, in order to form a Corporation under the
provisions of Title 30, Chapter 1, Idaho Code, submits
the following articles of incorporation:

Article 1: The name of the corporation shall be: _____

_____

Article 2: The number of shares the corporation is authorized to issue is:_____

Article 3: The street address of the registered office is: _____

_____ and the registered agent at such address is: _____

Article 4: The name and address of the incorporator are:_____

_____

Article 5: The mailing address of the corporation shall be: _____

_____

Optional articles:

Customer Acct #:

(if using pre-paid account)

Secretary of State use only

Revised 7/98

g:\corp\forms\ARTS.p65

Signature of an incorporator:

_____

INSTRUCTIONS

1. Complete and submit the application in duplicate original. The name of the corporation must contain the requirements of 30-1-401

2. The minimum information required by law is that in Articles 1 through 5. Other permissible provisions may be added in the area for optional articles and may be continued on attached sheets if necessary.

3. Enclose the appropriate fee:

   a. If the application is typed, the fee is $100.00.
   b. If the application is not typed, the fee is $120.00.
   c. If expedited service is requested, add $20.00 to the filing fee.
   d. If the fees are to be paid from the filing party's pre-paid customer account, conspicuously indicate the customer account number in the cover letter or transmittal document.

4. Mail or deliver to:

   Office of the Secretary of State
   700 West Jefferson
   PO Box 83720
   Boise ID 83720-0080
   (208) 334-2301

5. If you have questions or need help, call the Secretary of State's office at (208) 334-2301.

Form **BCA-2.10** | **ARTICLES OF INCORPORATION**

(Rev. Jan. 1995)

George H. Ryan
Secretary of State
Department of Business Services
Springfield, IL 62756
http://www.sos.state.il.us

Payment must be made by certified check, cashier's check, Illinois attorney's check, Illinois
C.P.A's check or money order,
payable to "Secretary of State."

This space for use by Secretary of State

SUBMIT IN DUPLICATE!

**This space for use by
Secretary of State**

Date

Franchise Tax $
Filing Fee $

Approved:

1. CORPORATE NAME: _____

_____

(The corporate name must contain the word "corporation", "company," "incorporated," "limited" or an abbreviation thereof.)

2. Initial Registered Agent: _____

| First Name | Middle Initial | Last name |

Initial Registered Office: _____

| Number | Street | Suite # |

IL

| City | Zip Code | County |

3. Purpose or purposes for which the corporation is organized:
(If not sufficient space to cover this point, add one or more sheets of this size.)

4. Paragraph 1: Authorized Shares, Issued Shares and Consideration Received:

Class	Par Value per Share	Number of Shares Authorized	Number of Shares Proposed to be Issued	Consideration to be Received Therefor
	$			$

TOTAL = $

Paragraph 2: The preferences, qualifications, limitations, restrictions and special or relative rights in respect of the shares of each class are:
(If not sufficient space to cover this point, add one or more sheets of this size.)

(over)

5. *OPTIONAL:* (a) Number of directors constituting the initial board of directors of the corporation:_____ .

(b) Names and addresses of the persons who are to serve as directors until the first annual meeting of shareholders or until their successors are elected and qualify:

Name	Residential Address	City, State, ZIP

6. *OPTIONAL:* (a) It is estimated that the value of all property to be owned by the corporation for the following year wherever located will be: $_____

(b) It is estimated that the value of the property to be located within the State of Illinois during the following year will be: $_____

(c) It is estimated that the gross amount of business that will be transacted by the corporation during the following year will be: $_____

(d) It is estimated that the gross amount of business that will be transacted from places of business in the State of Illinois during the following year will be: $_____

7. *OPTIONAL:* *OTHER PROVISIONS*

Attach a separate sheet of this size for any other provision to be included in the Articles of Incorporation, e.g., authorizing preemptive rights, denying cumulative voting, regulating internal affairs, voting majority requirements, fixing a duration other than perpetual, etc.

8. ## NAME(S) & ADDRESS(ES) OF INCORPORATOR(S)

The undersigned incorporator(s) hereby declare(s), under penalties of perjury, that the statements made in the foregoing Articles of Incorporation are true.

Dated _____ , 19 _____ .

Signature and Name	**Address**

1. _____   1. _____
   Signature   Street

   _____   _____
   (Type or Print Name)   City/Town   State   Zip Code

2. _____   2. _____
   Signature   Street

   _____   _____
   (Type or Print Name)   City/Town   State   Zip Code

3. _____   3. _____
   Signature   Street

   _____   _____
   (Type or Print Name)   City/Town   State   Zip Code

(Signatures must be in **BLACK INK** on original document. Carbon copy, photocopy or rubber stamp signatures may only be used on conformed copies.)

NOTE: If a corporation acts as incorporator, the name of the corporation and the state of incorporation shall be shown and the execution shall be by its president or vice president and verified by him, and attested by its secretary or assistant secretary.

FEE SCHEDULE

- The initial franchise tax is assessed at the rate of 15/100 of 1 percent ($1.50 per $1,000) on the paid-in capital represented in this state, with a minimum of $25.
- The filing fee is $75.
- The **minimum total due** (franchise tax + filing fee) is **$100.**
  (Applies when the Consideration to be Received as set forth in Item 4 does not exceed $16,667)
- The Department of Business Services in Springfield will provide assistance in calculating the total fees if necessary.
  Illinois Secretary of State   Springfield, IL 62756
  Department of Business Services   Telephone (217) 782-9522 or 782-9523

C-162.19

PAUL D. PATE
Secretary of State
State of Iowa

IOWA BUSINESS CORPORATION ACT

provisions relating to:

Filing Requirements
Incorporation
Purposes and Powers

PAUL D. PATE
SECRETARY OF STATE

Coporations Divisions

General Information.......515/281-5204
Certified Copies.............515/281-5204
Original Notices.............515/281-5204
Annual Reports.............515/281-7796

Fax...............................515/242-5953 or
                                        515/242-6556

Mailing Address:

Secretary of State
Hoover Building, 2nd Floor
Des Moines, IA 50319

490.120 Filing Requirements.

1. A document must satisfy the requirements of this section, and of any other section that adds to or varies these requirements, to be entitled to filing.

2. The document must be filed in the office of the secretary of state.

3. The document must contain the information required by this chapter. It may contain other information as well.

4. The document must be typewritten or printed.

5. The document must be in the English language. A corporate name need not be in English if written in English letters or Arabic or Roman numerals, and the certificate of existence required of foreign corporations need not be in English if accompanied by a reasonably authenticated English translation.

6. Except as provided in section 490.1622, subsection 2, the document must be executed by one of the following methods:

a. The chairperson of the board of directors of a domestic or foreign corporation, its president, or another of its officers.

b. If directors have not been selected or the corporation has not been formed, by an incorporator.

c. If the corporation is in the hands of a receiver, trustee, or other court-appointed fiduciary, by that fiduciary.

7. The person executing the document shall sign it and state beneath or opposite the person's signature, the person's name and the capacity in which the person signs. The document may, but need not, contain:

a. The corporate seals.

b. An attestation by the secretary or an assistant secretary.

c. An acknowledgment, verification, or proof.

The secretary of state may accept for filing a document containing a copy of a signature, however made.

8. If the secretary of state has prescribed a mandatory form for the document under section 490.121, the document must be in or on the prescribed form.

9. The document must be delivered to the office of the secretary of state for filing and must be accompanied by the correct filing fee.

10. The secretary of state may adopt rules for the electronic filing of documents and the certification of electronically filed documents.

89 Acts, ch 288, §3; 90 Acts, ch 1205, §16

490.201 Incorporators.

One or more persons may act as the incorporator or incorporators of a corporation by executing and delivering articles of incorporation to the secretary of state for filing.

89 Acts, ch 288, §18

490.202 Articles of incorporation.

1. The articles of incorporation must set forth all of the following:

a. A corporate name for the corporation that satisfies the requirements of section 490.401.

b. The number of shares the corporation is authorized to issue.

c. The street address of the corporation's initial registered office and the name of its initial registered agent at that office.

d. The name and address of each incorporator.

2. The articles of incorporation may set forth any or all of the following:

a. The names and addresses of the individuals who are to serve as the initial directors.

b. Provisions not inconsistent with law regarding:

(1) The purpose or purposes for which the corporation is organized.

(2) Managing the business and regulating the affairs of the corporation.

(3) Defining, limiting, and regulating the powers of the corporation, its board of directors, and shareholders.

(4) A par value for authorized shares or classes of shares.

(5) The imposition of personal liability on shareholders for the debts of the corporation to a specified extent and upon specified conditions.

c. Any provision that under this chapter is required or permitted to be set forth in the bylaws.

d. A provision consistent with section 490.832.

3. The articles of incorporation need not set forth any of the corporate powers enumerated in this chapter.

89 Acts, ch 288, §19

490.203 Incorporation.

1. Unless a delayed effective date or time is specified, the corporate existence begins when the articles of incorporation are filed.

2. The secretary of state's filing of the articles of incorporation is conclusive proof that the incorporators satisfied all conditions precedent to incorporation except in a proceeding by the state to cancel or revoke the incorporation or involuntarily dissolve the corporation.

89 Acts, ch 288, §20

490.204 Liability for preincorporation transactions.

All persons purporting to act as or on behalf of a corporation, knowing there was no incorporation under this chapter, are jointly and severally liable for all liabilities created while so acting.

89 Acts, ch 288, §21

490.205 Organization of corporation.

1. After incorporation:

a. If initial directors are named in the articles of incorporation, the initial directors shall hold an organizational meeting, at the call of a majority of the directors, to complete the organization of the corporation by appointing officers, adopting bylaws and carrying on any other business brought before the meeting.

b. If initial directors are not named in the articles, the incorporator or incorporators shall hold an organizational meeting at the call of a majority of the incorporators to do one of the following:

(1) Elect directors and complete the organization of the corporation.

(2) Elect a board of directors who shall complete the organization of the corporation.

2. Action required or permitted by this chapter to be taken by incorporators at an organizational meeting may be taken without a meeting if the action taken is evidenced by one or more written consents describing the action taken and signed by each incorporator.

3. An organizational meeting may be held in or out of this state.

89 Acts, ch 288, §22

490.206 Bylaws.

1. The incorporators or board of directors of a corporation shall adopt initial bylaws for the corporation.

2. The bylaws of a corporation may contain any provision for managing the business and regulating the affairs of the corporation that is not inconsistent with law or the articles of incorporation.

89 Acts, ch 288, §23

490.207 Emergency bylaws.

1. Unless the articles of incorporation provide otherwise, the board of directors of a corporation may adopt bylaws to be effective only in an emergency defined in subsection 4. The emergency bylaws, which are subject to amendment or repeal by the shareholders, may make all provisions necessary for managing the corporation during the emergency, including:

a. Procedures for calling a meeting of the board of directors.

b. Quorum requirements for the meeting.

c. Designation of additional or substitute directors.

2. All provisions of the regular bylaws consistent with the emergency bylaws remain effective during the emergency. The emergency bylaws are not effective after the emergency ends.

3. Corporate action taken in good faith in accordance with the emergency bylaws has both of the following effects:

a. The action binds the corporation.

b. The action shall not be used to impose liability on a corporate director, officer, employee, or agent.

4. An emergency exists for purposes of this section if a quorum of the corporation's directors cannot readily be assembled because of some catastrophic event.

89 Acts, ch 288, §24

490.301 Purposes.

1. A corporation incorporated under this chapter has the purpose of engaging in any lawful business unless a more limited purpose is set forth in the articles of incorporation.

2. A corporation engaging in a business that is subject to regulation under another statute of

this state may incorporate under this chapter only if permitted by, and subject to all limitations of, the other statute.

89 Acts, ch 288, §25

490.302 General powers.

Unless its articles of incorporation provide otherwise, a corporation has perpetual duration and succession in its corporate name and has the same powers as an individual to do all things necessary or convenient to carry out its business and affairs, including without limitation power to do all of the following:

1. Sue and be sued, complain, and defend in its corporate name.

2. Have a corporate seal, which may be altered at will, and use it, or a facsimile of it, by impressing or affixing it or in any other manner reproducing it.

3. Make and amend bylaws, not inconsistent with its articles of incorporation or with the laws of this state, for managing the business and regulating the affairs of the corporation.

4. Purchase, receive, lease, or otherwise acquire, and own, hold, improve, use, and otherwise deal with, real or personal property, or any legal or equitable interest in property, wherever located.

5. Sell, convey, mortgage, pledge, lease, exchange, and otherwise dispose of all or any part of its property.

6. Purchase, receive, subscribe for, or otherwise acquire, own, hold, vote, use, sell, mortgage, lend, pledge, or otherwise dispose of, and deal in and with shares or other interests in, or obligations of, any other entity.

7. Make contracts and guarantees, incur liabilities, borrow money, issue its notes, bonds, and other obligations, which may be convertible into or include the option to purchase other securities of the corporation, and secure any of its obligations by mortgage or pledge of any of its property, franchises, or income.

8. Lend money, invest and reinvest its funds, and receive and hold real and personal property as security for repayment.

9. Be a promoter, partner, member, associate, or manager of any partnership, joint venture, trust, or other entity.

10. Conduct its business, locate offices, and exercise the powers granted by this chapter within or without this state.

11. Elect directors and appoint officers, employees, and agents of the corporation, define their duties, fix their compensation, and lend them money and credit.

12. Pay pensions and establish pension plans, pension trusts, profit sharing plans, share bonus plans, share option plans, and benefit or incentive plans for any or all of its current or former directors, officers, employees, and agents.

13. Make donations for the public welfare or for charitable, scientific, or educational purposes.

14. Transact any lawful business that will aid governmental policy.

15. Make payments or donations, or do any other act, not inconsistent with law, that furthers the business and affairs of the corporation.

89 Acts, ch 288, §26

490.303 Emergency powers.

1. In anticipation of or during an emergency as defined in subsection 4, the board of directors of a corporation may do either or both of the following:

a. Modify lines of succession to accommodate the incapacity of any director, officer, employee, or agent.

b. Relocate the principal office, designate alternative principal offices or regional offices, or authorize the officers to do so.

2. During an emergency defined in subsection 4, unless emergency bylaws provide otherwise:

a. Notice of a meeting of the board of directors need be given only to those directors whom it is practicable to reach and may be given in any practicable manner, including by publication and radio.

b. One or more officers of the corporation present at a meeting of the board of directors may be deemed to be directors for the meeting, in order of rank and within the same rank in order of seniority, as necessary to achieve a quorum.

3. Corporate action taken in good faith during an emergency under this section to further the ordinary business affairs of the corporation shall both:

a. Bind the corporation.

b. Not be used to impose liability on a corporate director, officer, employee, or agent.

4. An emergency exists for purposes of this section if a quorum of the corporation's directors cannot readily be assembled because of some catastrophic event.

89 Acts, ch 288, §27

490.304 Ultra vires.

1. Except as provided in subsection 2, the validity of corporate action is not challengeable on the ground that the corporation lacks or lacked power to act.

2. A corporation's power to act may be challenged in any of the following proceedings:

a. By a shareholder against the corporation to enjoin the act.

b. By the corporation, directly, derivatively, or through a receiver, trustee, or other legal representative, against an incumbent or former director, officer, employee, or agent of the corporation.

c. By the attorney general under section 490.1430.

3. In a shareholder's proceeding under subsection 2, paragraph "a", to enjoin an unauthorized corporate act, the court may enjoin or set aside the act, if equitable and if all affected persons are parties to the proceeding, and may award damages for loss, other than anticipated profits, suffered by the corporation or another party because of enjoining the unauthorized act.

89 Acts, ch 288, §28

Ron Thornburgh
Secretary of State

2nd Floor, State Capitol
300 SW 10th Ave.
Topeka, KS 66612-1594
(785) 296-4564

Suggestions for Completing
Your Articles of Incorporation

The following suggestions are made to assist you in filing your articles of incorporation. If you have any questions, please feel free to contact the corporations division of this office. Remember that the advice of your attorney and tax preparer is most important and that these suggestions are not meant to substitute for that advice.

Generally: The Kansas General Corporation Code, found in the Kansas Statutes Annotated at 17-6001 and following sections, requires that you file articles of incorporation with this office. The original and one copy may be personally delivered or mailed to this office with a $75 filing fee. It would be helpful if you provide a name and phone number of the individual we may contact if we should have questions concerning your articles. We certify one copy and return it to you.

After the proper filing of the articles of incorporation a corporation must ascertain that all legal requirements of other government agencies have been met. Particular care should be taken to comply with requirements of the Internal Revenue Service, Kansas Department of Revenue, appropriate licensing agencies, and local zoning authorities. Private legal counsel may be retained to resolve any problems which you may encounter.

Your legal counsel can advise you about corporate meetings, elections and by-laws. By-laws and minutes of corporate meetings are not, however, filed with this office.

Article One: The name of your corporation must include one of the words of incorporation as set forth in K.S.A. 17-6002, such as Incorporated, Inc., Corporation, Corp., Company, Co., Limited and Ltd. The name cannot be the same as one already in use by a corporation in Kansas without that corporation's written consent, properly executed and acknowledged. The use of a different word of incorporation is not sufficient difference.

Article Two: Every corporation must have a **registered office and a resident agent** at that address. The address must include the Kansas county and must be more than a post office box. The resident agent may be either an individual or a Kansas domestic corporation, including the corporation itself.

(over)

Article Three: It is sufficient to state, either alone or with specific purposes, that the corporation is to engage in any lawful act or activity for which corporations may be organized under the Kansas General Corporation Code.

Article Four: The articles must set forth the total number of shares which the corporation is authorized to issue and the par value of each share. If the stock is to be without par value, this must be stated. If more than one class is to be authorized, this must be specified with the total number of shares and par value of each such class. A corporation does not have to issue all of its authorized shares.

Article Five: The names and addresses of the incorporators must be listed in the articles. Kansas statutes require only one incorporator. The articles must be signed by the incorporators **exactly** as listed and be acknowledged before a notary public.

Article Six: If the powers of the incorporators are to terminate upon filing of the articles and become vested in the directors, the names and addresses of these directors should be given.

Article Seven: The corporation may exist "perpetually" or for a specified term of years.

Articles of incorporation may contain other lawful provisions as desired by the corporation.

All corporations are required to file an annual report and pay an annual franchise fee to this office. Failure to do so will forfeit your corporate powers. We send a form letter to each new corporation requesting that we be notified of its tax closing date, which must be the same as used for income tax purposes. The first annual report will not be required until a corporation is at least six months old and is due at the time its income tax return is due prior to any extension. As a courtesy, we will send blank annual reports to an address you designate to receive them. Regardless of whether the corporation receives these blank reports, it is the corporation's responsibility to file annual reports in a timely manner.

We hope this information is helpful in preparing and filing your articles of incorporation. If you have any questions, please contact the articles clerk in our Corporation Division, (785) 296-4564.

Office of the Secretary of State/Corporation Division   Form

For Profit Articles of Incorporation CF

We, the undersigned incorporators, hereby associate ourselves together to form and establish a corporation FOR profit under the laws of the State of Kansas.

Article One: Name of the corporation

_____

_____

DO NOT WRITE IN THIS SPACE

Article Two: Address of registered office in Kansas _____
(Street Address or Rural Route)

_____   _____   _____
(City)   (County)   (Zip Code)

Name of resident agent at above address _____

Article Three: Nature of corporation business or purposes to be conducted or promoted is

_____

_____

Article Four: Total number of shares that this corporation shall be authorized to issue

_____ shares of _____ stock, class _____	par value of _____ dollars each
_____ shares of _____ stock, class _____	par value of _____ dollars each
_____ shares of _____ stock, class _____	without nominal or par value
_____ shares of _____ stock, class _____	without nominal or par value

If applicable, state any designations, powers, preferences, rights, qualifications, limitations or restrictions applicable to any class of stock or any special grant of authority to be given to the board of directors

_____

_____

Article Five: Name and mailing address of each incorporator is

_____

_____

_____

Article Six: Name and mailing address of each person who is to serve as a director until the first annual meeting of the stockholders or until a successor is elected and qualified is

_____

_____

_____

Article Seven: Is this corporation to exist perpetually? Yes ____ No ____
If *no*, the term for which this corporation is to exist is_____
 •Tax closing date, if known _____

In testimony whereof, we have hereunto subscribed our names this ____ day of _____ , A.D. 19 ___ .   (Signatures must correspond exactly to the names of the incorporators listed in Article Five.)

_____   _____

_____   _____

_____   _____

State of _____
County of _____ }ss.

 Before me, a notary public in and for said county and state, personally appeared

_____   _____

_____   _____

_____   _____

who are known to me to be the same persons who executed the foregoing Articles of Incorporation and duly acknowledged the execution of the same. In witness whereof, I have hereunto subscribed my name and affixed my official seal, this _____ day of_____ , A.D. 19 ____ .

(Seal)

_____
(Notary Public)

My appointment or commission expires _____ , 19 _____ .

**Submit document in duplicate
with $75 filing fee to:**
Corporation Division,
Office of the Secretary of State,
2nd Floor, State Capitol, Topeka, KS 66612-1594
(913) 296-4564

Rev. 5/95 ck

W. Fox McKeithen
Secretary of State

ARTICLES OF INCORPORATION
(R.S. 12:24)

Domestic Business Corporation
Enclose **$60.00 filing fee.**
Make remittance payable to:
Secretary of State
Do not send cash

Return to: **Corporations Division**
P.O. Box 94125
Baton Rouge, LA 70804-9125
Phone (504) 925-4704

STATE OF LOUISIANA

PARISH OF _____

1. The name of this corporation is: _____

2. This corporation is formed for the purpose of: (check one)

   ( )   Engaging in any lawful activity for which corporations may be formed.

   ( )   _____
         (use for limiting corporate activity)

3. The duration of this corporation is: (may be perpetual) _____

4. The aggregate number of shares which the corporation shall have authority to issue is: _____

5. The shares shall consist of one class only and the par value of each share is _____ (shares may be without par value) per share.

6. The full name and post office address of each incorporator is: _____
   _____
   _____

7. Other provisions: _____
   _____
   _____

8. The corporation's federal tax identification number is: _____

Sworn to and subscribed before me at _____, LA, on this the_____ day

of _____, 19_____.

Incorporator(s) Signature:

_____

_____

_____

_____
Notary

399 Rev. 8/97   (See instructions on back)

INSTRUCTIONS

NOTE:

A corporation is a complex form of business structure. This form contains only the minimum provisions required by law to be set forth in Articles of Incorporation Additional provisions may be advisable or necessary, depending on the specific needs of each corporation. Consideration should be given to the advantages and disadvantages of incorporating, and the legal and tax consequences. You are strongly advised to seek legal advice from an attorney and tax and other business advice from an accountant.

1. File the Articles of Incorporation, and the Domestic Corporation Initial Report (form 341) which contains an agent affidavit and the requisite $60 filing fee with the Secretary of State's office.

2. The Articles of Incorporation and the Initial Report may be delivered to the Secretary of State's office in advance, for filing as of any specified date (and any given time on such date) within thirty days after the date of delivery. Requests should be made in writing and must be submitted along with the Articles of Incorporation and the Initial Report.

3. The Articles of Incorporation cannot be accepted for filing unless an Initial Report (form 341) is also filed. Upon filing with our office, you will receive a certified copy of the Articles and a Certificate of Incorporation. Within thirty (30) days after filing the Articles of Incorporation with the Secretary of State's office, a multiple original of the Articles and the Initial Report (or a copy of each certified by the Secretary of State), and a copy of the Certificate of Incorporation must be filed with the office of the recorder of mortgages in the parish where the corporation's registered office is located.

4. Please call the Internal Revenue Service at (901) 546-3920 for information to obtain a corporation's federal tax identification number prior to incorporation.

5. If the Articles of Incorporation are filed within five (5) working days (exclusive of legal holidays) after acknowledgment, the corporate existence shall begin as of the time of such acknowledgment.

DOMESTIC BUSINESS CORPORATION INITIAL REPORT

(R.S. 12:25 and 12:101)

1. The name of this corporation is: _____

2. The location and municipal address (not a P.O. Box only) of this corporation's registered office:

   _____

   _____

3. The full name and municipal address (not a P.O. Box only) of each of this corporation's registered agent(s) is/are:

   _____

   _____

4. The names and municipal addresses (not a P.O. Box only) of the first directors are:

   _____

   _____

Incorporator(s) signature(s):

_____

_____

_____

_____

AGENT'S AFFIDAVIT AND ACKNOWLEDGEMENT OF ACCEPTANCE

I hereby acknowledge and accept the appointment of registered agent for and on behalf of the above named corporation.

Registered agent(s) signature(s):

_____

_____

Sworn to and subscribed before me this _____ day of _____, 19_____.

_____
Notary

INSTRUCTIONS

1. An Initial Report must be completed and filed with the Articles of Incorporation of a Domestic Business Corporation.

2. If no directors have been selected when the Initial Report and Articles of Incorporation are filed, a Supplemental Report, setting forth their names and addresses must be filed in accordance with R.S. 12:25.

3. The Affidavit of Acknowledgement and Acceptance contained on the bottom of this form must be signed by each registered agent before a notary public.

NOTE: Upon filing the Articles of Incorporation and Initial Report with our office, you will receive certified copies of both documents and a Certificate of Incorporation. Within thirty (30) days after filing with the Secretary of State's office, a multiple original of the Articles and the Initial Report (or a copy of each certified by the Secretary of State) and a copy of the Certificate of Incorporation must be filed with the office of the recorder of mortgages of the parish where the corporation's registered office is located.

**DOMESTIC
BUSINESS CORPORATION**

STATE OF MAINE

ARTICLES OF INCORPORATION

(Check box only if applicable)
☐ This is a professional service corporation
formed pursuant to 13 MRSA Chapter 22.

Minimum Fee $105. (See §1403 sub-§§1 and 2)

_____
Deputy Secretary of State

A True Copy When Attested By Signature

_____
Deputy Secretary of State

Pursuant to 13-A MRSA §403, the undersigned, acting as incorporator(s) of a corporation, adopt(s) the following Articles of Incorporation:

FIRST: The name of the corporation is _____

and its principal business location in Maine is _____
(physical location - street (not P.O. Box), city, state and zip code)

SECOND: The name of its Clerk, who must be a Maine resident, and the registered office shall be:

_____
(name)

_____
(physical location - street (not P.O. Box), city, state and zip code)

_____
(mailing address if different from above)

THIS FORM _MUST_ BE ACCOMPANIED BY FORM MBCA-18A (Acceptance of Appointment as Clerk §304.2-A.).

THIRD: ("X" one box only)

☐ A. 1. The number of directors constituting the initial board of directors of the corporation is _____ (See §703.1.A.)

2. If the initial directors have been selected, the names and addresses of the persons who are to serve as directors until the first annual meeting of the shareholders or until their successors are elected and shall qualify are:

NAME   **ADDRESS**

_____   _____

_____   _____

_____   _____

3. The board of directors ☐ is ☐ is not authorized to increase or decrease the number of directors.

4. If the board is so authorized, the minimum number, if any, shall be _____ directors, (See §703.1.A.) and the maximum number, if any, shall be _____ directors.

☐ B. There shall be no directors initially; the shares of the corporation will not be sold to more than twenty (20) persons; the business of the corporation will be managed by the shareholders. (See §701.2.)

FOURTH: ("X" one box only)

☐ There shall be only one class of shares (title of class) _____

    Par value of each share (if none, so state) _____ Number of shares authorized _____

☐ There shall be two or more classes of shares. The information required by §403 concerning each such class is set out in Exhibit ____ attached hereto and made a part hereof.

SUMMARY

The aggregate par value of all authorized shares (of all classes) **having a par value** is $ _____

The total number of authorized shares (of all classes) **without par value** is _____ shares

FIFTH: ("X" one box only) Meetings of the shareholders ☐ may ☐ may not be held outside of the State of Maine.

SIXTH: ("X" if applicable) ☐ There are no preemptive rights.

SEVENTH: Other provisions of these articles, if any, including provisions for the regulation of the internal affairs of the corporation, are set out in Exhibit ____ attached hereto and made a part hereof.

INCORPORATORS   **DATED** _____

_____   Street _____
(signature)   (residence address)

_____   _____
(type or print name)   (city, state and zip code)

_____   Street _____
(signature)   (residence address)

_____   _____
(type or print name)   (city, state and zip code)

_____   Street _____
(signature)   (residence address)

_____   _____
(type or print name)   (city, state and zip code)

For Corporate Incorporators*

Name of Corporate Incorporator _____

By _____   Street _____
(signature of officer)   (principal business location)

_____   _____
(type or print name and capacity)   (city, state and zip code)

---

*Articles are to be executed as follows:
If a corporation is an incorporator (§402), the name of the corporation should be typed and signed on its behalf by an officer of the corporation. The articles of incorporation must be accompanied by a certificate of an appropriate officer of the corporation, not the person signing the articles, certifying that the person executing the articles on behalf of the corporation was duly authorized to do so.

SUBMIT COMPLETED FORMS TO: CORPORATE EXAMINING SECTION, SECRETARY OF STATE, 101 STATE HOUSE STATION, AUGUSTA, ME 04333-0101
TEL. (207) 287-4195

DOMESTIC
BUSINESS CORPORATION

STATE OF MAINE

ACCEPTANCE OF APPOINTMENT
AS CLERK OF

_____

(name of domestic business corporation)

Pursuant to 13-A MRSA §304.2-A, the undersigned hereby accepts the appointment as clerk for the above named domestic business corporation.

CLERK   DATED _____

_____   _____

(signature)   (type or print name)

SUBMIT COMPLETED FORMS TO: CORPORATE EXAMINING SECTION, SECRETARY OF STATE,
101 STATE HOUSE STATION, AUGUSTA, ME 04333-0101
TEL. (207) 287-4195

FORM NO. MBCA-18A   97

OFFICE OF THE SECRETARY OF STATE
BUREAU OF CORPORATIONS, ELECTIONS AND COMMISSIONS
DIVISION OF CORPORATIONS

CHAPTER 250

RULES FOR BUSINESS CORPORATIONS UNDER TITLE 13-A

1. **Filing Requirements**

   A. The standard size of forms and all attachments shall be 8 1/2 x 11. Exceptions may be made for "Certificates of Good Standing" accompanying forms MBCA 2 and 12, which may be 8 1/2 x 14, as well as documents secured from other states.

   B. Forms which do not conform to the size and content of the suggested forms may be rejected by the Secretary of State.

   C. All documents must be dated by month, day and year.

   D. Forms will only be accepted if typed or printed in ink.

   E. All documents must be originally signed, i.e., bear original signatures, not rubber stamped or machine made copies of signatures.

   F. The Secretary of State may reject a document which does not contain the name and capacity of the signer or signers in a legible form in addition to the signatures.

   G. Document filing date shall be the date the document is first received in the Bureau of Corporations, Elections and Commissions in proper filing order with the appropriate filing fees. The Secretary of State is required to return documents that do not meet statutory or rule requirements. The Secretary of State reserves the right to determine that a document is in proper filing order. As a courtesy to filers, the Secretary of State may, in its discretion, correct typographical errors or make other corrections if authorized to do so by the filer. The Secretary of State may require written authorization from the filer as a condition to making such corrections.

   H. Zip code is requested with address of registered office, but documents will not be refused for filing if not given.

   I. When the names of officers are requested, as in Annual Reports, the names of the President, Treasurer, Clerk, or Registered Agent, and Directors or Shareholders (if there are no Directors) shall be furnished.

   J. When qualifying or registering a foreign corporation, a Certificate of Good Standing shall be an original certificate dated within 90 days of submission from the official having custody of the corporate records stating that the corporation has legal existence, good standing or similar language.

K. An excused foreign corporation, in order to resume doing business in Maine, must file a Certificate of Resumption in accordance with 13-A MRSA Section 1301, Subsection 5, accompanied by a Certificate of Good Standing, or equivalent, dated within 90 days of submission.

L. An amendment to the Articles of Incorporation shall be considered a change of purpose if it adds a new purpose, removes the old purpose in part or totally, or makes the old purpose more specific or more general.

M. Refunds of less than $2.00 will not be processed.

N. The address required by 13-A MRSA Section 304 or Section 1212, concerning the registered office of a clerk or registered agent, shall state the location address of such office. If, in addition, a different mailing address exists that information must also be included.

O. Principal business location in Maine, pursuant to 13-A MRSA Section 403.1.A., shall mean the municipality in Maine where the corporation is located. The street address and zip code are requested, but documents will not be refused for filing if not given.

2. Annual Reports

A. Each business corporation on file as of December 31st of a given calendar year must file an annual report no later than June 1st of the following year. The information contained in the annual report must be current as of the date the report is signed. Corporations previously excused from filing annual reports, which resume the transaction of business pursuant to 13-A MRSA §1301, sub-§5 are required to file an annual report beginning the next June 1st following resumption.

B. The Annual Report form issued by the Secretary of State, containing preprinted information about the corporation, must be used. Additional pages may be attached to include the variable information in items number 1, 2 and 3 of the report form (corporate purpose, name and address of officers and directors or shareholders). List the number of pages attached on the report. Use one side of the paper only. All attachments must contain the name and charter number of the corporation across the top of the page. Each page should be numbered consecutively.

3. List of Registered Agents

A. The Secretary of State will establish and maintain a list of corporations and individuals willing to serve as a registered agent for foreign corporations doing business in this State. Persons who would like to be included on the list may complete an application form setting forth contact information. The list will be updated monthly. Foreign corporations seeking to qualify in this State will be forwarded the list upon request.

STATUTORY AUTHORITY: 13-A MRSA Section 1303.

D

The Commonwealth of Massachusetts

William Francis Galvin
Secretary of the Commonwealth
One Ashburton Place, Boston, Massachusetts 02108-1512

ARTICLES OF ORGANIZATION
(General Laws, Chapter 156B)

ARTICLE I
The exact name of the corporation is:

ARTICLE II
The purpose of the corporation is to engage in the following business activities:

Examiner

Name
Approved

C
P
M
R.A.

P.C.

Note: If the space provided under any article or item on this form is insufficient. additions shall be set forth on one side only of separate 8 1/2 x 11 sheets of paper with a left margin of at least 1 inch. Additions to more than one article may be made on a single sheet so long as each article requiring each addition is clearly indicated.

ARTICLE III

State the total number of shares and par value, if any, of each class of stock which the corporation is authorized to issue.

WITHOUT PAR VALUE		WITH PAR VALUE		
TYPE	NUMBER OF SHARES	TYPE	NUMBER OF SHARES	PAR VALUE
Common:		Common:		
Preferred:		Preferred:		

ARTICLE IV

If more than one class of stock is authorized, state a distinguishing designation for each class. Prior to the issuance of any shares of a class, if shares of another class are outstanding, the corporation must provide a description of the preferences, voting powers, qualifications, and special or relative rights or privileges of that class and of each other class of which shares are outstanding and of each series then established within any class.

ARTICLE V

The restrictions, if any, imposed by the Articles of Organization upon the transfer of shares of stock of any class are:

ARTICLE VI

**Other lawful provisions, if any, for the conduct and regulation of the business and affairs of the corporation, for its voluntary dissolution, or for limiting, defining, or regulating the powers of the corporation, or of its directors or stockholders, or of any class of stockholders:

If there are no provisions state "None".
Note: The preceding six (6) articles are considered to be permanent and may ONLY be changed by filing appropriate Articles of Amendment.

ARTICLE VII

The effective date of organization of the corporation shall be the date approved and filed by the Secretary of the Commonwealth. If a *later* effective date is desired, specify such date which shall not be more than *thirty days* after the date of filing.

ARTICLE VIII

The information contained in Article VIII is not a permanent part of the Articles of Organization.

a. The street address (*post office boxes are not acceptable*) of the principal office of the corporation *in Massachusetts* is:

b. The name, residential address and post office address of each director and officer of the corporation is as follows:

	NAME	RESIDENTIAL ADDRESS	POST OFFICE ADDRESS
President:			
Treasurer:			
Clerk:			
Directors:			

c. The fiscal year (i.e., tax year) of the corporation shall end on the last day of the month of:

d. The name and business address of the resident agent, if any, of the corporation is:

ARTICLE IX

By-laws of the corporation have been duly adopted and the president, treasurer, clerk and directors whose names are set forth above, have been duly elected.

IN WITNESS WHEREOF AND UNDER THE PAINS AND PENALTIES OF PERJURY, I/we, whose signature(s) appear below as incorporator(s) and whose name(s) and business or residential address(es) *are clearly typed or printed* beneath each signature do hereby associate with the intention of forming this corporation under the provisions of General Laws, Chapter 156B and do hereby sign these Articles of Organization as incorporator(s) this _____ day of _____ , 19 _____ ,

_____

_____

_____

_____

Note: If an existing corporation is acting as incorporator, type in the exact name of the corporation, the state or other jurisdiction where it was incorporated, the name of the person signing on behalf of said corporation and the title he/she holds or other authority by which such action is taken.

THE COMMONWEALTH OF MASSACHUSETTS

ARTICLES OF ORGANIZATION
(General Laws, Chapter 156B)

I hereby certify that, upon examination of these Articles of Organization, duly submitted to me, it appears that the provisions of the General Laws relative to the organization of corporations have been complied with, and I hereby approve said articles; and the filing fee in the amount of $ _____ having been paid, said articles are deemed to have been filed with me this _____ day of _____ 19 _____ .

Effective date: _____

WILLIAM FRANCIS GALVIN
Secretary of the Commonwealth

FILING FEE: One tenth of one percent of the total authorized capital stock, but not less than **$200.00**. For the purpose of filing, shares of stock with a par value less than $1.00, or no par stock, shall be deemed to have a par value of $1.00 per share.

TO BE FILLED IN BY CORPORATION
Photocopy of document to be sent to:

_____

_____

_____

Telephone: _____

MICHIGAN DEPARTMENT OF CONSUMER AND INDUSTRY SERVICES
CORPORATION, SECURITIES AND LAND DEVELOPMENT BUREAU

Date Received			(FOR BUREAU USE ONLY)

Name	
Address	
City	State	Zip Code

☞ Document will be returned to the name and address you enter above ☜

EFFECTIVE DATE: _____

ARTICLES OF INCORPORATION
For use by Domestic Profit Corporations
(Please read information and instructions on the last page)

Pursuant to the provisions of Act 284, Public Acts of 1972, the undersigned corporation executes the following Articles:

ARTICLE I

The name of the corporation is:

ARTICLE II

The purpose or purposes for which the corporation is formed is to engage in any activity within the purposes for which corporations may be formed under the Business Corporation Act of Michigan.

ARTICLE III

The total authorized shares:

1. Common Shares _____

    Preferred Shares _____

2. A statement of all or any of the relative rights, preferences and limitations of the shares of each class is as follows:

ARTICLE IV

1. The address of the registered office is:

_____ , Michigan _____
(Street Address)   (City)   (ZIP Code)

2. The mailing address of the registered office, if different than above:

_____ . Michigan _____
(Street Address or P.O. Box)   (City)   (ZIP Code)

3. The name of the resident agent at the registered office is: _____

ARTICLE V

The name(s) and address(es) of the incorporator(s) is (are) as follows:

Name   Residence or Business Address

_____

_____

_____

_____

_____

ARTICLE VI (Optional. Delete if not applicable)

When a compromise or arrangement or a plan of reorganization of this corporation is proposed between this corporation and its creditors or any class of them or between this corporation and its shareholders or any class of them, a court of equity jurisdiction within the state, on application of this corporation or of a creditor or shareholder thereof, or on application of a receiver appointed for the corporation, may order a meeting of the creditors or class of creditors or of the shareholders or class of shareholders to be affected by the proposed compromise or arrangement or reorganization, to be summoned in such manner as the court directs. If a majority in number representing 3/4 in value of the creditors or class of creditors. or of the shareholders or class of shareholders to be affected by the proposed compromise or arrangement or a reorganization, agree to a compromise or arrangement or a reorganization of this corporation as a consequence of the compromise or arrangement, the compromise or arrangement and the reorganization, if sanctioned by the court to which the application has been made, shall be binding on all the creditors or class of creditors, or on all the shareholders or class of shareholders and also on this corporation.

ARTICLE VII (Optional. Delete if not applicable)

Any action required or permitted by the Act to be taken at an annual or special meeting of shareholders may be taken without a meeting, without prior notice, and without a vote, if consents in writing, setting forth the action so taken, are signed by the holders of outstanding shares having not less than the minimum number of votes that would be necessary to authorize or take the action at a meeting at which all shares entitled to vote on the action were present and voted. The written consents shall bear the date of signature of each shareholder who signs the consent. No written consents shall be effective to take the corporate action referred to unless, within 60 days after the record date for determining shareholders entitled to express consent to or to dissent from a proposal without a meeting, written consents dated not more than 10 days before the record date and signed by a sufficient number of shareholders to take the action are delivered to the corporation. Delivery shall be to the corporation's registered office, its principal place of business, or an officer or agent of the corporation having custody of the minutes of the proceedings of its shareholders. Delivery made to a corporation's registered office shall be by hand or by certified or registered mail, return receipt requested.

Prompt notice of the taking of the corporate action without a meeting by less than unanimous written consent shall be given to shareholders who would have been entitled to notice of the shareholder meeting if the action had been taken at a meeting and who have not consented in writing.

C&S 500

Name of person or organization
remitting fees:

Preparer's name and business
telephone number:

_____   _____

_____   (   ) _____

INFORMATION AND INSTRUCTIONS

1. The articles of incorporation cannot be filed until this form, or a comparable document, is submitted.

2. Submit one original of this document. Upon filing, the document will be added to the records of the Corporation, Securities and Land Development Bureau. The original will be returned to the address appearing in the box on the front as evidence of filing.

   Since this document will be maintained on optical disk media, it is important that the filing be legible. Documents with poor black and white contrast, or otherwise illegible, will be rejected.

3. This document is to be used pursuant to the provisions of Act 284, P.A. of 1972, by one or more persons for the purpose of forming a domestic profit corporation.

4. Article I - The corporate name of a domestic profit corporation is required to contain one of the following words or abbreviations: "Corporation", "Company", "Incorporated", "Limited", "Corp.", "Co.", "Inc.", or "Ltd.".

5. Article II - State, in general terms, the character of the particular business to be carried on. Under section 202(b) of the Act, it is sufficient to state substantially, alone or with specifically enumerated purposes, that the corporation may engage in any activity within the purposes for which corporations may be formed under the Act. The Act requires, however, that educational corporations state their specific purposes.

6. Article III - Indicate the total number of shares which the corporation has authority to issue. If there is more than one class or series of shares, state the relative rights, preferences and limitations of the shares of each class in Article III(2).

7. Article IV - A post office box may not be designated as the address of the registered office.

8. Article V - The Act requires one or more incorporators. Educational corporations are required to have at least three (3) incorporators. The address(es) should include a street number and name (or other designation), city and state.

9. The duration of the corporation should be stated in the articles only if not perpetual.

10. This document is effective on the date endorsed "filed" by the Bureau. A later effective date, no more than 90 days after the date of delivery, may be stated as an additional article.

11. The articles must be signed by each incorporator. The names of the incorporators as set out in article V should correspond with the signatures.

12. **FEES:** Make remittance payable to the State of Michigan. Include corporation name on check or money order.

    NONREFUNDABLE FEE $10.00
    ORGANIZATION FEE: first 60,000 authorized shares or portion thereof $50.00
    TOTAL MINIMUM FEE **$60.00**
    ADDITIONAL ORGANIZATION FEE FOR AUTHORIZED SHARES OVER 60,000:
        each additional 20,000 authorized shares or portion thereof $30.00
        maximum fee per filing for first 10,000,000 authorized shares $5,000.00
        each additional 20,000 authorized shares or portion thereof in excess of 10,000,000 shares $30.00
        maximum fee per filing for authorized shares in excess of 10,000,000 shares $200,000.00

13. Mail form and fee to: The office is located at:

    Michigan Department of Consumer & Industry Services   6546 Mercantile Way
    Corporation, Securities and Land Development Bureau   Lansing, MI 48910
    Corporation Division   Telephone: (517) 334-6302
    P O Box 30054
    Lansing, MI 48909-7554

Use space below for additional Articles or for continuation of previous Articles. Please identify any Article being continued or added. Attach additional pages if needed.

I, (We), the incorporator(s) sign my (our) name(s) this _____ day of _____, 19 _____

_____   _____

_____   _____

_____   _____

_____   _____

_____   _____

STATE OF MINNESOTA
SECRETARY OF STATE

ARTICLES OF INCORPORATION
Business and Nonprofit Corporations

PLEASE TYPE OR PRINT LEGIBLY IN BLACK INK.

Please read the directions on the reverse side before completing this form. All information on this form is public information.

The undersigned incorporator(s) is an (are) individual(s) 18 years of age or older and adopt the following articles of incorporation to form a (mark ONLY one):

☐ FOR-PROFIT BUSINESS CORPORATION (Chapter 302A)   ☐ NONPROFIT CORPORATION (Chapter 317A)

ARTICLE I   NAME

The name of the corporation is:

_____

(Business Corporation names must include a corporate designation such as Incorporated, Corporation, Company, Limited or an abbreviation of one of those words.)

ARTICLE II   REGISTERED OFFICE ADDRESS AND AGENT

The registered office address of the corporation is:

_____

(A complete street address or rural route and rural route box number is required; the address cannot be a P.O. Box) City State Zip

The registered agent at the above address is:

_____

Name   (**Note:** You are not required to have a registered agent.)

ARTICLE III   SHARES

The corporation is authorized to issue a total of _____ shares.
(If you are a business corporation you must authorize at least one share. Nonprofit corporations are not required to have shares.)

ARTICLE IV   INCORPORATORS

I (We), the undersigned incorporator(s) certify that I am (we are) authorized to sign these articles and that the information in these articles is true and correct. I (We) also understand that if any of this information is intentionally or knowingly misstated that criminal penalties will apply as if I (we) had signed these articles under oath. (Provide the name and address of each incorporator. Each incorporator must sign below. List the incorporators on an additional sheet if you have more than two incorporators.)

Name	Street	City	State	Zip	Signature
Name	Street	City	State	Zip	Signature

Print name and phone number of person to be contacted if there is a question about the filing of these articles.

_____   (_____)_____

Name   Phone Number   03930254 Rev. 11/98

DIRECTIONS

THIS FORM MUST BE TYPEWRITTEN OR PRINTED IN BLACK INK.

Choose which type of corporation you are filing. A for-profit business corporation's goal is to make money for its shareholders.

A nonprofit corporation's goal is generally to return something to the community, not the financial gain of the members. In addition, a nonprofit corporation cannot pay members dividends.

ARTICLE I. State the exact corporate name. Business corporations MUST choose one of the following words or abbreviation of these words as part of the name of the business: Incorporated, Corporation, Limited or Company. The word "company" cannot be immediately preceded by "and" or "&". Nonprofit corporations may use these words but are not required to do so. Name availability may be checked on a preliminary basis by calling the Business Information Line at (651)296-2803 between 8:00 a.m. and 4:30 p.m. (CT) on any working day.

ARTICLE II. State the complete street address or rural route and rural route box number for the registered office address. Post office box numbers are NOT acceptable.

ARTICLE III. State the number of shares the corporation will be authorized to issue. Business corporations must be authorized to issue at least one share. Nonprofit corporations may (but are not required to) issue shares.

ARTICLE IV. Only one incorporator is required. If you have more than one incorporator you must state the name and complete address for each incorporator. Each incorporator must sign. List the incorporators on an additional sheet if you have more than two incorporators.

NOTE: This form is intended merely as a guide in the formation of a Minnesota corporation. It is not intended to cover all situations. If this form does not meet the specific needs and requirements of the corporation, the incorporators should draft their own articles.

A nonprofit corporation that wishes to apply to the Internal Revenue Service (IRS) for tax exempt status (501(c)(3) **cannot use this form for its articles**. The IRS has additional language requirements. That language is available from the IRS by calling (800)829-1040. After combining the IRS language with the requirements on the front of this form, submit the articles to this Office for filing. Once the articles have been filed and returned to the corporation, the application for tax exempt status can be made to the IRS.

FILING FEES: Make checks payable to the Secretary of State.

> **Business Corporations - $135**
> **Nonprofit Corporations - $70**

SEND FORM AND FEE TO:

Secretary of State
Business Services Section
180 State Office Bldg.
100 Constitution Ave.
St. Paul, MN 55155-1299
(651)296-2803

All of the information on this form is public and required in order to process this filing. Failure to provide the requested information will prevent the Office from approving or further processing this filing.

This document can be made available in alternative formats, such as large print, Braille or audio tape, by calling (651)296-2803/Voice. For TTY communication, contact Minnesota Relay Service at 1-800-627-3529 and ask them to place a call to (651)296-2803. The Secretary of State's Office does not discriminate on the basis of race, creed, color, sex, sexual orientation, national origin, age, marital status, disability, religion, reliance on public assistance, or political opinions or affiliations in employment or the provision of services.

OFFICE OF THE MISSISSIPPI SECRETARY OF STATE
P.O. BOX 136, JACKSON, MS 39205-0136   (601) 359-1333
Instructions for Articles of Incorporation

Our forms have been designed to be scanned by computer equipment. There are several simple rules to follow in completing this form to ensure that the form, when completed, can be processed correctly.

1. The areas marked ① (the computer barcode area and the right margin) are reserved areas. Make no marks or notations in these areas.

2. The form contains alignment marks (⇨) for your typewriter. The alignment marks are in the left margin of the form on each line, indicated by ②. Align your typewriter to print an upper case X directly on this '⇨' symbol. Then normal typing, spacing, and line indexing will automatically position your typewriter within the typeable areas on the form. Please use a new black ribbon when completing the form.

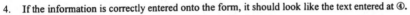

3. Typeable areas, which are the boxes (like the box indicated by ③), are the only places where you should be making any marks. With the exception of areas reserved for signatures, all information provided should be typewritten in these boxes or printed in black ink. Signatures should always be completely contained within the boundaries of the box set aside for the signature.

4. If the information is correctly entered onto the form, it should look like the text entered at ④.

5. Where a choice needs to be indicated, please make your selection by entering an upper case 'X' in the box to the left of the selection you want to make.

6. Enter numeric information **without commas**. Three thousand, for example, should be entered as '3000' not '3,000'.

7. All dates **must** be entered in the MM/DD/YYYY format, that is, using the 4 digit year. For example, January 4th, 1997 should be entered as '1/4/1997'. Although not required, a leading zero in the month and day is acceptable (like '01/04/1997').

8. In order to ensure mail is deliverable, do not combine post office box numbers and Street Address in one box. Please enter the actual physical street location in the box labeled Physical Address, and/or post office box numbers in the boxes labeled P.O. Box. Where necessary, use directional indicators (like '123 W Main St' instead of '123 Main St'). It is not necessary to enter the text 'PO BOX' when specifying a P.O. Box. Our system will supply this text automatically.

9. States must be entered as the two character approved US Post Office state code. For example, Mississippi should be entered as 'MS' without periods, not 'Miss.', or using other abbreviations.

10. Boxes set aside for ZIP codes contain enough space to enter both five digit and four digit ZIP code values, separated by a dash. Please ensure the five digit ZIP is entered to the **left** of the dash, and the four digit zip is to the **right** of the dash.

11. The following rules apply to the data entry areas on the form.

    Type of Corporation - Check the appropriate box to indicate the type of corporation.

    Name of Corporation - Enter the Corporation name or names, up to 60 characters per line for a maximum of two lines. Profit corporation names must contain the word "Corporation", "Incorporated", "Company,"or "Limited" or the abbreviation "Corp", "Inc.", Co.", or "Ltd.". This does not apply to nonprofit corporations.

    Future Effective Date - The filing will be effective as of the actual date filed, unless this date is filled in. Note that this date must be in the future. This date is not to exceed 90 days from the date of filing of this form.

    Duration - Complete only if Non-Profit. Either enter the number of years of duration, or X the perpetual box.

Rev. 03/96

OFFICE OF THE MISSISSIPPI SECRETARY OF STATE
P.O. BOX 136, JACKSON, MS 39205-0136   (601) 359-1333
Instructions for Articles of Incorporation

Shares - Complete only if Profit. Enter a textual description of the type of shares issued. Examples include COMMON, PREFERRED, etc. Limit to 5 characters.

Name and Address of Registered Agent - The name and street address of the Registered Agent. Limit the name of the agent to 40 characters. Do not exceed 45 characters per address line, 20 characters for city, 2 characters for state, and 9 digits for zip code.

Name and Address of Each Incorporator - The name and address of each incorporator. Limit the name of the incorporator to 40 characters. Do not exceed 45 characters per address line, 20 characters for city, 2 characters for state, and 9 digits for zip code.

Other Provisions - If there are other provisions under which the incorporation is taking place, check this box, and attach a sheet containing the provisions.

Keep all signatures within the blocks allocated for them.

Enclose the $50 filing fee, payable to the Secretary of State, with this document

Thank you for your assistance. Please call us at the above number if there are any questions.

Rev. 03/96

OFFICE OF THE MISSISSIPPI SECRETARY OF STATE
P.O. BOX 136, JACKSON, MS 39205-0136   (601) 359-1333
Articles of Incorporation

The undersigned, pursuant to Section 79-4-2.02 (if a profit corporation) or Section 79-11-137 (if a nonprofit corporation) of the Mississippi Code of 1972, hereby executes the following document and sets forth:

1. Type of Corporation

⇨   ☐ Profit   ☐ Nonprofit

2. Name of the Corporation

⇨

3. The future effective date is
    (Complete if applicable)

⇨ **4. FOR NONPROFITS ONLY:** The period of duration is ☐ years or ☐ perpetual

5. FOR PROFITS ONLY: The Number (and Classes) if any of shares the corporation is authorized to issue is (are) as follows

Classes	# of Shares Authorized	If more than one (1) class of shares is authorized, the preferences, limitations, and relative rights of each class are as follows:
⇨		(See Attached)
⇨		

6. Name and Street Address of the Registered Agent and Registered Office is

⇨   Name

⇨   Physical
     Address

⇨   P.O. Box

⇨   City, State, ZIP5, ZIP4   -

7. The name and complete address of each incorporator are as follows

⇨   Name

⇨   Street

Rev. 01/96

OFFICE OF THE MISSISSIPPI SECRETARY OF STATE
P.O. BOX 136, JACKSON, MS 39205-0136   (601) 359-1333
Articles of Incorporation

⇨ City, State, ZIP5, ZIP4 ☐ ☐ -

⇨ Name ☐

⇨ Street ☐

⇨ City, State, ZIP5, ZIP4 ☐ ☐ -

⇨ Name ☐

⇨ Street ☐

⇨ City, State, ZIP5, ZIP4 ☐ ☐ -

⇨ Name ☐

⇨ Street ☐

⇨ City, State, ZIP5, ZIP4 ☐ ☐ -

⇨ **8. Other Provisions** ☐ See Attached

9. Incorporators' Signatures (please keep writing within blocks)

Rev. 01/96

ARTICLES OF INCORPORATION

The undersigned acting as incorporator(s) to form a corporation under the New Mexico Business Corporation Act (53-11-1 to 53-18-12 NMSA 1978), adopt(s) the following Articles of Incorporation for such corporation:

ARTICLE ONE: The name of the corporation_____

_____

ARTICLE TWO:
The period of its duration is_____

_____

ARTICLE THREE: The purpose or purposes for which the corporation is organized are:

ARTICLE FOUR: The aggregate number of shares which the corporation shall have authority to issue: (ATTACH SCHEDULE, IF NEEDED)

ARTICLE FIVE: Any provision limiting or denying to shareholders the preemptive right to acquire unissued or treasury shares, or securities convertible into such shares or carrying a right to subscribe to or to acquire shares is:

ARTICLE SIX: The name of its initial registered agent is:

_____

and the street address (P.O. BOX IS UNACCEPTABLE UNLESS GEOGRAPHICAL LOCATION IS GIVEN), city and zip code of its initial registered office in New Mexico.

_____

ARTICLE SEVEN: The number constituting the initial board of directors is____ and the names and addresses of the persons who have consented to serve as directors until the first annual meeting of shareholders or until their successors are elected and qualify are:

        NAME   ADDRESS

ARTICLE EIGHT: The name and address of each incorporator is:

        NAME   ADDRESS

Dated:_____

_____

_____

_____
           Signature of Incorporator(s)

(File Duplicate Originals)

NMSCC-CD
DPR-NC
(REV 10/97)

**AFFIDAVIT OF ACCEPTANCE OF APPOINTMENT
BY DESIGNATED INITIAL REGISTERED AGENT**

TO: THE STATE CORPORATION COMMISSION
     STATE OF NEW MEXICO

STATE OF_____

COUNTY OF_____

On this_____day of_____, 19____, before me a Notary Public in
and for the State and County aforesaid, personally appeared_____
_____, who is to me known to be the
person and who acknowledged to me that the undersigned individual or corporate
entity does hereby accepts the appointment as the Initial Registered Agent of
_____

_____

_____

the corporation which is named in the annexed Articles of Incorporation, and
which is applying for a Certificate of Incorporation pursuant to the provisions
of the Business Corporation Act of the State of New Mexico.

1)_____
   Registered Agent's Signature (Individual Designation)

OR

2)_____
   Registered Agent's Corporate Name

By_____
   Signature of Agent's President/Vice President

(NOTARY SEAL)

_____
          NOTARY PUBLIC

My Commission Expires:_____

NMSCC-CD
DPR-NCAA
REV 10/97

(This form must be printed or typed in black ink)

CERTIFICATE OF INCORPORATION
OF

_____

(Insert corporate name)

Under Section 402 of the Business Corporation Law

FIRST: The name of the corporation is: _____

_____

SECOND: This corporation is formed to engage in any lawful act or activity for which a corporation may be organized under the Business Corporation Law, provided that it is not formed to engage in any act or activity requiring the consent or approval of any state official, department, board, agency or other body.

THIRD: The county within this state, in which the office of the corporation is to be located is:_____

FOURTH: The total number of shares which the corporation shall have authority to issue and a statement of the par value of each share or a statement that the shares are without par value are: 200 No Par Value

FIFTH: The secretary of state is designated as agent of the corporation upon whom process against the corporation may be served. The **post office address** to which the Secretary of State shall mail a copy of any process accepted on behalf of the corporation is:

_____

_____

_____

SIXTH: *(optional)* The name and **street address in this state** of the registered agent upon whom process against the corporation may be served is:

_____

_____

_____

SEVENTH: *(optional—if this provision is used, a specific date must be stated which is not before, nor more than 90 days after the date of filing)* The date corporate existence shall begin, if other than the date of filing, is:_____

IN WITNESS WHEREOF, this certificate has been subscribed this _____ day of _____ 19___, by the undersigned, who affirms that the statements made herein are true under the penalties of perjury.

X_____
(Signature)

_____
(Type or print name)

_____
(Street address)

_____
(City, State, Zip code)

This form may not contain any attachments or riders
except an original receipt evidencing reservation of name.

- -

CERTIFICATE OF INCORPORATION
OF

Under Section 402 of the Business Corporation Law

- -

Filed by: _____
(Name)

_____
(Mailing address)

_____
(City, State and Zip code)

Application for Reservation of Name
Under §303 of the Business Corporation Law

NYS Department of State
DIVISION OF CORPORATIONS, STATE RECORDS and UCC
41 State Street
Albany, NY 12231-0001

PLEASE TYPE OR PRINT

APPLICANT'S NAME AND ADDRESS

NAME TO BE RESERVED

RESERVATION IS INTENDED FOR (CHECK ONE)

G New domestic corporation

G Foreign corporation intending to apply for authority to do business in New York State*

G Proposed foreign corporation, not yet incorporated, intending to apply for authority to conduct business in New York State

G Change of name of an existing domestic or an authorized foreign corporation*

G Foreign corporation intending to apply for authority to do business in New York State whose corporate name is not available for use in New York State*

G Authorized foreign corporation intending to change its fictitious name under which it does business in this state*

G Authorized foreign corporation which has changed its corporate name in its jurisdiction, such new corporate name not being available for use in New York State*

X_____

Signature of applicant, applicant's attorney or agent

(If attorney or agent, so specify)

_____

Typed/printed name of signer

INSTRUCTIONS:
1. Upon filing this application, the name will be reserved for 60 days and a certificate of reservation will be issued.
2. The certificate of reservation must be returned with and attached to the certificate of incorporation or application for authority, amendment or with a cancellation of the reservation.
3. The name used must be the same as appears in the reservation.
4. A $20 fee payable to the Department of State must accompany this application.
5. Only names for business, transportation, cooperative and railroad corporations may be reserved under §303 of the Business Corporation Law.

*If the reservation is for an existing corporation, domestic or foreign, the corporation must be the applicant.

STATE OF NORTH CAROLINA
Department of the Secretary of State

ARTICLES OF INCORPORATION

Pursuant to Section 55-2-02 of the General Statutes of North Carolina, the undersigned does hereby submit these Articles of Incorporation for the purpose of forming a business corporation.

1. The name of the corporation is: _____

2. The number of shares the corporation is authorized to issue is: _____

   These shares shall be: *(check either a or b)*

   a.____ all of one class, designated as common stock; or

   b.____ divided into classes or series within a class as provided in the attached schedule,

   with the information required by N.C.G.S. Section 55-6-01.

3. The street address and county of the initial registered office of the corporation is:

   Number and Street _____

   City, State, Zip Code_____ County _____

4. The mailing address *if different from the street address* of the initial registered office is:

   _____

5. The name of the initial registered agent is: _____

6. Any other provisions which the corporation elects to include are attached.

7. The name and address of each incorporator is as follows:

8. These articles will be effective upon filing, unless a date and/or time is specified: _____

This the____day of _____, 19____

_____

_____
Signature

_____
Type or Print Name and Title

NOTES:
1. Filing fee is $125. This document and one exact or conformed copy of these articles must be filed with the Secretary of State. *(Revised October, 1997)*

CORPORATIONS DIVISION   **300 N. SALISBURY ST.**   **RALEIGH, NC 27603-5909**

ARTICLES OF INCORPORATION

Item 1   Enter the complete corporate name which must include a corporate ending required by N.C.G.S. §55-4-01(a) (corporation, company, limited, incorporated, corp., co., ltd., or inc.).

Item 2   Enter the number of shares the corporation will have the authority to issue.

Check (a) or (b), whichever is applicable. If (b) is checked, add an attachment that includes the description of the designations, preferences, limitations, and relative rights of the shares.

Item 3   Enter the complete street address of the registered office and the county in which it is located.

Item 4   Enter the complete mailing address of the registered agent only if mail is not delivered to the street address stated in Item 3 or if you prefer to receive mail at a P.O. Box or Drawer.

Item 5   Enter the name of the registered agent. The registered agent must be either a North Carolina resident at least 18 years old, an existing business or nonprofit corporation, or a foreign business or nonprofit corporation authorized to transact business or conduct affairs in North Carolina.

Item 6   See form.

Item 7   Enter the name and address of each incorporator. Only one incorporator is required in order to file.

Item 8   The document will be effective on the date and at the time of filing, unless a delayed date or an effective time (on the day of filing) is specified. If a delayed effective date is specified without a time, the document will be effective at 11:59:59 p.m. on the day specified. If a delayed effective date is specified with a time, the document will be effective on the day and time so specified. A delayed effective date may be specified up to and including the 90th day after the day of filing.

Date and Execution

Enter the date the document was executed.

In the blanks provided enter:

- The name of the entity executing the Articles of Incorporation; if an individual, leave blank.
- The signature of the incorporator or representative of the incorporating entity.
- The name of the incorporator or name and title of the above signed representative.

ATTENTION: Corporations wishing to render a professional service as defined in N.C.G.S. §55B-2(6) shall contact the appropriate North Carolina licensing board to determine whether compliance with additional licensing requirements may be mandated by law.

**ARTICLES OF INCORPORATION - NORTH DAKOTA BUSINESS
OR FARMING CORPORATION**
NORTH DAKOTA SECRETARY OF STATE
SFN 16812 (6-89)

SEE PAGE 4 FOR FILING AND MAILING INSTRUCTIONS

FOR OFFICE USE ONLY

Validation #

FILE NO. _____

    We, the undersigned natural persons of the age of eighteen years or more, acting as incorporators of a corporation organized under North Dakota _____ Corporation Act, adopt the following Articles of Incorporation for such Corporation:

Article 1. The name of said Corporation shall be: _____

_____

Article 2. The period of its duration is perpetual, OR _____

Article 3. The purpose for which the Corporation is organized are general business purposes, OR:

Article 4.

A. Aggregate number of shares the corporation has authority to issue		
B. Par value per share authorized by corporation		
C. If shares are divided into classes, they are identified as folows:		
CLASS	NO. OF SHARES	PAR VALUE PER SHARE

Article 5.

A. Name of Registered Agent			
B. Social Security or Federal ID # of Registered Agent			
C. Address of Registered Office	City	State	Zip Code
D. Address of Executive Office (if different than "C"	City	State	Zip Code
E. The articles of incorporation are accompanied by a signed consent of the registered agent with a filing fee of $10.			

Article 6.   Other provisions by which this corporation shall be governed: (If none, insert "none")

Article 7. A. The name, social security number, and address of each incorporator:

NAME	SOCIAL SECURITY NUMBER	ADDRESS	CITY	STATE	ZIP

B. SIGNATURES

I (We), the above named incorporator(s), have read the foregoing Articles of Incorporation, know the contents, and believe the statements made therein to be true.

Dated _____ , 19 _____ .

_____   _____

_____   _____

_____   _____

_____   _____

_____   _____

8. FEES:

Filing	$30.00
Consent of Registered Agent	$10.00
Minimum License Fee	$50.00
Additional License Fees	
(Equal to $10.00 for every additional $10,000 in excess of $50,000)	

SEE INSTRUCTIONS ON PAGE 4.

OFFICE USE ONLY

Certificate No.
Date Filed
Fee Paid
Filed By

INSTRUCTIONS

Articles of incorporation for business and farm corporations are filed pursuant to the provisions of Chapter 10-19.1 of the North Dakota Century Code. Farm corporations are also subject to the provisions of Chapter 10-06 of the North Dakota Century Code. Specify in the paragraph preceding Article 1 whether the corporation is a business corporation or a farm corporation. Articles of Incorporation, and the consent of the registered agent must be submitted in duplicate original format, two forms of each bearing original signatures.

ARTICLE 1. The corporate name must be in the English language. It must contain the word "corporation", "company", "incorporated", or "limited", or an abbreviation of one of such words, but that word or abbreviation may not be immediately preceded by the word "and" or the character "&". The corporate name cannot be the same as, or deceptively similar to, any other corporate name, trade name, limited partnership name, fictitious partnership name, trademark, or any name reserved in the office of the Secretary of State. A filing in the same or similar name is only permitted if articles of incorporation are submitted with the signed consent of the alternate name holder. That consent is required in duplicate originals with an additional filing fee of $10.00.

ARTICLE 2. Corporations are afforded perpetual existence by law, however, should limited existence be intended, specify the date on which the corporate existence is to expire.

ARTICLE 3. Articles of incorporation can be filed with general business purposes. If specific purposes are intended, specify those purposes in this section.

ARTICLE 4.
- A. Give the aggregate, or total, number of shares being authorized.
- B. Give the par value authorized for each share, or if the shares are being authorized without par value, state "None" in this section.
- C. If shares are being classified in different classes or series, summarize the shares by class, the number of shares in each class, and the par value of each class.

ARTICLE 5.
- A. A corporation must continuously maintain a registered agent. That agent may be an individual residing in North Dakota, another domestic corporation, or a foreign corporation authorized to transact business in North Dakota. A corporation cannot serve as its own registered agent.
- B. The social security number or the individual, or the Federal ID number of the corporation, appointed as the registered agent is required.
- C. The address of the registered office must be the business address of the registered agent. A registered office need not be the same as the principal place of business or the principal executive office of the corporation. A complete physical address is required for service of process. If that address does not serve as the mailing address, a post office address is required to insure delivery of all legal notices and reports.
- D. The address of the corporation's principal executive office is required.
- E. The signed consent of the registered agent to serve in that capacity must accompany the articles of incorporation. The consent must be submitted in duplicate originals, two forms bearing original signatures.

ARTICLE 6. This article provides special provisions, if any, to govern the corporation in the absence of bylaws, or unless otherwise modified in the articles of incorporation.

ARTICLE 7.
- A. A corporation may be incorporated by one or more natural persons of the age of eighteen years or more. Corporations cannot serve as incorporators. Give the names of the incorporators, their social security numbers, and complete mailing addresses.
- B. All incorporators listed in Article 7A must sign the articles of incorporation.

8. FEES. The minimum fee to incorporate is $90.00 which includes the filing fee of $30.00, the consent of agent filing fee of $10.00, and the minimum license fee of $50.00. License fees are computed by multiplying the number of shares by the authorized par value, or by $.10 if shares are authorized without par value. License fees are equal to $10.00 for every $10,000 of capitalization, or fraction, except that all corporations are subject to a minimum of $50.00 in license fees for $50,000 when they incorporate.

MAILING INSTRUCTIONS. Send duplicate originals of the articles of incorporation, the consent of the registered agent, and fees to:

Secretary of State
Capitol Building
600 E. Boulevard Avenue
Bismarck, ND 58505-0500

SPECIAL NOTE. All corporations must file an annual report in order to maintain their corporate existence. Business corporations must file their first annual report on or before August 1st in the year following that in which their certificate of incorporation was issued. Farm corporations must file their first annual report on or before April 15th in the year following that in which their certificate of incorporation was issued.

Additional information or forms may be obtained by contacting the Corporations Division of the Secretary of State's Office at 701-224-4284 or writing to the address given above. The Secretary of State's Office has telecopier service available (701-224-2992).

Prescribed by
Bob Taft, Secretary of State
30 East Broad Street, 14th Floor
Columbus Ohio 43266-0418
Form AFR (December 1990)

ARTICLES OF INCORPORATION
(Under Chapter 1701 of the Ohio Revised Code)
Profit Corporation

The undersigned, desiring to form a corporation, for profit, under Sections 1701.1 et seq. Of the Ohio Revised Code, do hereby state the following:

FIRST. The name of said corporation shall be _____

_____ .

SECOND. The place in Ohio where its principal office is to be located is _____

_____, _____ County Ohio.
     (city, village or township)

THIRD. The purpose(s) for which this corporation is formed is:

FOURTH. The number of share which the corporation is authorized to have outstanding is: (Please state whether share are common or preferred, and their par value, if any. Shares will be recorded as common with no par value unless otherwise indicated.)

IN WITNESS WHEREOF, we have hereunto subscribed our names, this _____ day of _____, 19 _____.

By: _____, Incorporator

By: _____, Incorporator

By: _____, Incorporator

Print or type incorporators' names below their signatures.

INSTRUCTIONS

1. The minimum fee for filing Articles of Incorporation for a profit corporation is $85.00. If Article Fourth indicates more than 850 shares of stock authorized, please see Section 111.16(A) of the Ohio Revised Code or contact the Secretary of State's office (614-466-3910) to determine the correct fee.

2. Articles will be returned unless accompanied by an Original Appointment of Statutory Agent. Please see Section 1701.07 of the Ohio Revised Code.

Prescribed by
Bob Taft, Secretary of State
30 East Broad Street, 14th Floor
Columbus Ohio 43266-0418

ORIGINAL APPOINTMENT OF STATUTORY AGENT

The undersigned, being at least a majority of the incorporators of _____

_____ , hereby appoint

(name or corporation)

_____ to be statutory agent upon whom any

(name of agent)

process, notice or demand required or permitted by statute to be served upon the corporation may

be served. The complete address or the agent is:

_____

(street address)

_____ , Ohio _____

(city)   (zip code)

NOTE: P.O. Box addresses are not acceptable.

_____

(incorporator)

_____

(incorporator)

_____

(incorporator)

ACCEPTANCE OF APPOINTMENT

The undersigned, _____ , named herein as the statutory agent for

_____ , hereby acknowledges and accepts the

(name of corporation)

appointment of statutory agent for said corporation.

_____

Statutory Agent

INSTRUCTIONS

1) Profit and no-profit articles or incorporation must be accompanied by and original appointment of agent. R.C. 1701.07(B), 1702.06(B).

2) The statutory agent for a corporation may be (a) a natural person who is a resident of Ohio, or (b) an Ohio corporation or a foreign profit corporation licensed in Ohio which has a business address in this state and is explicitly authorized by its articles of incorporation to act as a statutory agent. R.C. 1701.07(A), 1702.06(A).

3) An original appointment of agent form must be signed by at least a majority of the incorporators of the corporation. R.C. 1701.07(B), 1702.06(B). These signatures must be the same as the signatures on the articles of incorporation.

ISD STATAG

MINIMUM FEE: $50.00
Fee is $1.00 per $1,000.00
on Total Authorized Capital

FILE IN DUPLICATE

PRINT-CLEARLY

CERTIFICATE OF INCORPORATION

Oklahoma Secretary of State, 2300 N. Lincoln Blvd., Room 101, State Capitol Building, Oklahoma City, OK 73105-4897
Telephone (405)-522-4560

The undersigned, for the purpose of forming an Oklahoma profit corporation pursuant to the provisions of Title 18, Section 1001, do hereby execute the following certificate of incorporation:

1.   The name of the corporation is:

_____

(**NOTE**: Please refer to procedure sheet for statutory words required to be included in the corporate name.)

2.   The name of the registered agent and the street address of the registered office in the State of Oklahoma is:

_____

Name	Street Address	City	County	Zip Code

(P.O. BOXES ARE NOT ACCEPTABLE)

3.   The duration of the corporation is:_____
(Perpetual unless otherwise stated)

4.   The purpose of purposes for which the corporation is formed are:

5.   The aggregate number of shares which the corporation shall have the authority to issue, the designation of each class, the number of shares of each class, and the par value of the shares of each class are as follows:

NUMBER OF SHARES	SERIES (If any)	PAR VALUE PER SHARE (Or, if without par value, so state)
COMMON_____		_____
PREFERRED_____		_____

6.   If the powers of the incorporator(s) are to terminate upon the filing of the certificate of incorporation, the names and mailing addresses of the persons who are to serve as director(s):

NAME	**MAILING ADDRESS**	**CITY**	**STATE**	**ZIP CODE**

7.   The name and mailing address of the undersigned incorporator(s):

NAME	**MAILING ADDRESS**	**CITY**	**STATE**	**ZIP CODE**

Signed and dated this_____day of_____,_____.

SIGNATURE OF ALL INCORPORATORS

_____
SIGNATURE

_____
SIGNATURE

PROCEDURES FOR COMPLETING THE CERTIFICATE OF INCORPORATION

This information is intended as an aid in completing the certificate of incorporation forms provided by the Secretary of State's office. Title 18 of the Oklahoma Statutes, commonly known as the Oklahoma General Corporation Act, applies to all corporations except those expressly excluded and those for which special statutes are in existence with which the provisions of Title 18 may conflict. **PLEASE CONSULT THE STATUTES CAREFULLY.**

It may be to your benefit to contact the **INTERNAL REVENUE SERVICE** concerning federal tax requirements, and the **OKLAHOMA TAX COMMISSION** concerning state tax requirements prior to filing with the Secretary of State.

The availability of the proposed corporate name may be checked by telephoning in advance the **BUSINESS FILING DIVISION** of the Secretary of State's office directly at **(405)-522-4560. PRIOR** to incorporating, a name may be reserved for a period of sixty (60) days by filing a name reservation application and paying a fee of $10.00.

PROCEDURES

1. Prepare and file with the Secretary of State **TWO** signed certificates of incorporation.

2. **Pay** to the Secretary of State a filing fee of $1.00 per $1,000.00 on the total authorized capital (number of shares multiplied by the par value); No Par Value Stock is valued at $50.00 per share for determining filing fees only. The **MINIMUM FEE** is **$50.00**. (Title 18, Section 1142)

3. Make the check or money order **payable** to the Oklahoma Secretary of State. The certificate of incorporation may be mailed or delivered in person to: **Secretary of State, 2300 N Lincoln Blvd., Room 101, Oklahoma City, Oklahoma 73105-4897.** Documents to be **PROCESSED in person** must be delivered to the Secretary of State's office between the hours of **8:00 a.m. and 4:00 p.m. (Monday-Friday).**

INSTRUCTIONS

1. **NAME** - The name of the corporation **MUST** contain one of the following words: **association, company, corporation, club, foundation, fund, incorporated, institute, society, union, syndicate** or **limited** or one of the abbreviations **co., corp., inc.** or **ltd.**, or words or abbreviations of like import in other languages provided that such abbreviations are written in Roman characters or letters. (Title 18, Section 1006)

2. **REGISTERED AGENT AND REGISTERED OFFICE** - **Every** corporation **must** maintain a registered office and a registered agent. The agent may be either the corporation itself, an individual resident of this state, a domestic or qualified foreign corporation, limited liability company, or limited partnership. Each registered agent shall maintain a business office **identical** with the registered office which is open during regular business hours to accept service of process and otherwise perform the functions of a registered agent. The registered office address must be a physical address and cannot be a post office address. (Title 18, Section 1021 and Section 1022)

3. **DURATION** - The duration of the corporation is the life span of the corporation. Perpetual means continuous. All domestic corporations shall have a perpetual duration unless otherwise stated.

4.   **PURPOSE** - The purpose of the corporation is the type of business the corporation intends to conduct. It shall be sufficient to state, either alone or with other business purposes, that the purpose of the corporation is **to engage in any lawful act or activity for which corporations may be organized under the general corporation law of Oklahoma.**

5.   **AUTHORIZED CAPITAL** - Every business corporation must have authorized capital consisting of shares of stock and par value. The par value is the value assigned to each share. A definition of **Common Stock** and **Preferred Stock** may be found in a dictionary.

6.   **DIRECTORS** - If the incorporators are not to continue as the directors once the certificate of incorporation is filed, the name(s) and addresses of the first board of directors must be set out. A minimum of one director is required. (Title 18, Section 1011)

7.   **INCORPORATORS** - Any person, partnership, association or corporation, **singly** or **jointly** with others, and without regard to his or their residence, domicile or state of incorporation, may incorporate or organize a corporation pursuant to the provisions of the Oklahoma General Corporation Act. The incorporators are the original signers of the certificate of incorporation. The incorporators are not necessarily officers, directors or shareholders, although it does not exclude them from being such. A minimum of one incorporator is required for a profit corporation. (Title 18, Section 1005)

Phone: (503) 986-2200
Fax: (503) 378-4381

Secretary of State
Corporation Division
255 Capitol St. NE, Suite 151
Salem, OR 97310-1327

Articles of Incorporation—Business/Professional

Check the appropriate box below:

☐ BUSINESS CORPORATION
(Complete only 1, 2, 3, 4, 5, 6, 7, 9, 10, 11)

☐ PROFESSIONAL CORPORATION
(Complete all items)

For office use only

Registry Number: _____

Attach Additional Sheet if Necessary
Please Type or Print Legibly in **Black** Ink

1) **NAME** _____

NOTE: For a BUSINESS CORPORATION, the name must contain the word "Corporation," "Company," "Incorporated," or "Limited," or an abbreviation of one of such words. For a PROFESSIONAL CORPORATION, the name must contain the words "Professional Corporation," or abbreviations thereof, i.e., "P.C.," or "Prof. Corp."

☐ CHECK HERE TO INDICATE ON YOUR REGISTRATION THAT YOU DO NOT WANT MAIL SOLICITATION.

2) **REGISTERED AGENT**

_____

3) **ADDRESS OF REGISTERED AGENT** (Must be an **Oregon Street Address** which is identical to the registered agent's business office. Must include city, state, zip; no PO Boxes.)

_____
_____
_____

4) **MAILING ADDRESS OF REGISTERED AGENT** (Address, city, state, zip)

_____
_____
_____

5) **ADDRESS FOR MAILING NOTICES**

_____
_____
_____

6) **OPTIONAL PROVISIONS** (Attach a separate sheet.)

7) **NUMBER OF SHARES THE CORPORATION WILL HAVE THE AUTHORITY TO ISSUE**

_____

PROFESSIONAL CORPORATION ONLY

8) **PROFESSIONAL/BUSINESS SERVICES** (List professional service(s) and other business services to be rendered.)

_____
_____
_____
_____
_____

9) **INCORPORATORS** (List names and addresses of each incorporator. Attach a separate sheet if necessary.)

_____
_____
_____
_____

10) **EXECUTION** (All incorporators **must** sign. Attach a separate sheet if necessary.)

Printed Name   Signature

_____   _____
_____   _____
_____   _____

11) **CONTACT NAME**   **DAYTIME PHONE NUMBER**

_____   _____

FEES

Business Corporation $ 50
Professional Corporation $ 40

Make check payable to "Corporation Division."

NOTE: Filing fees may be paid with VISA or MasterCard. The card number and expiration date should be submitted on a separate sheet for your protection.

CR111 (Rev. 8/97)

Department of State
Corporation Bureau
P.O. Box 8722
Harrisburg, PA 17105-8722

Instructions for Completion of Form:

A. One original of this form is required. The form shall be completed in black or blue-black ink in order to permit reproduction. The filing fee for this form is $100 made payable to the Department of State. PLEASE NOTE: A separate check is required for each form submitted.

B. Under 15 Pa.C.S. ' 135(c) (relating to addresses) an actual street or rural route box number must be used as an address, and the Department of State is required to refuse to receive or file any document that sets forth only a post office box address.

C. The following, in addition to the filing fee, shall accompany this form:

   (1) Three copies of a completed form DSCB:15-134A (Docketing Statement).
   (2) Any necessary copies of form DSCB:17.2 (Consent to Appropriation of Name) or form DSCB:17.3 (Consent to Use of Similar Name).
   (3) Any necessary governmental approvals.

D. For general instructions relating to the incorporation of business corporations see 19 Pa. Code Ch. 23 (relating to business corporations generally). These instructions relate to such matters as corporate name, stated purposes, term of existence, nonstock status, authorized share structure and related authority of the board of directors, inclusion of names of first directors in the Articles of Incorporation, ptional provisions on cumulative voting for election of directors, etc.

E. For required provisions in the Articles of a management corporation, see 15 Pa.C.S. '2703 (relating to additional contents of articles of management corporations).

F. For restrictions on the stated purposes of professional corporations, see 15 Pa.C.S. '2903 (relating to formation of professional corporations).

G. Articles for a nonprofit cooperative corporation should be filed on Form DSCB:15-7102B (Articles of Incorporation Nonprofit Cooperative Corporation).

H. One or more corporations or natural persons of full age may incorporate a business corporation.

I. 15 Pa.C.S. ' 1307 (relating to advertisement) requires that the incorporators shall advertise their intention to file or the corporation shall advertise the filing of articles of incorporation. Proofs of publication of such advertising should not be submitted to, and will not be received by or filed in, the Department, but should be filed with the minutes of the corporation.

J. This form and all accompanying documents shall be mailed to:

Department of State
Corporation Bureau
P.O. Box 8722
Harrisburg, PA 17105-8722

K. To receive confirmation of the file date prior to receiving the microfilmed original, send either a self-addressed, stamped postcard with the filing information noted or a self-addressed, stamped envelope with a copy of the filing document.

Microfilm Number_____

Entity Number_____

Filed with the Department of State on_____

_____
Secretary of the Commonwealth

ARTICLES OF INCORPORATION-FOR PROFIT
OF

_____
Name of Corporation
A TYPE OF CORPORATION INDICATED BELOW

Indicate type of domestic corporation:

___ Business-stock (15 Pa.C.S. ' 1306)

___ Business-nonstock (15 Pa.C.S. ' 2102)

___ Business-statutory close (15 Pa.C.S. ' 2303)

___ Cooperative (15 Pa.C.S. ' 7102)

___ Management (15 Pa.C.S. ' 2702)

___ Professional (15 Pa.C.S. ' 2903)

___ Insurance (15 Pa.C.S. ' 3101)

DSCB:15-1306/2102/2303/2702/2903/3101/7102A (Rev 91)

In compliance with the requirements of the applicable provisions of 15 Pa.C.S. (relating to corporations and unincorporated associations) the undersigned, desiring to incorporate a corporation for profit hereby, state(s) that:

1. The name of the corporation is: _____

_____

2. The (a) address of this corporation's initial registered office in this Commonwealth or (b) name of its commercial registered office provider and the county of venue is:

(a) _____
    Number and Street   City   State   Zip   County

(b) c/o: _____
    Name of Commercial Registered Office Provider   County

For a corporation represented by a commercial registered office provider, the county in (b) shall be deemed the county in which the corporation is located for venue and official publication purposes.

3. The corporation is incorporated under the provisions of the Business Corporation Law of 1988.

4. The aggregate number of shares authorized is: _____ (other provisions, if any, attach 8 1/2 x 11 sheet)

5. The name and address, including number and street, if any, of each incorporator is:

    Name   Address

_____   _____

_____   _____

6. The specified effective date, if any, is:_____.____

                                      month   day   year   hour, if any

7. Additional provisions of the articles, if any, attach an 8 1/2 x 11 sheet.

8. Statutory close corporation only: Neither the corporation nor any shareholder shall make an offering of any of its shares of any class that would constitute a "public offering" within the meaning of the Securities Act of 1933 (15 U.S.C. ' 77a et seq.).

9. Cooperative corporations only: (Complete and strike out inapplicable term) The common bond of membership

    among its members/shareholders is: _____

    IN TESTIMONY WHEREOF, the incorporator(s) has (have) signed these Articles of Incorporation this _____day of_____ , 19 _____ .

_____
(Signature)

_____
(Signature)

DOCKETING STATEMENT DSCB:15-134A (Rev 95)
DEPARTMENTS OF STATE AND REVENUE

FILING FEE: NONE

BUREAU USE ONLY:
Dept. of State Entity Number _____

Revenue Box Number _____

Filing Period _____ Date 3 4 5 _____

SIC _____ Report Code _____

This form (file in triplicate) and all accompanying documents shall be mailed to:
COMMONWEALTH OF PENNSYLVANIA
DEPARTMENT OF STATE
CORPORATION BUREAU
P.O. BOX 8722
HARRISBURG, PA 17105-8722

Check proper box:

____ Pa. Business-stock   ____ Pa. Business-nonstock   ____ Pa. Business-Management   ____ Pa. Professional

____ Pa. Business-statutory close   ____ Pa. Business-cooperative   ____ Pa. Nonprofit-stock   ____ Pa. Nonprofit-nonstock

____ Foreign-business   ____ Foreign-nonprofit   ____ Motor Vehicle for Hire   ____ Insurance

____ Foreign-Certificate of Authority to D/B/A _____

____ Business Trust

____ Pa. Limited Liability Company   ____ Pa. Restricted Professional Limited Liability Company

____ Foreign Limited Liability Company   ____ Foreign Restricted Professional Limited Liability Company

Association registering as a result of (check box):

____ Incorporation (Pa.)   ____ Domestication   ____ Consolidation

____ Authorization of a foreign association   ____ Division   ____ Summary of Record

____ Organization (Pa.)

1. Name of entity: _____

   _____

2. Location of (a) initial registered office in Pennsylvania or (b) the name and county of the commercial registered office provider:

   (a) _____
       Number and Street/RD number and Box   City   State   Zip code   County

   (b) c/o: _____
       Name of commercial registered office provider   County

3. State or Country of Incorporation/Organization: _____

4. Specified effective date, if applicable: _____

5. Federal Identification Number: _____

6. Describe principal Pennsylvania activity to be engaged in, within one year of this application date: _____

   _____

   _____

7. Names, residences and social security numbers of the chief executive officer, secretary and treasurer or individual responsible for maintaining financial records:

Name   Address   Title   Social Security #

_____

_____

_____

If professional association, include officer's professional license numbers with the respective Pennsylvania Professional Board.

8. Location of principal place of business:

_____
Number and Street/RD number and Box   City   State   Zip

9. Mailing address if different than #8 (Location where correspondence, tax report form, etc. are to be sent):

_____
Number and Street/RD number and Box   City   State   Zip

10. This entity is organized or incorporated under the General Association Act of 1988. (Not applicable if a foreign entity)

11. Act of General Assembly or authority under which you are organized or incorporated (foreign entity only):

_____

12. Date and state of incorporation or organization (foreign association only): _____

13. Date business started in Pennsylvania (foreign association only): _____

14. Is the entity authorized to issue capital stock?_____ YES _____ NO

15. Entity's fiscal year ends: _____

16. Has the association solicited or does it intend to solicit contributions with the Commonwealth of Pennsylvania? ___YES ___NO

This statement shall be deemed to have been executed by the individual who executed the accompanying submittal. See 18 Pa.C.S. §4904 (relating to unsworn falsification to authorities).

Instructions for Completion of Form:

A. A separate completed set of copies of this form shall be submitted for each entity or registration resulting from the transaction.

B. The Bureau of Corporation Taxes in the Pennsylvania Department of Revenue should be notified of any address changes. Notification should be sent to the Processing Division, Bureau of Corporation Taxes, Pa. Department of Revenue, Dept. 280705, Harrisburg, PA 17128-0705.

C. All Pennsylvania corporate tax reports, except those for motor vehicle for hire, must be filed with the Commonwealth on the same fiscal basis as filed with the U.S. government. Motor vehicle for hire, i.e., gross receipts tax reports, must be filed on a calendar year basis only.

D. The disclosure of the social security numbers of the corporate officers in Paragraph 7 is voluntary. The numbers are used to assure the proper identification of corporation officers by the Department of Revenue in accordance with the Fiscal Code.

Filing Fee: $150.00   ID Number: _____

STATE OF RHODE ISLAND AND PROVIDENCE PLANTATIONS
Office of the Secretary of State
Corporations Division
100 North Main Street
Providence, Rhode Island 02903-1335

BUSINESS CORPORATION

ORIGINAL ARTICLES OF INCORPORATION

The undersigned acting as incorporator(s) of a corporation under Chapter 7-1.1 of the General Laws, 1956, as amended, adopt(s) the following Articles of Incorporation for such corporation:

1. The name of the corporation is_____

_____
(This is a close corporation pursuant to § 7-1.1-51 of the General Laws, 1956, as amended) (strike if inapplicable)

2. The period of its duration is (if perpetual, so state) _____

3. The specific purpose or purposes for which the corporation is organized are:

_____

_____

_____

_____

_____

_____

4. The aggregate number of shares which the corporation shall have authority to issue is:

    (a) *If only one class:* Total number of shares _____ (If the authorized shares are to consist of one class only state the par value of such shares or a statement that all of such shares are to be without par value.):

_____

or

    (b) *If more than one class:* Total number of shares _____ (State (A) the number of shares of each class thereof that are to have a par value and the par value of each share of each such class, and/or (B) the number of such shares that are to be without par value, and (C) a statement of all or any of the designations and the powers, preferences and rights, including voting rights, and the qualifications, limitations or restrictions thereof, which are permitted by the provisions of Chapter 7-1.1 of the General Laws in respect of any class or classes of stock of the corporation and the fixing of which by the articles of association is desired, and an express grant of such authority as it may then be desired to grant to the board of directors to fix by vote or votes any thereof that may be desired but which shall not be fixed by the articles.):

_____

_____

5. Provisions (if any) dealing with the preemptive right of shareholders pursuant to § 7-1.1-24 of the General Laws, 1956, as amended:

_____

_____

Form No. 11A
Revised 3/97

6. Provisions (if any) for the regulation of the internal affairs of the corporation:

_____

_____

7. The address of the initial registered office of the corporation is _____
   (Street)

_____,RI_____ and the name of its initial registered agent at such address is
   (City/Town)   (Zip Code)

_____.

8. The number of directors constituting the initial board of directors of the corporation is _____ and the names and addresses of the persons who are to serve as directors until the first annual meeting of shareholders or until their successors are elected and shall qualify are: (If this is a close corporation pursuant to Section 7-1.1-51 of the General Laws, 1956, as amended, and there shall be no board of directors, state the titles of the initial officers of the corporation and the names and addresses of the persons who are to serve as officers until the first annual meeting of shareholders or until their successors be elected and qualify.)

Title	Name	Address
_____	_____	_____
_____	_____	_____
_____	_____	_____
_____	_____	_____

9. The name and address of each incorporator is:

Name	Address
_____	_____
_____	_____
_____	_____

10. Date when corporate existence to begin: _____
    (not more than 30 days after filing of these articles of incorporation)

Dated_____, 19____   _____

                                               _____

                                               _____
                                               Signature of each Incorporator

STATE OF
COUNTY OF

     In _____, on this _____ day of _____, 19____, personally appeared
before me _____,
each and all known to me and known by me to be the parties executing the foregoing instrument, and they severally
acknowledged said instrument by them subscribed to be their free act and deed.

                                               _____
                                               Notary Public
                                               My Commission Expires:_____

Filing Fee: $150.00   ID Number: _____

 STATE OF RHODE ISLAND AND PROVIDENCE PLANTATIONS
Office of the Secretary of State
Corporations Division
100 North Main Street
Providence, Rhode Island 02903-1335

BUSINESS CORPORATION

DUPLICATE ORIGINAL ARTICLES OF INCORPORATION

The undersigned acting as incorporator(s) of a corporation under Chapter 7-1.1 of the General Laws, 1956, as amended, adopt(s) the following Articles of Incorporation for such corporation:

1. The name of the corporation is_____

_____
(This is a close corporation pursuant to § 7-1.1-51 of the General Laws, 1956, as amended) (strike if inapplicable)

2. The period of its duration is (if perpetual, so state)_____

3. The specific purpose or purposes for which the corporation is organized are:

_____

_____

_____

_____

_____

4. The aggregate number of shares which the corporation shall have authority to issue is:

(a) *If only one class:* Total number of shares _____ (If the authorized shares are to consist of one class only state the par value of such shares or a statement that all of such shares are to be without par value.):

_____

or

(b) *If more than one class:* Total number of shares _____ (State (A) the number of shares of each class thereof that are to have a par value and the par value of each share of each such class, and/or (B) the number of such shares that are to be without par value, and (C) a statement of all or any of the designations and the powers, preferences and rights, including voting rights, and the qualifications, limitations or restrictions thereof, which are permitted by the provisions of Chapter 7-1.1 of the General Laws in respect of any class or classes of stock of the corporation and the fixing of which by the articles of association is desired, and an express grant of such authority as it may then be desired to grant to the board of directors to fix by vote or votes any thereof that may be desired but which shall not be fixed by the articles.):

_____

_____

5. Provisions (if any) dealing with the preemptive right of shareholders pursuant to § 7-1.1-24 of the General Laws, 1956, as amended:

_____

_____

Form No. 11B
Revised 3/97

6. Provisions (if any) for the regulation of the internal affairs of the corporation:

_____

_____

7. The address of the initial registered office of the corporation is _____
(Street)

_____,RI_____ and the name of its initial registered agent at such address is
(City/Town)   (Zip Code)

_____.

8. The number of directors constituting the initial board of directors of the corporation is _____ and the names and addresses of the persons who are to serve as directors until the first annual meeting of shareholders or until their successors are elected and shall qualify are: (If this is a close corporation pursuant to Section 7-1.1-51 of the General Laws, 1956, as amended, and there shall be no board of directors, state the titles of the initial officers of the corporation and the names and addresses of the persons who are to serve as officers until the first annual meeting of shareholders or until their successors be elected and qualify.)

Title	Name	Address
_____	_____	_____
_____	_____	_____
_____	_____	_____
_____	_____	_____

9. The name and address of each incorporator is:

Name	Address
_____	_____
_____	_____
_____	_____

10. Date when corporate existence to begin_____
(not more than 30 days after filing of these articles of incorporation)

Dated_____, 19____   _____

                                               _____

                                               _____
Signature of each Incorporator

STATE OF
COUNTY OF

    In _____, on this _____ day of _____, 19____, personally appeared before me _____,
each and all known to me and known by me to be the parties executing the foregoing instrument, and they severally acknowledged said instrument by them subscribed to be their free act and deed.

                                         _____
Notary Public
My Commission Expires: _____

STATE OF RHODE ISLAND AND PROVIDENCE PLANTATIONS

Office of the Secretary of State
Corporations Division
100 North Main Street
Providence, Rhode Island 02903-1335
(401) 222-3040

INSTRUCTIONS FOR FILING
ARTICLES OF INCORPORATION
FOR A DOMESTIC BUSINESS CORPORATION

Section 7-1.1-48 of the General Laws of Rhode Island, as amended

1. To incorporate, you must file duplicate original Articles of Incorporation (Forms 11A and 11B) with the Office of the Secretary of State, Corporations Division, at the above address. When the Articles are properly completed, signed and submitted with the correct filing fee, a Certificate of Incorporation, together with the file stamped duplicate original Articles of Incorporation affixed thereto, shall be returned to you. *(If you are filing as a Professional Service Corporation pursuant to Section 7-5.1-2, or if the corporation falls under the jurisdiction of a regulatory agency, please call this office for further instructions prior to submitting the Articles of Incorporation.)*

2. The minimum filing and license fee is $150.00 for up to 8,000 shares of authorized stock. The fee is prorated beyond 8,000 shares. Call the Corporations Division at the above telephone number for the appropriate fee if the number of authorized shares is greater than 8,000.

3. The corporate name shall contain the word "corporation," "company," "incorporated," or "limited," or shall contain an abbreviation of one of the words. A proposed name cannot be the same as, or deceptively similar to, the name of any entity, name reservation or registration on file with the Corporations Division. Availability of the corporation's name should be checked prior to submission of the Articles by calling the above telephone number. This is only a preliminary clearance and does not ensure that the name will be acceptable upon filing the Articles of Incorporation. It is suggested that you do not make any financial expenditures or execute documents utilizing the name based upon this preliminary clearance. The final determination as to availability of the name will be made when the documents are submitted for filing.

4. If the corporation elects to organize as a close corporation pursuant to the provisions of Section 7-1.1-51 of the General Laws, as amended, No. 8 of the Articles of Incorporation must be completed to reflect the number of initial directors together with the names and addresses of each director. However, if a close corporation elects not to have a board of directors, then No. 8 should be completed to reflect the number as "Zero" and the corporation must list the title(s), name(s) and address(s) of the initial corporate officer(s).

5. Each corporation shall have and continuously maintain in this state a registered office, which may be, but need not be, the same as its place of business, and a registered agent, which agent may be either an individual resident in this state whose business office is identical with the registered office, or a domestic corporation, or a foreign corporation authorized to transact business in this state, having a business office identical with the registered office. However, in the case where the registered agent of a corporation is an attorney, the business address of the agent need not be identical with the registered office, but may be the usual business address of the attorney. The registered agent so appointed by a corporation shall be an agent of the corporation upon whom any process, notice or demand required or permitted by law to be served upon the corporation may be served.

6. The corporation is responsible for filing an Annual Report each calendar year between January 1 and March 1, beginning with the year following the year of incorporation. An Annual Report form will be mailed to the Registered Agent prior to January 1 each year. Be sure to follow up with your Registered Agent concerning the filing of this report.

7. Failure to comply with Nos. 5 and 6 above may result in the revocation of the Certificate of Incorporation pursuant to the provisions of Section 7-1.1-87 of the General Laws, as amended.

If you have any questions or wish to receive additional forms, please call us at (401) 222-3040, Monday through Friday, between 8:30 a.m. and 4:30 p.m

Form No. 11D
Revised 1/98

Secretary of State
State Capitol
500 E. Capitol Ave.
Pierre SD 57501
Phone 605-773-4845
Fax 605-773-4550

Articles of Incorporation

Executed by the undersigned for the purpose of forming a South Dakota Business Corporation under Chapter 47 of SDCL.

Article I

The name of the corporation is _____

Article II

The period of existence is _____

Article III

The purposes for which the corporation is organized.

Article IV

The number of shares which it shall have authority to issue, itemized by class, par value of shares, shares without par value, and series, if any, within a class:

Number	Class	Series	Par value per share or statement that shares are without par value

Article V

The preferences, limitations, designation and relative rights of each class or series of stock:

Article VI

The corporation will not commence business until consideration of the value of at least One Thousand Dollars ($1,000.00) has been received for the issuance of shares.

Article VII

The complete address, including the street address or a statement that there is no street address, of its registered office is _____

_____ZIP _____

and the name of its registered agent at such address is_____.

Article VIII

The number of directors constituting the initial board of directors is _____ and the names and addresses of the persons who are to serve as directors:

Name	Address
_____	_____
_____	_____
_____	_____
_____	_____
_____	_____

Article IX

The names and addresses of the incorporators:

ame   Address

_____   _____
_____   _____
_____   _____
_____   _____
_____   _____
_____   _____

Article X
(Other provisions)

These Articles may be amended in the manner authorized by law at the time of amendment.

All Incorporators must sign below and signatures must be notarized.

Dated_____ 19 _____

_____   _____

_____   _____

STATE OF _____

COUNTY OF _____

On this the _____ day of _____ 19 _____, before me personally appeared_____
_____ known to me or satisfactorily proven to be
the person(s) who are described in, and who executed the within instrument and acknowledged to me that
she/he/they executed the same.

My Commission Expires _____   _____
                                                                    Notary Public

Notarial Seal

The Consent of Appointment below must be signed by the registered agent.

Consent of Appointment by the Registered Agent
I, _____, hereby give my consent to serve as the (Name of Registered Agent) registered agent for _____ (Corporate Name) Dated _____ 19 ____   _____ (Signature of Registered Agent)

dbartinc.pdf

The proper filing fee must accompany the application. Make checks payable to the Secretary of State.

Fee Schedule

Authorized capital stock of	$ 25,000	or less	$ 90
Over $25,000 and not exceeding	100,000		110
Over $100,000 and not exceeding	500,000		130
Over $500,000 and not exceeding	1,000,000		150
Over $1,000,000 and not exceeding	1,500,000		200
Over $1,500,000 and not exceeding	2,000,000		250
Over $2,000,000 and not exceeding	2,500,000		300
Over $2,500,000 and not exceeding	3,000,000		350
Over $3,000,000 and not exceeding	3,500,000		400
Over $3,500,000 and not exceeding	4,000,000		450
Over $4,000,000 and not exceeding	4,500,000		500
Over $4,500,000 and not exceeding	5,000,000		550

For each additional $500,000, $40 in addition to $550.

For purposes only of computing fees under this section, the dollar value of each authorized share having a par value shall be equal to par value and the value of each authorized share having no par value shall be equal to one hundred dollars per share. The maximum amount charged under this subdivision may not exceed sixteen thousand dollars ($16,000).

Filing Instructions:

Article VII - South Dakota law requires the corporation to continuously maintain a resident of this state as the registered agent. The registered agent's address is considered the registered office address of the corporation.

The Consent of Appointment must be signed by the registered agent.

The articles must be originally signed by each incorporator in the presence of a notary public.

One originally signed and one exact copy (photocopy) of the articles of incorporation must be submitted along with the proper filing fee to the Secretary of State's Office.

C H A R T E R

O F

_____

The undersigned person(s) under the Tennessee Business Corporation Act adopt(s) the following charter for the above listed corporation:

1. The name of the corporation is _____

_____.

[NOTE: Pursuant to Tennessee Code Annotated Section 48-14-101(a)(1), each corporation name must contain the word "corporation", "incorporated" or "company" or the abbreviation "corp.", "inc." or "co.".]

2. The number of shares of stock the corporation is authorized to issue is

_____.

3. (a) The complete address of the corporation's initial registered office in Tennessee is

_____

Street Address   City   State, Zip Code
County of _____.
[NOTE: A street address, a zip code and the county are required by Tennessee Code Annotated Section 48-12-102(a)(3).]

   (b) The name of the initial registered agent, to be located at the address listed in 3(a), is

_____.

4. The name and complete address of each incorporator is:

_____

Name   Address   Zip Code

_____

Name   Address   Zip Code

_____

Name   Address   Zip Code

[NOTE: An address and zip code are both required by Tennessee Code Annotated Section 48-12-102(a)(4).]

5. The complete address of the corporation's principal office is:

_____

Street Address   City   State/Country   Zip Code

[NOTE: A street address and a zip code are both required by Tennessee Code Annotated Section 48-12-102(a)(5).]

5. The complete address of the corporation's principal office is:

_____

Street Address   City   State/Country   Zip Code

[NOTE: A street address and a zip code are both required by Tennessee Code Annotated Section 48-12-102(a)(5).]

6. The corporation is for profit.

7. Other provisions:
   [NOTE: Insert here any provision(s) desired and permitted by law. **Examples:** names and addresses of persons serving as the initial board of directors, business purpose(s) of the corporation, management or regulation of affairs of the corporation, provision limiting the personal liability of directors for monetary damages for breach of fiduciary duty, etc. See Tennessee Code Annotated Section 48-12-102(b).]

_____   _____

Signature Date   Incorporator's Signature

                                            _____

                                            Incorporator's Name (typed or printed)

SS-4417
(Rev. 5/89)

RDA 1678

Office of the
Secretary of State

Corporations Section

P.O. Box 13697
Austin, Texas 78711-3697

INCORPORATION OF A
BUSINESS CORPORATION

The Texas Business Corporation Act governs the formation of corporations organized for profit. The secretary of state does not provide forms for articles of incorporation and cannot provide legal advice. In view of the legal complexities involved, it is recommended that you consult the attorney of your choice for information and advice concerning incorporation as well as information on state taxes and applicable licensing requirements.

To incorporate, you must file articles of incorporation pursuant to article 3.02 of the Texas Business Corporation Act (Volume 3A, Vernon's Texas Civil Statutes). The articles of incorporation must minimally set forth:

1. The name of the corporation.

2. The period of duration, which may be perpetual.

3. A lawful purpose, which may be stated to be, or to include, the transaction of any or all lawful business for which corporations may be incorporated under the Texas Business Corporation Act.

4. The number of shares that the corporation is authorized to issue and a statement of the par value of the shares, or that the shares are to have "no par value."

5. The following statement: "The corporation will not commence business until it has received for the issuance of its shares consideration of the value of a stated sum which shall be at least one thousand dollars ($1,000.00)."

6. The street address of the registered office and the name of the registered agent located at such address. (The phrases "registered agent" and "registered office" must be used when setting forth this information in the articles.)

7. The number of directors constituting the initial board of directors and their names and addresses. Only one director is required.

8. The name and address of the incorporator.

The incorporator must sign the articles of incorporation. After signing, <u>two copies</u> of the articles of incorporation and the filing fee should be delivered to the secretary of state. We will place one document on record and return a file stamped copy to you for your files.

<u>Prior to signing, please review carefully the statements set forth in the document. A person commits an offense under the Texas Business Corporation Act, the Texas Limited Liability Company Act or the Texas Non-Profit Corporation Act if the person signs a document the person knows is false in any material respect with the intent that the document be delivered to the secretary of state for filing. The offense is a Class A misdemeanor.</u>

The filing fee is $300.00. Checks should be made payable to the secretary of state. Questions concerning franchise taxes should be directed to Tax Assistance Section, Comptroller of Public Accounts, Austin, Texas 78774-0100, (512) 463-4600, or (800) 252-1381.

Availability of the corporation's name may be checked prior to submission of the articles by calling (512) 463-5555. This is only a preliminary clearance and does not ensure that the name will be acceptable upon filing the articles of incorporation. Do not make any financial expenditures or execute documents utilizing the name based upon this preliminary clearance. The final determination as to availability of the name is made when the document is submitted for filing.

Under article 10.03 of the Texas Business Corporation Act, a business corporation may choose to make the filing of certain documents effective as of a date not more than 90 days after the date of filing. This can be accomplished by stating within the document a future effective date or by describing a future event when the articles are to become effective. Please refer to article 10.03 of the TBCA for the specific requirements necessary for filing documents with a future effective date.

Two copies of the form along with the filing fee should be mailed to the address shown in the heading of this form. The delivery address is James Earl Rudder Office Building, 1019 Brazos, Austin, Texas 78701. We will place one document on record and, *if a duplicate copy has been provided for such purpose*, return a file stamped copy. The telephone number is (512) 463-5555, TDD: (800) 735-2989, FAX: (512) 463-5709.

Form No. 201
Revised 9/97

The Office of the Secretary of State does not discriminate on the basis of race, color, national origin, sex, religion, age or disability in employment or the provision of services.

ARTICLES OF INCORPORATION
(Vermont profit)

Corporate name _____

(the name must end with one of these endings <u>corporation</u>, <u>incorporated</u>, <u>company</u>, <u>limited</u> or an abbrev. thereof)

Name of registered agent _____

A registered agent is an individual or a domestic or foreign corporation, profit or non-profit, whose business office is identical to the address of the registered office. The registered office must be located in Vermont. A registered agent receives various kinds of legal notices, including service of process for the corporation. A corporation cannot act as its own registered agent.

Address of registered office _____ VT _____

(street and box # of place of business)   (city)   (zip)

The fiscal year ends the month of: _____ *(DEC will be designated as the month your year ends unless you state differently.)*

Every corporation has perpetual duration, unless otherwise stated _____

<u>Please check the box that applies for your corporation:</u>

[ ] General corporation *(T.11A)*   [ ] Professional Corporation *(T.11,Ch.3)*   [ ] Close corporation *(T.11A,Ch.20)*

Number of shares the corporation is authorized to issue:

_____

Classes of shares (common/preferred/etc.) & number of shares authorized to issue, in each class:

_____

One or more classes of shares that together have unlimited voting rights:

_____

One or more classes of shares (which may be the same class with voting rights) that together are entitled to receive the net assets of the corporation upon dissolution.

CLOSE CORPORATIONS   *(11VSA, Chapter 20)*

The provisions of title 11A, other than those set forth in Chapter 20, shall apply to close corporations in the absence of a contrary or inconsistent provision in Chapter 20. A corporation whose status as a close corporation terminates shall immediately become subject to the obligations and rights of a general corporation.

In addition to the other information required herein a close corporation must include the following information in its articles: (1)"this corporation is a close corporation"; (2) that all the corporation's issued and outstanding stock of all classes shall be held by not more than a specified number of persons, not exceeding 35; (3) that each certificate for shares shall conspicuously note the fact that the corporation is a close corporation; (4) provisions, if any, setting forth restrictions on shares transfer; (5) whether dissolution occurs upon the occurrence of a specified event or contingency; (6) whether are limited or whether the corporation will be managed without a board of directors; (7) provide that there shall be no offering of any of its shares for "public offering"; and (8) that all issued and outstanding shares of all classes be represented by certificates.

_____

_____

_____

_____

_____

_____

ANNUAL REPORT: EACH CORPORATION UNDER THIS TITLE IS REQUIRED TO FILE AN ANNUAL REPORT WITHIN 2-1/2 MONTHS OF THE CLOSE OF ITS FISCAL YEAR END. FAILURE TO FILE THIS REPORT WILL RESULT IN TERMINATION OF THE CORPORATE CHARTER. A PRE-PRINTED REPORT FORM WILL BE MAILED TO YOUR AGENT WHEN THE REPORT IS DUE.

PURPOSE: Every corporation is considered as being organized for the purpose of engaging in any lawful business unless a more limited purpose is set forth in the articles of incorporation. Corporations engaging in businesses that are subject to regulation by certain State agencies may incorporate only if permitted by, and subject to all limitations of the statutes which control these businesses. These corporations include: (1) banks, savings and loan associations, credit unions, and other financial institutions regulated under Title 8; (2) insurance companies regulated under Title 8; (3) public service utilities regulated under Title 30; (4) railroad companies regulated under Title 19; and (5) professional corporations regulated under chapter 3 of Title 11.

State the purpose here.

_____

_____

PROFESSIONAL CORPORATIONS: (11 VSA, Chapter 3) Professional corporations must provide the following additional information: the name, address, license number and expiration date of license for each incorporator, officer, director and shareholder. (A certificate from the proper regulating board must be attached)

_____
name, title, license #, expiration date, address

_____
name, title, license #, expiration date, address

_____
name, title, license #, expiration date, address

DIRECTORS: Names and addresses of the individuals who will serve as the initial board of directors. A board of directors of a corporation which is not a close corporation dispensing with a board of directors must consist of three or more individuals. If the number of shareholders in any corporation is less than three, the number of directors may be as few as the shareholders. Listing the names of the initial directors is optional.

_____
name and address

_____
name and address

_____
name and address

One or more natural persons of majority age (18) may act as incorporator by signing below.

Signature of incorporator _____

Address _____

Signature of incorporator _____

Address _____

In order to develop a data base which highlights trends in Vermont business, the Department of Economic Development has requested that we include the list below to assist them in determining which most closely reflects your corporation. Your participation will enable them to serve emerging businesses more effectively. Please circle the most appropriate category. Completion of this section is voluntary.

01. Agricultural Crops	26. Apparel, Textile Products	51. Miscellaneous Retail
02. Agricultural Livestock	27. Paper, Allied Products	52. Depository Institution
03. Agricultural Services	28. Printing, Publishing	53. Nondepository Institution
04. Forestry	29. Chemicals, Allied Products	54. Security/Commodity Broker
05. Fishing, Hunting, Trapping	30. Petroleum & Coal Products	55. Insurance Carrier
06. Metal Mining	31. Rubber & Misc. Plastic	56. Insurance Agent/Broker
07. Coal Mining	32. Leather/Leather Products	57. Real Estate
08. Oil, Gas extraction	33. Railroad Transportation	58. Holding, Investment Office
09. Nonmetallic Minerals	34. Local Passenger Transit	59. Hotel, Other Lodging
10. Building Contractor	35. Trucking & Warehousing	60. Personal Services
11. Heavy Construction	36. Water Transportation	61. Business Services
12. Special Trade Contractors	37. Air Transportation	62. Auto Repair, Services, Parking
13. Lumber, Wood Products	38. Pipelines, (not natural gas)	63. Miscellaneous Repairs
14. Furniture, Fixtures	39. Transportation Services	64. Motion Pictures
15. Stone, Clay, Glass	40. Communications	65. Amusement/Recreation
16. Primary Metal Industry	41. Electric, Gas & Sanitary	66. Health Services
17. Fabricated Metal	42. Durable Goods/Wholesale	67. Legal Services
18. Industrial Machinery	43. Nondurable Goods/Wholesale	68. Educational Services
19. Electronic Equipment	44. Building & Garden	69. Social Services
20. Transportation Equipment	45. Gen. Merchandise Store	70. Museums
21. Instruments/Related Prod.	46. Food Stores	71. Membership Organizations
22. Miscellaneous Mfg.	47. Auto Dealers/Stations	72. Engineering/Mgmt. Services
23. Food, Kindred Products	48. Apparel & Accessories	73. Private Households
24. Tobacco Products	49. Furniture/Furnishings	74. Services, not elsewhere clsfd.
25. Textile Mill Products	50. Eating/Drinking Places	

****

$75.00 FILING FEE MUST BE ATTACHED TO THIS APPLICATION.
THE ARTICLES MUST BE TYPEWRITTEN OR PRINTED AND FILED IN DUPLICATE.
UNLESS A DELAYED EFFECTIVE DATE IS SPECIFIED, THE DOCUMENT IS EFFECTIVE ON THE DATE IT IS APPROVED. A DELAYED EFFECTIVE DATE CANNOT BE LATER THAN THE 90TH DAY AFTER FILING.

ARTICLES OF INCORPORATION

OFFICE OF SECRETARY OF STATE

FILED_____

_____

fee of $_____ has been paid.

GUIDE FOR ARTICLES OF INCORPORATION
VIRGINIA STOCK CORPORATION

The undersigned, pursuant to Chapter 9 of Title 13.1 of the Code of Virginia, state(s) as follows:

1. The name of the corporation is:

    _____.

2. The number (and classes, if any) of shares the corporation is authorized to issue is (are):

    Number of shares authorized   **Class(es)**

    _____   _____

    _____   _____

3. A. The name of the corporation's initial registered agent is

    _____.

    B. The initial registered agent is (mark appropriate box):
        (1)   An **individual** who is a **resident of Virginia** and
                [ ]   an initial director of the corporation
                [ ]   a member of the Virginia State Bar
                            OR
        (2)   [ ]   a professional corporation or professional limited liability company of attorneys
                        registered under Section 54.1-3902, Code of Virginia

4. A. The corporation's initial registered office address which is the business address of the initial
        registered agent is:

        _____ VA _____,
            (number/street)   (city or town)   (ZIP code)

    B. The registered office is physically located in the [ ] City **or** [ ] County of

        _____.

5. The initial directors are:
            NAME(S)   **ADDRESS(ES)**

    _____   _____
                                       _____
    _____   _____
                                       _____
    _____   _____
                                       _____

6. INCORPORATOR(S):

    _____   _____

    _____   _____

    _____   _____
            SIGNATURE(S)   PRINTED NAME(S)

See instructions on the reverse.

NOTE

When preparing articles of incorporation, the information should be typewritten.

This form contains the minimum number of provisions required by Virginia law to be set forth in the articles of incorporation. If additional provisions are desired, then the **complete** articles of incorporation, including the additional provisions, should be typewritten on white, opaque paper 8 1/2" by 11" in size, using only one side of a page. A minimum of a 1" margin must be provided on the left, top and bottom margins of a page and 1/2" at the right margin.

INSTRUCTIONS

1. **Name:** The corporate name must contain the word "corporation," "incorporated," "company" or "limited"; or the abbreviation "corp.," "inc.," "co." or "ltd." See Virginia Code Section 13.1-630.

2. **Shares:** List the total number of shares the corporation is authorized to issue. If more than one class of shares is to be authorized, list the number of authorized shares of each class and a distinguishing designation for each class (e.g., common, preferred, etc.) and state the relative rights, limitations & preferences of each class. See Sections 13.1-619, 13.1-638.

3. **Registered agent:** A. Provide the name of the registered agent, whose business address is the same as the corporation's registered office address. See Sections 13.1-619, 13.1-634. B. Check one of the boxes to indicate the status of the registered agent. The qualifications of the initial registered agent are set forth on the front of this form - no other person or entity may serve as the registered agent.

4. **Registered office:** A. Provide the complete post office address (which must include a street address, if any, or a rural route and box number in rural areas) of the corporation's registered office which is the same as the business address of the registered agent. B. Provide the name of the city **or** county where the registered office is physically located. (Cities and counties in Virginia are separate local jurisdictions.) See Sections 13.1-619, 13.1-634.

5. **Directors:** If the registered agent's status in 3.B. is that of initial director, then the names and addresses of the initial directors must be included in the articles of incorporation. A corporation can have directors immediately upon formation **only** if they are named in the articles.

6. **Incorporator(s):** One or more persons must sign the articles of incorporation in this capacity. See Section 13.1-604.

SEND THE ARTICLES OF INCORPORATION, ALONG WITH THE CHARTER AND FILING FEES, TO THE CLERK OF THE STATE CORPORATION COMMISSION, P. O. BOX 1197, RICHMOND, VA 23218-1197. (Street address: 1300 East Main Street, Richmond, VA 23219) (804) 371-9733.

Charter fee: 1,000,000 or fewer authorized shares - $50 for each 25,000 shares or fraction thereof; more than 1 million shares - $2,500. Filing fee: $25.
SEND BOTH FEES IN THE SAME CHECK, MADE PAYABLE TO THE STATE CORPORATION COMMISSION.

STATE OF WASHINGTON
SECRETARY OF STATE

Ralph Munro, Secretary of State

APPLICATION TO FORM A PROFIT CORPORATION

(Per Chapter 23B.02 RCW)

FEE: $175

EXPEDITED (24-HOUR) SERVICE AVAILABLE – $20 PER ENTITY INCLUDE FEE AND WRITE "EXPEDITE" IN BOLD LETTERS ON OUTSIDE OF ENVELOPE

• Please PRINT or TYPE in black ink
• Sign, date and return original **and one copy** to:

CORPORATIONS DIVISION
505 E. UNION • PO BOX 40234
OLYMPIA, WA 98504-0234

• **Be sure to include filing fee.** Checks should be made payable to "Secretary of State"

FOR OFFICE USE ONLY

FILED: / /	UBI:
CORPORATION NUMBER:	

IMPORTANT! Person to contact about this filing	Daytime Phone Number (with area code)

ARTICLES OF INCORPORATION

NAME OF CORPORATION *(Must contain the word "Corporation" "Incorporated" or "Limited" or the abbreviation "Corp." "Inc." "Co." or "Ltd.")*

NUMBER OF SHARES THE CORPORATION IS AUTHORIZED TO ISSUE *(Minimum of one (1) share must be listed)*

CLASS OF SHARES *(If "preferred" class is checked, please attach description)*
☐ Common ☐ Preferred

EFFECTIVE DATE OF INCORPORATION *(Specified effective date may be up to 90 days after receipt of the document by the Secretary of State)*
☐ Specific Date: _____ ☐ Upon filing by the Secretary of State

>>> PLEASE ATTACH ANY OTHER PROVISIONS THE CORPORATION ELECTS TO INCLUDE <<<

NAME AND ADDRESS OF WASHINGTON STATE REGISTERED AGENT

Name _____

Street Address *(Required)* _____ City _____ State _____ ZIP _____

PO Box *(Optional – Must be in same city as street address)* _____ ZIP *(If different than street ZIP)* _____

I consent to serve as Registered Agent in the State of Washington for the above named corporation. I understand it will be my responsibility to accept Service of Process on behalf of the corporation; to forward mail to the corporation; and to immediately notify the Office of the Secretary of State if I resign or change the Registered Office Address.

_____   _____   _____
Signature of Agent   Printed Name   Date

NAMES AND ADDRESSES OF EACH INCORPORATOR *(If necessary, attach additional names and addresses)*

Name _____

Address _____ City _____ State _____ ZIP _____

Name _____

Address _____ City _____ State _____ ZIP _____

Name _____

Address _____ City _____ State _____ ZIP _____

SIGNATURE OF INCORPORATOR

This document is hereby executed under penalties of perjury, and is, to the best of my knowledge, true and correct.

_____   _____   _____   _____
Signature of Incorporator   Printed Name   Title   Date

CORPORATIONS INFORMATION AND ASSISTANCE – 360/753-7115 (TDD – 360/753-1485)

005-001 (5/97)

18

KEN HECHLER
Secretary of State
State Capitol, W-139
1900 Kanawha Blvd. East
Charleston, WV 25305-0770

Penney Barker, Supervisor
CORPORATIONS DIVISION
Tel: (304) 558-8000
Fax: (304) 558-0900
Hours: 8:30 a.m. - 4:30 p.m. ET

INSTRUCTIONS FOR FILING ARTICLES OF INCORPORATION

BEFORE you fill out the application: The corporate name you select will be approved **only** if it is available-- that is, if the name is not the same as and is distinguishable from any other name which has been reserved or filed. If you prepare corporate papers without applying for and receiving a name reservation, you do so at your own risk. A telephone check on availability of a name is NOT a guarantee.

You may apply for a name reservation in writing, accompanied by a $15 fee payable to the Secretary of State, mailed to the address shown above. Once approved, you are guaranteed exclusive use of the name for 120 days, enough time to prepare and submit the articles. A name reservation may be renewed only once for an additional 120 days.

If you plan to do business under <u>any other name</u>, other than the name on your certificate of incorporation, you must register that trade name with the Secretary of State. Failure to do so could result in a fine or imprisonment.

FILLING OUT THE APPLICATION:

Section 1.   Enter the exact **name** of the corporation, and be sure to include one of the required terms, 'corporation', 'company', 'incorporated', 'limited', or an abbreviation of one of these terms. The name **may not** contain any word or phrase which implies that it is organized for any purposes other than those contained in these articles of incorporation. [W. Va. Code 31-1-11]

Section 2.   The **principal office** may be located within West Virginia or another state. Be sure to give the street address of the building in which the principal office is located.

Section 3.   A West Virginia domestic corporation must have a physical location as the **principal place of business** within the state. Give the street address, city, zip and county in W. Va.

Section 4.   Unless you name a person or business as "**agent of process**" who can receive service of a summons or complaint and annual report forms, legal process and forms will go to the address listed in #2. If you change your agent of process, W. Va. Code 31-1-15 requires you to notify the Secretary of State in writing.

Section 5.   In a **non-profit corporation**, no funds of the corporation may be distributed to members, directors or officers. In a **for-profit corporation**, the assets and profits of the corporation "belong to" the shareholders, and can be distributed to them. Check the appropriate box. Non-profit status will not be granted by the Tax Department until IRS 501(c) status is approved.

Section 6.   When a for-profit corporation is formed, this statement sets the aggregate (total) value of all authorized capital stock, and how it is divided into shares. It does not necessarily reflect the money put into the corporation. The number of shares <u>must be listed</u>, but may be increased later on. If you are just starting out and want to begin at the lowest license tax category, the total value must be $5,000 or less. The par value is calculated this way:

$$\frac{\text{Total value}}{\text{No. of shares}} = \text{Par value} \qquad \text{or, for example} \qquad \frac{\$5000}{100 \text{ shares}} = \$50 \text{ per share}$$

Now here's the tricky part! What if you list the **shares** as having **'no par value'?** <u>For the purpose of calculating the license tax</u>, these 'no par value' shares are <u>presumed</u> to have the par value of $25. If you list the number of shares as 200, for example, the total value is 200 x $25 = $5,000, the maximum total value allowed for the lowest license tax category. If you make the number of shares 1,000, then the license tax category is determined by 1,000 x $25 = $25,000, two tax categories higher.

If the corporation will have more than one class of shares, preferred or special classes in series, consult W. Va. Code 31-1-78 through 31-1-84 and attach the necessary provisions to the Articles.

Section 7.   It is important to describe the **purposes** of the corporation clearly to insure you receive all the necessary information about registering with the required state agencies. Attach an extra page if needed.

Section 8. The **provisions for the regulation of internal affairs** refers to the specific rules adopted by the corporation for its operation, either through by-laws or as attached. For a non-profit corporation, this may include any provisions for the distribution of assets on dissolution or liquidation. Non-profits must attach the statement required by IRS and must get IRS 501(c) status before the Tax Department will classify the corporation as non-profit.

Section 9. **Preemptive rights** deal with the priority of current stockholders to purchase unissued "treasury" shares in the corporation. If preemptive rights are granted, your current stockholders will be given first refusal on the purchase of any additional shares the corporation may want to sell.

Section 10. The **incorporators** (one or more persons or a domestic or foreign corporation)are the persons who set up the corporation. They need not own shares in or run the corporation.

Section 11. If the **directors** or officers are known when you set up the corporation, enter them here. If not, enter the **number of directors** to be elected. A president and a secretary, who are not the same person, are required to conduct the affairs of the corporation.

Section 12. The Secretary of State may accept filings only from persons recorded as having authority to act for the corporation. Enter those names here, and remember, these persons must sign any filings until the officers names are filed.

Section 13. If any pages are attached, give the number to make sure all intended provisions are included in the filing.

Section 14. Each incorporator must sign in the presence of the notary on duplicate originals. Unless two original "Articles" with original signatures are filed, the filing will be rejected.

FILING THE ARTICLES --TWO ORIGINALS REQUIRED-- AND PAYING THE FEE

• Calculate fee below -- be sure to calculate the fee based on the month the filing will be received by the Secretary of State
• Make check payable to **Secretary of State** •Mail fee & two original Articles to address on application.

Registration Fee _____

For profit corporations -- $50
Non-profit corporations -- $25
All corporations now pay this fee. Find amount for month of filing--see bottom row on chart.

+ **Attorney-In-Fact Fee** _____

Subtotal _____

Non-profit corporations, pay this amount

+ **License Tax Fee (Profit only)** _____

(See chart below for for fee based on value of authorized stock and month filing received by the Sec. of State)

Total _____

For profit corporations, pay this amount

TOTAL VALUE OF AUTHORIZED CAPITAL STOCK	JULY 100%	AUG. 100%	SEPT. 100%	OCT. 90%	NOV. 80%	DEC. 70%	JAN. 60%	FEB. 50%	MAR. 40%	APR. 30%	MAY** 120%	JUNE** 100%
0 - 5.000	20	20	20	18	16	14	12	10	10	10	30	30
5,001 - 10.000	30	30	30	27	24	21	18	15	12	10	40	40
10,001- 25.000	40	40	40	36	32	28	24	20	16	12	50	50
25,001- 50.000	50	50	50	45	40	35	30	25	20	15	60	60
50,001- 75.000	80	80	80	72	64	56	48	40	32	24	96	90
75,001- 100.000	100	100	100	90	80	70	60	50	40	30	120	110
100,001- 125.000	110	110	110	99	88	77	66	55	44	33	132	121
125,001- 150.000	120	120	120	108	96	84	72	60	48	36	144	132
150,001- 175.000	140	140	140	126	112	98	84	70	56	42	158	154
175,001- 200.000*	150	150	150	135	120	105	90	75	60	45	180	165
Attorney-in-Fact	10	10	10	9	8	7	6	5	4	3	12	11

* If value of authorized capital stock is over $200,000: fee (100%) is $180 + $.20 for each added $1,000 or fraction thereof, up to $1 million.
  If value over $1 million, fee (100%) is $340 + $.15 for each added $1,000 or fraction thereof, up to $15 million.
** May and June rates include advance payment of next fiscal year license taxes.

COUNTY FILING REQUIREMENTS: After you receive your certificate and one original copy of the Articles, file that within six months with the county clerk in the W.Va. county where your principal place of business is located.

DISSOLUTION: A corporation is a legal entity which can only be dissolved through formal action -- not by a letter or phone call. You remain liable for all taxes, assessments, fines, penalties and interest until you receive a certificate of dissolution from the Secretary of State. Contact us for more information.

Penney Barker, Supervisor
Corporations Division
Tel: (304) 558-8000
Fax: (304) 558-0900
Hrs: 8:30 am - 4:30 pm ET
FILE **TWO** ORIGINALS

ID: SS 000 __ __ __ __

WEST VIRGINIA
ARTICLES OF INCORPORATION

We, the undersigned, acting as incorporators according to West Virginia Code §31-1-27, adopt the following Articles of Incorporation for a West Virginia Domestic Corporation, which shall be perpetual:

1. The **name** of the **West Virginia corporation** shall be:
[The name must contain one of the words 'corporation', 'company', incorporated', 'limited', or an abbreviation of one of those words. WV Code §31-1-11]

_____

_____

2. The **physical address** (not a PO box) of the **principal office** of the corporation will be:

    located in the County of:

The mailing address of the above location, if different, will be:

Street: _____

City/State/Zip: _____

County: _____

Street/Box: _____

City/State/Zip: _____

3. The **physical address** (not a PO box) of the **principal place of business in West Virginia** of the corporation will be:
    located in the County of:

The mailing address of the above location, if different, will be:

Street: _____

City/State/Zip: _____ WV _____

County: _____

Street/Box: _____

City/State/Zip: _____

4. The name and address of the **person to whom notice of process may be sent** is:

Name: _____

Street: _____

City/State/Zip: _____

5. This corporation is organized as: (check one below)

☐ NON-PROFIT, NON-STOCK (complete sections 7, 8, 10, 11, 12 & 13)

☐ FOR PROFIT (complete sections 6, 7, 8, 9, 10, 11, 12 & 13)

6. FOR PROFIT ONLY:
    The total value of all authorized capital stock of the corporation will be $_____.

    The capital stock will be divided in _____ shares at the par value of $_____ per share.

☐ Check here if the shares are to be divided into more than one class or if the corporation is to issue shares in any preferred or special class in series. [Additional statements are required within the articles of incorporation, and are attached.]

7. The **purposes** for which this corporation is formed are as follows:
   (Describe the type(s) of business activity which will be conducted, for example, "agricultural production of grain and poultry", "construction of residential and commercial buildings", "manufacturing of food products", "commercial printing", "retail grocery and sale of beer and wine". Purposes may conclude with words "... including the transaction of any or all lawful business for which corporations may be incorporated in West Virginia.")

8. The provisions for the regulation of the internal affairs of the corporation (optional, check one if applicable):
   [Non-profit organizations must attach statement required by IRS for 501(c) status approval.]
   ☐ are set forth in the bylaws   ☐ are attached and hereby set forth in
      of the corporation;   the articles of incorporation.

9. The provisions granting, limiting or denying preemptive rights to shareholders, if any, (check if applicable):
   ☐ are set forth in the bylaws   ☐ are attached and hereby set forth in
      of the corporation;   the articles of incorporation.

10. The full names and addresses of the incorporators, and the number of shares subscribed for by each are:
    Name   **Address: No. & Street / City, State, Zip**   **No. of Shares**

11. The number of directors constituting the initial board of directors of the corporation is _____, and the names and addresses of the persons who will serve as directors until the first annual meeting, or until their successors are elected and shall qualify are (attach additional page if necessary):
    Name   **Address: No. & Street / City, State, Zip**

12. The names of the individuals who will have signature authority on documents filed with the Secretary of State until the names of the president and secretary are filed on the annual report are:

13. The number of pages attached and included in these Articles is _____.

14. **ACKNOWLEDGMENT:** [All incorporators must sign **two originals**, with names & signatures the same throughout the Articles. **Documents with photocopied signatures cannot be accepted.**]
    We, the undersigned, for the purpose of forming a corporation under the laws of the State of West Virginia, do make and file this "Articles of Incorporation." In witness whereof, we have accordingly set our hands:

    Date _____   Signatures: _____   _____

                                         _____   _____

    STATE OF _____, COUNTY OF _____;

    I, _____, a Notary Public, hereby certify that _____

    _____, whose names are signed to the foregoing Articles of Incorporation, this day personally appeared before me and acknowledged their signatures.

    My commission expires _____   _____, Notary Public

    Articles prepared by _____, (address)_____

    SEAL

State of Wisconsin
Department of Financial Institutions

ARTICLES OF INCORPORATION (Stock, for profit Corporation)

Executed by the undersigned for the purpose of forming a Wisconsin for-profit corporation under Ch. 180 of the Wisconsin Statutes:

Article 1. Name of the corporation: _____

Article 2. The corporation is organized under Ch. 180 of the Wisconsin Statutes.

Article 3. The corporation shall be authorized to issue _____ shares.
(see FEE information in the instructions)

Article 4. Name of the initial registered agent:_____

Article 5. Street address of the initial registered
office: (The complete address, including street and _____
number, if assigned, and ZIP code. P O Box address
may be included as part of the address, but is _____
insufficient alone.)

Article 6. Other provisions (OPTIONAL):

Article 7. **Name** and **complete address** of each incorporator:

_____   _____
Incorporator's signature   Incorporator's signature

This document was drafted by _____
(name of the individual who drafted the document)

FILING FEE - $90.00, or more SEE instructions, suggestions, and procedures on
following pages.

ARTICLES OF INCORPORATION (Ch. 180, stock, for-profit)

Γ

Please indicate here where you would like the acknowledgment copy of the filed document sent. Please include complete name and mailing address.

L

Your phone number during the day: (   ) _____ - _____

INSTRUCTIONS (Ref. sec. 180.0202 Wis. Stats. for document content)

Submit one original and one exact copy to Dept. of Financial Institutions, P O Box 7846, Madison WI, 53707-7846, together with a **FILING FEE of $90.00**, or more, payable to the department. (If sent by Express or Priority U.S. mail, address to 345 W. Washington Av, 3rd Floor, Madison WI, 53703). The original must include an original manual signature, per sec. 180.0120(3)(c), Wis. Stats. This document can be made available in alternate formats upon request to qualifying individuals with disabilities. Upon filing, the information in this document becomes public and might be used for purposes other than that for which it was originally furnished. If you have any questions, please contact the Division of Corporate & Consumer Services at 608-261-7577.

Article 1. The name must contain "corporation", "incorporated", "company", or "limited" or the abbreviation "corp.", "inc.", "co." or "ltd." or comparable words or abbreviations in another language. If you wish to provide a second choice name that you would accept if your first choice is not available, indicate it here:

_____

Article 3. Some quantity of shares must be authorized. For the minimum filing fee, up to 9,000 shares may be authorized. If more than one class of shares is authorized, state the designation of each class, and the number of shares of each class that the corporation is authorized to issue.

Articles 4 & 5. The corporation must have a registered agent located at a registered office in Wisconsin. The address of the registered office is to describe the physical location where the registered agent maintains their business office. Set forth the street number and name, city and ZIP code in Wisconsin. P O Box addresses may be included as part of the address, but are insufficient alone. The corporation may not name itself as its own registered agent.

Article 6. This space is provide for insertion of any desired material, such as grant or limit of preemptive rights, or other information not inconsistent with law.

Article 7. Print or typewrite the name and complete address of each incorporator. At least one incorporator is required to sign the document, although all incorporators may sign.

If the document is executed in Wisconsin, sec. 182.01(3), Wis. Stats., provides that it shall not be filed unless the name of the drafter (either an individual or a governmental agency) is printed in a legible manner. If the document is not executed in Wisconsin, please so state.

This document may declare a delayed effective date. To do so, enter a remark under Article 6: "This document has a delayed effective date of (enter the future date) ." The delayed effective date may not before, or more than 90 days after, the document is received by the Department of Financial Institutions for filing.

FILING FEE - Minimum fee is **$90.00** which is sufficient to authorized 9,000 shares. If the articles authorized the issuance of more than 9,000 shares, provide an additional filing fee equal to 1 cent for each additional share over 9,000. Shares may be, but are not required to be, designated as with or without a par value.

DFI/CORP/2I(R12/98)   2 of 2

Articles of Incorporation

Wyoming Secretary of State   Phone (307) 777-7312/7311
Corporation Division   Fax: (307) 777-5339
The State Capitol   E-Mail: Corporations@missc.state.wy.us
Cheyenne, WY 82002-0020

1)   **Corporate Name**_____

2)   **Registered Agent Name**_____

3)   **Address of Registered Agent** (Must be a Wyoming Street Address which is identical to the registered agent's business office. Must include street address/city/ state/ zip. **No Post Office Boxes or Mail Drop Boxes.**)

_____
_____

4)   **Number and Class of Shares the Corporation Will Have the Authority to Issue**

_____

       Number and Class of Shares Which Are Entitled to Receive the Net Assets upon Dissolution

_____

5)   **Address for Mailing Annual Report Form**

_____
_____
_____

6)   **Incorporators** (List names and addresses of each incorporator.)

_____   _____   _____
_____   _____   _____
_____   _____   _____

7)   **Execution** (All incorporators must sign.)
        Printed Name   Signature   Date

_____   _____   _____
_____   _____   _____
_____   _____   _____

8)   Contact Name   Daytime Phone Number

_____   _____

Rev. 7/96

1) Fee: $100.00
2) Make Check Payable to Secretary of State.
3) Articles must be accompanied by a written consent to appointment executed by the registered agent.

HOW TO REGISTER A DOMESTIC CORPORATION

To incorporate your company in the state of Wyoming you must file articles of incorporation in the Secretary of State's office and it shall be accompanied by one (1) exact or photo copy. The articles must be in compliance with Wyoming statutes 17-16-120 and 17-16-202. In addition the articles must be accompanied by a written consent to appointment manually signed by the registered agent.

Should you require further information concerning corporations, please do not hesitate to contact the Corporations division at (307) 777-7311. Corporations can also be contacted by e-mail: Corporations@missc.state.wy.us

Other Required Filing:

Annual Reports due on or before the first day of your registration month.

INSTRUCTIONS:

1. The Articles of Incorporation shall be accompanied by a written consent to appointment executed by the registered agent. The registered agent must have a **physical address** in Wyoming.

2. Articles of Incorporation shall be accompanied by one (1) exact or photo copy.

3. **Please review form prior to submitting to the Secretary of State to ensure all areas have been cmpleted to avoid a delay in the processing of your documents.**

CONSENT TO APPOINTMENT
BY REGISTERED AGENT

I, _____, voluntarily consent to serve as the registered

agent for _____

on the date shown below.

The registered agent certifies that he is: (circle one)

    (a)   *An individual who resides in this state and whose business office is identical with the registered office;*

    (b)   *A domestic corporation or not-for-profit domestic corporation whose business office is identical with the registered office; or*

    (c)   *A foreign corporation or not-for-profit foreign corporation authorized to transact business in this state whose business office is identical with the registered office.*

Dated this _____ day of _____, 19____.

_____
Signature of Registered Agent

raconsen - Revised: 4/97

INDEX